EMPLOYED for
LIFE

DAILY JOB SEEKER
ENCOURAGE-MINTS

"Oh, taste and see that the Lord is Good!" (Ps 34:8)

BARBARA
RARDEN

Cover Design & Layout by CAL Design Group
Printed in the United States of America

Published by: Virtual Workplace Publications,
A Division of Clarion Consulting Group, Inc.
6103 Johns Rd, Suite 5-6, Tampa, FL 33634
www.employed4life.com

ISBN: 978-0-9842738-0-5
Category: Religious / Christian Living / Self Help

IV

PREFACE

Do you know the story of Mephibosheth and King David? You'll find it in chapter nine of the book of Second Samuel and it goes like this:

One day David asked, "Is anyone in Saul's family still alive—anyone to whom I can show kindness for Jonathan's sake?" He summoned a man named Ziba, who had been one of Saul's servants. "Are you Ziba?" the king asked. "Yes sir, I am," Ziba replied. The king then asked him, "Is anyone still alive from Saul's family? If so, I want to show God's kindness to them." Ziba replied, "Yes, one of Jonathan's sons is still alive. He is crippled in both feet." "Where is he?" the king asked. "In Lo-debar," Ziba told him, "at the home of Makir son of Ammiel." So David sent for him and brought him from Makir's home. His name was Mephibosheth; he was Jonathan's son and Saul's grandson. When he came to David, he bowed low to the ground in deep respect. David said, "Greetings, Mephibosheth." Mephibosheth replied, "I am your servant." "Don't be afraid!" David said. "I intend to show kindness to you because of my promise to your father, Jonathan. I will give you all the property that once belonged to your grandfather Saul, and you will eat here with me at the king's table!" Mephibosheth bowed respectfully and exclaimed, "Who is your servant, that you should show such kindness to a dead dog like me?" Then the king summoned Saul's servant Ziba and said, "I have given your master's grandson everything that belonged to Saul and his family. You and your sons and servants are to farm the land for him to produce food for your master's household. But Mephibosheth, your master's grandson, will eat here at my table." (Ziba had fifteen sons and twenty servants.) Ziba replied, "Yes, my lord the king; I am your servant, and I will do all that you have commanded." And from that time on, Mephibosheth ate regularly at David's table, like one of the king's own sons. Mephibosheth had a young son named Mica. From then on, all the members of Ziba's household were Mephibosheth's servants. And Mephibosheth, who was crippled in both feet, lived in Jerusalem and ate regularly at the king's table.

This could well be the story of the typical Christian job seeker. If you go back a few chapters you will read that Mephibosheth became crippled when his nurse dropped him. One minute he is safe in her arms, but the next minute he's crippled. Sounds like our view of what happens when someone loses a job, doesn't it? One minute they're safe and secure, working in some organization, and then suddenly they're out on the street. Most of us find that to be a rather crippling experience. We become excruciatingly aware of our shortcomings, limitations and past failures. We might even feel shame or blame about being unemployed. So, like Mephibosheth, many of us go into hiding and struggle with how we will ever find our way out of the circumstances we've been thrust into. Is that you? If so, keep reading because now comes the good part.

You might feel like you've been rejected and abandoned by the workplace; you might be staring at want ads wondering where to go; and you might think you've been forgotten. But I have great news for you. There's a King who is looking for you and His intention is to find you and bless you! In writing this book I get to play the part of the servant who brings you from your Lo Debar to the palace.

I can tell you a few more things that I've observed from my years in the job ministry. Sometimes when believers are called into God's presence they become frightened. They don't know that God is Love and that He desires only to bless them. They've been told so many lies, and taught so much that is in error, that they think God is the one who crippled them; they think He caused their current painful situation. If you're thinking that, you'll need to spend some serious time getting to know your King. You have to discover that He is good and only good and that you can trust Him with your entire life. That's why the scriptures tell us to "Seek first the Kingdom..." Once you find the Kingdom and become personally acquainted with the King, you will find everything else you need in Him.

Chances are also good that it will take you a while to get this truth into your mind and spirit. When you first encounter the message of good news you may well respond like Mephibosheth and declare that you're not good enough. You might want to point out all your shortcomings to God and tell Him why you will never find a great job. Rest assured that even thinking of yourself as a "dead dog" won't stop God now that He's got your attention. He's called you into His presence and He won't let you go. You'll have to put this book down and run away if you don't want to be blessed. (And even then, I bet He'll come after you!). Your King has determined that you are to dine with Him from now on. He will feed you. He will provide for you. He will restore all that you have lost and give you an inheritance you never knew you possessed.

I like what King David did when he couldn't get Mephibosheth to rise up and accept his gifts. He turned to a faithful servant and told him to go farm the land, bring in the harvest, and give it to Mephibosheth. And that's what God will do for you too. "For he will order his angels to protect you wherever you go. They will hold you up with their hands so you won't even hurt your foot on a stone." (Psalm 91:11-12, NLT) If you'll stay and dwell with Him, He'll assign helpers and servants to you. They'll bring you favor and open doors you never expected. The King will find a way to bring your blessings to you. That doesn't mean you won't have to work at finding a job and presenting yourself effectively. It just means you'll have supernatural support and guidance on the journey.

So here's what I recommend. Decide to accept what the King is offering. Seek Him first and decide to live in His Kingdom before, and above, anything else you plan to do. Let this devotional guide you day-by-day into a closer, richer relationship with Him. And do not miss the end of Mephibosheth's story. He never fully recovered from the experience that crippled him. Yet despite his limitations, King David took care of him for all the rest of his days. If you decide to stay with the King, the same can be true for you. God will show Himself strong in your weaknesses and you'll be victorious in spite of your shortcomings. But perhaps you will choose to go beyond Mephibosheth and become completely healed, strong and confident. Then you will be able to demonstrate the goodness of God and lead others into the palace!

This I can promise you. If you follow God's "Ask, Seek and Knock" strategy for your job search, your life will never be the same. Believe it or not, you may someday say that this time of unemployment was the best thing that ever happened to you.

INTRODUCTION

If you're in a job search now, you already know how very lonely and very frustrating it can be as you try to find your next place of employment. To add to the challenge, nowadays the typical job search has become much more like a marathon than a sprint. Today the time between jobs can be so long that it is easy to lose heart, become discouraged, and succumb to fear. Through it all you've certainly discovered that there is no shortage of voices bringing bad news and painting pictures of unemployment disaster and tragedy.

But God has an extraordinary plan for His people. He has provided real, specific direction for this time. Better than that, His plan is a "gospel" plan for unemployment — good news for job seekers.

This devotional will show you a new, spiritual way to travel through the job search experience. God never intended for any of His children to barely survive; to just make it through unemployment by the skin of their teeth. As you use this devotional day-by-day you'll discover the true heart of God. He has prepared a victorious journey for all of us and He's ready to walk it out with everyone who will take Him up on His promises.

While most people believe that a job seeker should focus on getting a new job, any job, as rapidly as possible, before the money runs out — God has a different agenda. He wants to use this time to show us not a new way to make a living, but a new way of life. Believe it or not, He can use this situation, a crisis in the eyes of the world, to enrich your life, renew your mind, provide for you (even when you're not drawing a paycheck), and prepare you for new work. If you're willing, you'll be led to discover the good works which God has prepared for you to do. (Ephesians 2:10) It's true! God has a five-fold blessing for every believer. If you'll receive it, He will give you:

A greater understanding and love of Him,

A greater understanding and love of yourself,

Better relationships and love for others,

Freedom from fear in your life — forever!

A new, wonderful assignment in the workplace.

This devotional follows a four-part pattern every month to guide you into all that God has for you and to support and encourage you during your search. Every month you will be reminded to **Choose** God's way and then put the His **Ask, Seek** and **Knock** strategy into action.

- **Choose:** The first ten days of each month will center you and remind you that you are a child of the King. Because you are His you have all the rights and privileges Christ purchased for believers at Calvary. But the manifestation of God's blessing will not happen automatically. You must choose citizenship in the kingdom of God, over citizenship in the world. This is a decision you will have to make, and then stick with, no matter what comes.

- **Ask:** Then, for five days every month, you'll be reminded to ask God about yourself. How does your Father, your Creator, view you? This will help you determine who you really are and how important you are in the Kingdom of God. You can't be successful if you go into the marketplace trying to sell a product you don't believe in. You have to get to know yourself and what you have to offer if you expect to find a "buyer."

- **Seek:** Next you'll spend five days learning how to seek and listen for the leading of the Holy Spirit. Do you want to know where you should look for a job? Do you need help knowing how to effectively conduct your job search? Let God put you in touch with divine connections and open doors before you.

- **Knock:** The last ten devotionals of the month will remind you that whenever you knock at a door, or meet someone new, you will be representing the Kingdom of God. You are an ambassador for Christ and you are never off-duty. Wherever you go as you look for work and for however long it takes, God— your Father, your employer and your provider— will be with you. But, it's up to you to claim your Kingdom identity *by faith* and stay in step with Him.

When you put God's strategy to work in your life, you will see how faithful, powerful, gracious, patient, radical and amazing He truly is.

For believers, this journey will confirm the character of God in many awesome ways. If you haven't personally encountered Jesus yet, this process could be a real eye-opener. God's loving kindness, shown in the many ways He cares for His children and sustains them at all times, just might compel you to question any reasons you might have for walking through life without Him. Let this devotional be your guide to the more abundant life Christ died to give you. Receive your inheritance and experience a victorious job search!

XVI

JANUARY

GOOD NEWS

DECEMBER 31
KNOCK AND BE AT PEACE

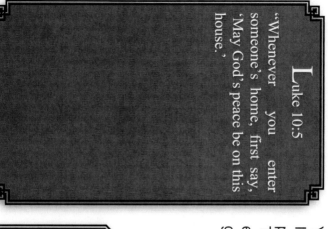

Luke 10:5

"Whenever you enter someone's home, first say, 'May God's peace be on this house.'"

You have the ability, even the assignment, to bring peace with you wherever you go. Imagine going into the workplaces of prospective employers and bringing the blessing of peace with you. Imagine the difference it could make in the lives of all who work there. That's an interesting idea, isn't it? Be the bearer of good tidings. Pray as you enter into every workplace. Bring joy, peace, and blessing with you and give that gift wherever you go, for the sake of the Kingdom and the glory of God.

DECLARE THIS:

- I am a blessing to everyone I meet.
- I bring peace and good will wherever I go.
- I will pray for peace and release the hand of God over every place I enter today.

JANUARY 1
CHOOSE YOUR KINGDOM

Without a doubt, this is the most radical... and the most important... piece of advice a job seeker will ever receive. Seek the Kingdom of God above all else. Radical? Yes! In fact, it's totally opposed to the advice you'll get from the world. But when God is in the absolute center of your job search He can guide you and open doors that wouldn't have opened any other way. Of course, you will still have to work very hard. But if you give God your full attention he will direct, manage, and bless the rest of the process for you.

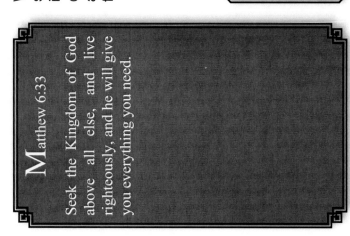

DECLARE THIS:

- I am a citizen in the Kingdom of God.
- I live by the laws of His Kingdom and I serve His will and purposes only.
- I am not moved by what I see in the world; I am not part of that kingdom.

Matthew 6:33

Seek the Kingdom of God above all else, and live righteously, and he will give you everything you need.

DECEMBER 30
KNOCK AND KEEP KNOCKING

> 1 Corinthians 10:13
>
> The temptations in your life are no different from what others experience. And God is faithful. He will not allow the temptation to be more than you can stand. When you are tempted, he will show you a way out so that you can endure.

The difference between believers and the rest of the world is that we know we have a faithful God who will never leave us. God is going to do a work with us. He is going to give us the strength to avoid temptation. So when the job search seems unending and your resources are disappearing, don't despair. Avoid every temptation to look for "an easy way out", fall back into a bad habit, or try to escape responsibility and run away. Remember, you're not on your own to make things work. Don't try to rely on your own strengths, talents, or will power. Let God do the "heavy lifting". He will show you a way out.

DECLARE THIS:

- I stand in faith that God is able to make a way out for me.
- I believe that God will never leave me or forsake me.
- In Christ I can withstand the temptation to look for my own shortcuts and escape routes. I will follow as the Lord leads me.

JANUARY 2
CHOOSE YOUR THOUGHTS

We do not belong to ourselves! Now that's an interesting piece of information. I used to hear my daughter tell her brother, "You are not the boss of me." Well, don't say that to God. Because God owns us — body, mind and spirit. It's time to throw out all thoughts and beliefs that do not agree with the Word of God. We need to think His thoughts and seek His ways. This time between jobs is God's time to do some serious work on us. Let's cooperate and behave as if we know that the Holy Spirit of God is inside us every moment of this day and every place that we go.

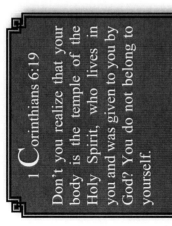

1 Corinthians 6:19

Don't you realize that your body is the temple of the Holy Spirit, who lives in you and was given to you by God? You do not belong to yourself.

DECLARE THIS:

- I belong totally to God who created me.
- My thoughts line up with His word.
- My body belongs to God and reflects His glory.

I saiah 32:20

Happy and fortunate are you who cast your seed upon all waters [when the river overflows its banks; for the seed will sink into the mud and when the waters subside, the plant will spring up; you will find it after many days and reap an abundant harvest], you who safely send forth the ox and the donkey [to range freely]. (The Amplified Bible)

Do you feel like you have sent out resumes and talked to everyone on the planet? If you've "cast your seed on all waters" then it's time to be encouraged. This Word promises that you will be happy and fortunate, no matter what the situation looks like. Remember — seed time and harvest is a Kingdom law. It will never fail as long as the earth remains. Look with excitement at this promise about the seed you've planted — "You will find it after many days and reap an abundant harvest!" Set your heart on it. Don't let anything persuade you otherwise. Then stay close to Him and listen. He will tell you where and when to reap. Get ready now to amaze your family and friends with your awesome job search testimony. Prepare yourself to tell how the Lord sustained you, guided you and brought you to your great new job!

DECLARE THIS:

- I am happy because I know my efforts will produce a great return.
- By faith I believe that God will deliver an abundant harvest for the seed I have planted as I follow His lead.
- I thank God for His promises and the confidence I have that His Word is true!

JANUARY 3
CHOOSE YOUR FUTURE

What do you feel when you think about your last job? The instruction here is clear — "forget all that." There is nothing about your past that can stop the future God has for you! Accept this and rejoice in your freedom from sadness, shame, guilt, anger, and resentment. Turn all your attention to the new thing God is about to do with and through you. Watch for the new path He has carved out for you. Watch to see how He will fill your present "wasteland" with rivers of flowing water! Focus on this alone — God has a wonderful future for you.

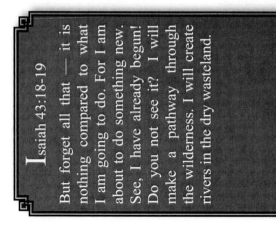

Isaiah 43:18-19

But forget all that — it is nothing compared to what I am going to do. For I am about to do something new. See, I have already begun! Do you not see it? I will make a pathway through the wilderness. I will create rivers in the dry wasteland.

DECLARE THIS:

- I willingly and completely release the past; it has no hold on me.
- I am focused on the future God has for me.
- By faith I receive the new thing God is doing in my life.

DECEMBER 28
KNOCK AND FAINT NOT!

P salm 27:13

I would have lost heart, unless I had believed. That I would see the goodness of the LORD In the land of the living. (NKJV)

I've been there, in that place of complete emptiness, with no hope in sight. So many times in that dark time of my life I said, "I know God's promises are true. They may be radical and nearly too good to be believed, but I do believe God's Word and I still believe I will experience what He has promised. What God says is true, even though I don't see it." I had to believe that I would see the goodness of the Lord, in this lifetime, or I too would have lost heart and would have been crushed. So I stood as so many have stood, and waited. It was a marathon of standing on the Word. But I can now tell you from my own experience that when you stand in faith you will see the goodness of the Lord. How about you? Are you there now? Perhaps it is time for your once-and-for-all quality decision. No matter what it looks like right now, decide that God is who He says He is and He will do for you what He has done for others. As soon as you decide to stand if it takes forever, you will find that your wait won't be long. Stand in faith! Your breakthrough is coming!

DECLARE THIS:

- I will not lose heart. I believe I will see the goodness of the Lord in my life.
- By faith I believe the awesome and wonderful promises of God and I won't change my mind about His Word.
- I am not moved by what I see or what I have. My faith is in the Word alone.

JANUARY 4
CHOOSE YOUR BOSS

This may be one of the most important revelations a job seeker could ever receive. Your employer is Almighty God and you work, full time, for Him. You can never be unemployed and you will never run out of provision. Think of the children in a royal family. They have work to do but they never need to be concerned about their provision. That's you! God has already met all your needs and now He's trying to get you to receive His provisions by faith. Turn all your attention on getting to know your new employer, your Father the King, and see what He has in store for you.

> **Matthew 6:30-33**
>
> If God gives such attention to the appearance of wildflowers — most of which are never even seen — don't you think He'll attend to you, take pride in you, do His best for you? What I'm trying to do here is to get you to relax, to not be so preoccupied with getting, so you can respond to God's giving. People who don't know God and the way he works fuss over these things, but you know both God and how he works. Steep your life in God-reality, God-initiative, God-provisions. Don't worry about missing out. You'll find all your everyday human concerns will be met. (Message)

DECLARE THIS:

- I work for my Father, the King over all things.
- I am a royal child and my provision is assured.
- I have the power and authority of the name of Jesus to use as I serve Him.

DECEMBER 27
KNOCK AND OVERCOME

Numbers 13:30

Then Caleb quieted the people before Moses, and said, "Let us go up at once and take possession, for we are well able to overcome it." (NKJV)

So what if we have to face the "giants" of hiring freezes, lay-offs, economic downturns, and financial failures? We are well able to overcome them. God has given His power and authority to us. We own this world and the workplace and it's time to act like it. There's important work to be done for the Kingdom. So check your motives and determine what your goal is. If you want to receive your blessing so you can bless others, you're ready to claim your victory. If you desire to be a "city set on a hill that cannot be hid" you're positioned to succeed and bring glory to God. Align with God's will and purposes and you cannot fail. Go into the workplace determined to win a great new job and bring the light of Christ with you. Remember that you are a conqueror and not a grasshopper!

DECLARE THIS:

- I believe the Word of God that says that all power and authority has been given by God to Christ Jesus and He has given it to His body.
- By faith I receive the power to go into the workplace and take the position that will enable me to be a blessing and bring God glory.
- I thank God that I work for Him and I will never be unemployed.

JANUARY 5
CHOOSE YOUR BENEFITS

Are you still trying to decide if you want to do your job search "God's way" or handle it yourself? Are you persuaded that you need to get God involved or do you still think you're okay on your own? Pause right here and meditate on this word. The God who sees all of eternity is telling you that He has a great future and hope for you. Doesn't it make sense to put him in charge? He promises only good to those who trust Him. Can you do better than that for yourself?

DECLARE THIS:

- I choose God's plan for my life because it is better than anything I could create.
- I acknowledge that I need God to determine my steps.
- In faith I surrender all my plans to God and listen for what He has in mind for me.

Jeremiah 29:11

For I know the plans I have for you," says the LORD. "They are plans for good and not for disaster, to give you a future and a hope.

DECEMBER 26
KNOCK AND WITNESS FOR THE KINGDOM

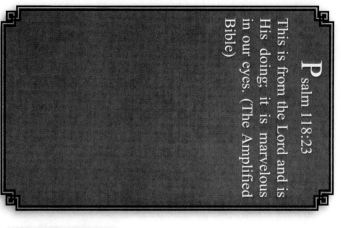

P salm 118:23

This is from the Lord and is His doing; it is marvelous in our eyes. (The Amplified Bible)

Many people know about God but they don't know His character. They are ready to believe that hurricanes and devastating wildfires are acts of God. They don't recognize His giving and loving nature in the wonderful blessings happening all around. That makes it our job to tell everyone this truth. Besides, it's fun to point out the marvelous things that God has done! Make a personal commitment to notice every time God acts on your behalf, bringing blessing and deliverance and provisions. Then talk it up! His actions truly are marvelous in our eyes and every good gift comes from Him. Let's spread the word.

DECLARE THIS:

- I love to tell others of the goodness of God.
- I know every good and perfect gift is from above. I thank God for them.
- By faith I recognize God's work in my life and I give Him praise.

JANUARY 6
CHOOSE YOUR WORK

To put it simply, it's time to get your house in order. Let's assume you know that Jesus is the Lord and you want to serve Him... but you're not sure how. Here's your starting point. Go to the last thing God told you to do and do it. Did He tell you to forgive someone? Is there a habit you need to break? Maybe there's some project you've put off or a volunteer assignment you haven't yet accepted. Now's the time. Go to the Lord and tell him you're willing to do anything He tells you and then just do it.

DECLARE THIS:

- I receive my righteousness by faith in Jesus.
- By faith I have the ability to choose to do what is right in God's sight.
- I'm quick to do what God tells me.

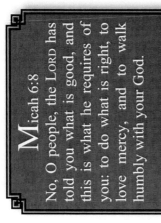

Micah 6:8
No, O people, the LORD has told you what is good, and this is what he requires of you: to do what is right, to love mercy, and to walk humbly with your God.

DECEMBER 25
KNOCK AND EXERCISE YOUR FAITH

Ecclesiastes 1:13
And I set my heart to seek and search out by wisdom concerning all that is done under heaven; this burdensome task God has given to the sons of man, by which they may be exercised. (NKJV)

Obviously Solomon isn't talking about the experience of unemployment here but "this burdensome task" sure sounds like a description of the job search process! And we know God is not the creator of joblessness. Yet, He certainly has been known to use it as a way "by which" (we) may be exercised". If you'll permit a personal note here — I can say that without a doubt my faith would not be what it is today if it had not been for my times of transition and unemployment. Solomon was searching for understanding. Maybe that's what we need to do too. If a season of unemployment sends us running to God, if it causes us to search His Word for our answers, and if it requires us to put our faith to work for us, then it may be the very "work out" we need. As tougher and tougher times come upon us, we'll be really grateful for this faith fitness program!

DECLARE THIS:

- My faith is working for me and I exercise it daily.
- My confidence is not in what is done under heaven because I am not a citizen here. I belong to the Kingdom of God.
- By faith I receive the fruit of my exercise program; I have strong faith!

JANUARY 7
CHOOSE YOUR PAY

Apparently, Solomon was really on to something when he chose wisdom above everything else. Most of us would try to get our basic needs met and then seek wisdom. But just look at what wisdom holds in her hands — long life, riches and honor! What an amazing concept! When we seek wisdom, which is just another name for the Word of God, we are guaranteed to get all her gifts. In the book of James, we find that God will give wisdom to anyone who asks for it. That certainly seems like the way to go, doesn't it?

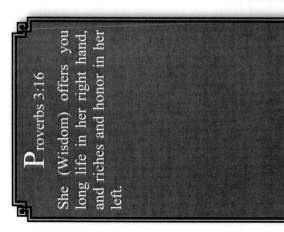

Proverbs 3:16

She (Wisdom) offers you long life in her right hand, and riches and honor in her left.

DECLARE THIS:

- I choose wisdom and seek it diligently.
- I know that Wisdom is God's word and I will find all my answers there.
- By faith I receive the wealth and honor that wisdom brings.

DECEMBER 24
KNOCK AND BRING GIFTS

> ℞omans 12:8
>
> If your gift is to encourage others, be encouraging. If it is giving, give generously. If God has given you leadership ability, take the responsibility seriously. And if you have a gift for showing kindness to others, do it gladly.

Whatever our gifts are, we need to practice and use them while we're unemployed. We may not be working in a job, but we can still make a contribution to others with our skills and talents. Have you checked to see where you might be able to volunteer service to your church? Could the church use someone to answer phones, care for the grounds, paint a room or visit members? For some of us, giving encouragement, praise and kindness is our special gift and calling. Whether we have a job or not, every one of us has the ability to give a smile and offer a helping hand. Some of us are called to lead and some to follow but all of us are called to give what God has designed us to give. So take whatever ability you have and give it gladly. Then watch for the harvest that will most assuredly come.

DECLARE THIS:

- I am designed to give to the body of Christ and the glory of God.
- By faith I receive God's direction about how and where to serve.
- I make a difference in the Kingdom of God.

JANUARY 8
CHOOSE YOUR TRAINING

"Let Him do what He thinks best." Are you able to say that? Can you tell God to train you however He chooses? What if God wants to deal with something in your heart before He opens up a place of new employment for you? Can you be okay with that? Are you willing to obediently spend your time volunteering or seeking the Kingdom first? Listen to what God has in mind. He knows what you really need. Decide to trust Him, no matter what. His will for you is far better and greater than anything you could plan for yourself.

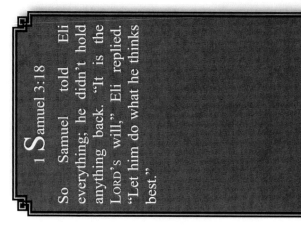

1 Samuel 3:18

So Samuel told Eli everything; he didn't hold anything back. "It is the LORD's will," Eli replied. "Let him do what he thinks best."

DECLARE THIS:

- I trust God's timing. He sees the future and has my very best in mind.
- I know God is perfect Love and He is altogether trustworthy and good.
- By faith I am committed to follow God's plan for my life.

DECEMBER 23
KNOCK WITH CONFIDENCE

> 1 Thessalonians 1:5
>
> For when we brought you the Good News, it was not only with words but also with power, for the Holy Spirit gave you full assurance that what we said was true.

Has God ever done something extraordinary for you? Have you ever personally experienced His intervention in your life? If so, then you have already seen Almighty God in action. During this season of searching, put yourself in places where you can witness God's power. Listen to the life-changing testimonies of others. Surround yourself with like-minded believers who will remind you of the God we serve. Build your confidence by focusing on God as He acts in and around you every day. He's here and He will get you through this season. Keep your confidence in His mighty power.

DECLARE THIS:

- I am assured that God's Word is true and His promises are meant for me.
- By faith I receive all that God intends for me to have.
- I thank God that my job search is in His hands and He will labor with me.

JANUARY 9
Choose Your Behavior

A job search is a full time job. It takes training and preparation and yet few people do the work required to master the process. What about you? Do you know how to conduct a job search so well that God would approve? If not, get busy. Learn to interview well. Spend your time in a planned and disciplined way. Show up on temporary assignments as if you are there to work for the Lord himself. Joseph was a great worker when he was a slave in Potiphar's house. And he continued to behave with excellence even in prison. Now it's your turn. Be the best job seeker out there.

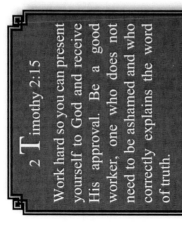

2 Timothy 2:15

Work hard so you can present yourself to God and receive His approval. Be a good worker, one who does not need to be ashamed and who correctly explains the word of truth.

DECLARE THIS:

- I am a good worker in all my endeavors. I am never off duty.
- I delight in learning new ways to serve God with excellence.
- I represent the truth to a dark world. I will be faithful in this assignment.

DECEMBER 22
KNOCK WITH THANKSGIVING

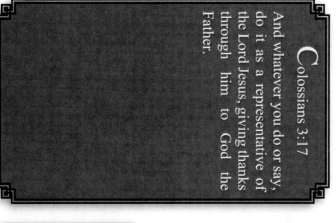

Colossians 3:17
And whatever you do or say, do it as a representative of the Lord Jesus, giving thanks through him to God the Father.

Nothing in this scripture suggests that we get a break from our Kingdom assignment as God's representatives just because we have no job. In fact, right now, in the "pressure cooker" of joblessness, all eyes are on us. Everyone is watching to see how we, as believers, handle this challenging time. Are we behaving any differently than unemployed unbelievers? We can praise God and give Him thanks so that the world can see our faith and His love... or we can keep a low profile and hope that no one sees us succumb to fear and panic. The decision is ours. We have the gospel of unemployment — good news. We serve the Lord who gives us victory in every life circumstance. I say let's give thanks and make a lot of noise when we do it!

DECLARE THIS:

- I give God thanks and praise because He is good.
- By faith I take my stand against the enemy and praise God for my victory before I see it.
- I know that I represent the Kingdom and I behave fearlessly because I trust the Word of God.

JANUARY 10
CHOOSE YOUR BATTLE

Don't miss this vital point. A huge battle is raging and we are not on the sidelines! Like it or not, it's time to become "armed and dangerous." If you've been going into the job market without prayer, without the direction of the Holy Spirit, and without the sword of the spirit, it's no wonder you're struggling. Stop stumbling around the battlefield bewildered and defenseless. Put on the whole armor of God! The devil may not want you to find your place in the workforce but God does! So suit up and claim your place with spiritual force.

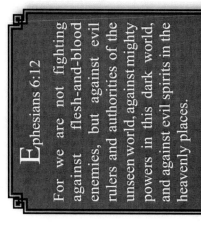

Ephesians 6:12

For we are not fighting against flesh-and-blood enemies, but against evil rulers and authorities of the unseen world, against mighty powers in this dark world, and against evil spirits in the heavenly places.

DECLARE THIS:

- I declare war on the enemies of Christ.
- By faith I take up the weapons of war to fight for the Kingdom of God.
- I never go out unarmed. The shield of faith protects me and the sword of the spirit brings victory.

DECEMBER 21
KNOCK WITH BOLDNESS

Deuteronomy 31:6

"So be strong and courageous! Do not be afraid and do not panic before them. For the LORD your God will personally go ahead of you. He will neither fail you nor abandon you."

Consider the story of the prodigal son... a story of boldness without wisdom. The younger son believed that his Father's inheritance belonged to him and he claimed it. But he didn't have the wisdom or character to manage what he received. How about us? Is there a kingdom purpose behind our demands for our inheritance? What's our plan of action once we are prosperous? Boldness without character is selfishness. When we understand that we, like Jesus, are here to accomplish our Father's business then we will be ready to receive it. If there is willful disobedience in our lives or a desire to satisfy only ourselves, God does us a great favor to withhold our inheritance and keep us out of the pig pens of life!

DECLARE THIS:

- I am a child of God and joint heir with Christ Jesus.
- I know that my inheritance is given to serve the Kingdom of God and bring Him glory.
- By faith I receive my inheritance and the character of Christ that I might manage it as God desires.

JANUARY 11
ASK EXPECTING RESULTS

When we're sick most of us have no problem taking a prescription medication that promises to help us recover. We'll take the medication three times a day for months if that's what the doctor tells us to do. We don't stop taking it if the symptoms persist after a dose or two. We just follow the directions on the bottle, believing relief will come. Why do we have such trouble doing the same thing with the promises of God? The Word is clear — if we keep on, we will receive. We'll find what we seek and end up right where we need to be. So keep on.

Matthew 7:7-8

Keep on asking, and you will receive what you ask for. Keep on seeking, and you will find. Keep on knocking, and the door will be opened to you. For everyone who asks, receives. Everyone who seeks, finds. And to everyone who knocks, the door will be opened.

DECLARE THIS:

- I know God's word is true and His promises are real.
- I am single-minded in my determination to receive God's promises.
- My eyes are ever open. I expect to see results for every prayer that lines up with His will.

DECEMBER 20

SEEK TO STAY FOCUSED ON JESUS

Hebrews 6:11-12

Our great desire is that you will keep on loving others as long as life lasts, in order to make certain that what you hope for will come true. Then you will not become spiritually dull and indifferent. Instead, you will follow the example of those who are going to inherit God's promises because of their faith and endurance.

Wouldn't it be great to become much more like Jesus before you enter into your next job assignment? What happens when we lean upon the Lord and practice patient endurance? We are "transformed into the same image, from glory to glory." We will inherit God's promises. Our part is simple — we just have to keep our eyes on Jesus and our hearts attuned to hear His voice within us. The more we focus on Him the more we become like Him. Where His Spirit is, there is complete freedom. Imagine the storms we'll be able to subdue and the peace we'll bring into the workplace as we walk in His image.

DECLARE THIS:

- I am the being transformed into the image of Jesus Christ, my Lord.
- By faith I receive the promise that "as He is, so am I in this life."
- I experience true liberty because I am in Christ.

JANUARY 12
FOR FIRST THINGS FIRST

Say this request out loud right now — "Lord, make me aware of your presence within me. Teach me to be led by your Spirit." Now you're ready to look for a job. Sadly, most job seekers never find this internal source of direction. They go to bed every night wondering if they spent their time well. Did they do all they could do to get back to work, they wonder? How about you? Do you recognize God's voice when He speaks to you? Can you lie down at night confident that you were always in the right place doing the right things? If not, ask Him to teach you to listen.

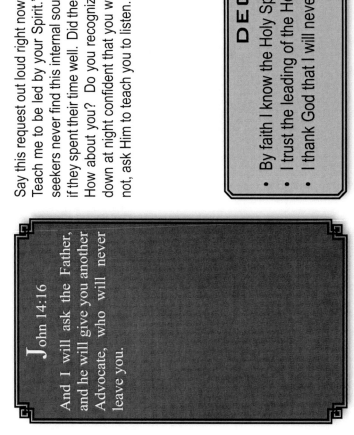

John 14:16

And I will ask the Father, and he will give you another Advocate, who will never leave you.

DECLARE THIS:

By faith I know the Holy Spirit of God is an indwelling presence in my life.

- I trust the leading of the Holy Spirit and I listen for His voice.
- I thank God that I will never be left alone or without direction.

DECEMBER 19
SEEK HIDDEN TREASURES

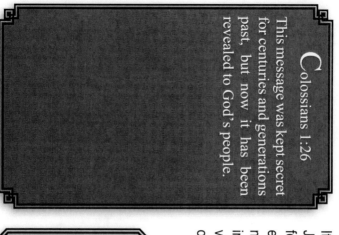

Colossians 1:26

This message was kept secret for centuries and generations past, but now it has been revealed to God's people.

It's hard to imagine but right now we are standing in the end of the age. The return of Jesus is imminent. Throughout the ages the saints of God have been waiting and praying for this very time! We have been given the highest level of revelation that believers have ever received. We have all the power and authority of God Almighty! He invested in the name of Jesus and gave us, the body of Christ, a legal right to use His name. We walk in the knowledge of the Word of God that has been hidden from the rest of the world. It is visible only to those with the spiritual eyes to see. Praise God for the gift of the knowledge of Him!

DECLARE THIS:

- I have a revelation of God that has never before been given to the body of Christ.
- By faith I walk in the Kingdom of God and have His Spirit as my Guide and Teacher.
- I thank God that I may know Him through His Word.

JANUARY 13
ASK ABOUT YOUR GIFTS

Have you ever experienced the great joy of doing something you really love? Amazingly, when we use our God-given gifts and talents we do our best work and we are satisfied. Doesn't it show the love of God that He would make us good at something and use those same gifts to make us happy? But notice the purpose here. Our talents and gifts were given for service to others. If we try to use them selfishly or hoard them until the "offer is right" they'll produce no fruit. So use your gifts — give them away for a while if you have to — and they'll produce a harvest for both you and the Kingdom.

1 Peter 4:10

Each one should use whatever gift he has received to serve others, faithfully administering God's grace in its various forms. (NIV)

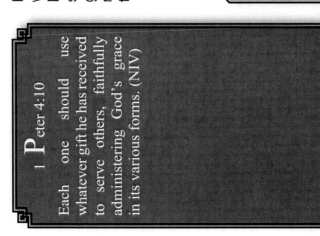

DECLARE THIS:

- I thank God for my gifts and talents. I dedicate them to His service.
- All that I am and all that I am capable of achieving is because of God and I am grateful.
- By faith I receive empowerment to use all my gifts for God's glory.

DECEMBER 18
SEEK DIVINE CONNECTIONS

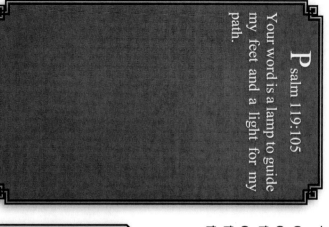

Psalm 119:105
Your word is a lamp to guide my feet and a light for my path.

The Bible is no ordinary book. It is actually the living Word of God. Though it was written countless years ago it has answers to meet your needs today. As you read it, with the help of the Holy Spirit, it will begin to talk to you. But you have to make the investment of your time and energy to seek its treasures. No prize this valuable was ever obtained without effort. Commit to spend time in the Word. Ask God to draw you to it. Let it reveal secrets to you and pour out the wisdom you need to have victory in this life. Don't try to navigate the job search without consulting the ultimate guidebook of all time!

DECLARE THIS:

- I am a child of the Kingdom of God and I want to learn His ways.
- By faith I receive revelation from the Holy Spirit.
- I trust that God will draw near to me each time I open His Word eagerly seeking to meet Him there.

JANUARY 14
ASK ABOUT YOUR DESIGN

God made you so you've got to be good! He doesn't make mistakes. No matter what you may have been told, you aren't an accident. In fact, God designed you as a unique part of His master plan with no one else to stand in for you. Do you understand your design? Have you discovered your gifts and talents? This would be a great time to find out what you have to contribute to the Kingdom of God. Don't be like the servant who buried his talents. Figure out what you're designed to do and invest your gifts and talents for the purposes of God.

DECLARE THIS:

- I know that I am wonderfully made and that God has a purpose for my life.
- I have a unique contribution to make to the Kingdom of God.
- I dedicate my gifts and design to God for His use.

Psalm 139: 13-15

You made all the delicate, inner parts of my body and knit me together in my mother's womb. Thank you for making me so wonderfully complex! Your workmanship is marvelous — how well I know it. You watched me as I was being formed in utter seclusion, as I was woven together in the dark of the womb.

DECEMBER 17

SEEK THE DIRECTION OF THE HOLY SPIRIT

Isaiah 63:11

Then they remembered those days of old when Moses led his people out of Egypt. They cried out, "Where is the one who brought Israel through the sea, with Moses as their shepherd? Where is the one who sent his Holy Spirit to be among his people?

When the going gets tough it's easy to think that God has run out of miracles or has tired of providing for us. That's when we need to revisit His Word. He always leads us out of trouble, just as a shepherd leads His flock. When we follow His guidance He keeps us from stumbling and falling. Don't become concerned if the path is long and the way is rocky. He's still the God who will guide you out of the wilderness. He's the One who will provide for you during the journey. So as you climb over the obstacles in your path, just see them as a way to rise higher in your faith.

DECLARE THIS:

- I know my God is with me and He will never leave or forsake me.
- By faith I trust in the provisions of God and His never-ending supply for me.
- My God performed miracles in the past and He will do that for me if the need arises.

JANUARY 15
Ask About Your Purpose

Many job seekers complain that they don't know what their purpose is. There's no mystery. The life purpose of every believer is to bring God glory! This scripture makes it pretty clear that we were created in Christ to do good works. Those works have been laid out before us and God will walk us right into them. The trouble comes when we start looking for careers that will give us satisfaction and fulfillment; jobs to make us feel important and respected. That's the purpose that motivates non-believers. We're here to serve God. Period. So find a way to bring God's love and light wherever you go. Ask God to open doors to the places where you can be the greatest blessing. There's your purpose, now go for it!

Ephesians 2:10

For we are His workmanship, created in Christ Jesus for good works, which God prepared beforehand that we should walk in them. (NKJV)

DECLARE THIS:

- I am ready and available to perform good works.
- I accept the commandment to love as my top priority in life.
- Because God designed me I know I am capable of greatness.

DECEMBER 16
SEEK SELF AWARENESS

1 John 4:18

And we have known and believed the love that God has for us. God is love, and he who abides in love abides in God, and God in him.

There is no fear in love; but perfect love casts out fear, because fear involves torment. But he who fears has not been made perfect in love. (NKJV)

What torments you — lack, resentment, strife, hurt feelings, shame? Where there is torment there is fear, and that points to one thing... the need for more of God's love. This scripture doesn't condemn us. Far from it. It's a promise. It tells us that it is possible to dwell in love and be completely free of fear. What an amazing truth! When we fill ourselves up with the love of God, fear is driven out of our hearts. Rather than taking anti-anxiety medications or exercising intense mind control, we can just turn our thoughts to God's love. For once we truly experience His love, and the power that it makes available to us, fear doesn't stand a chance!

DECLARE THIS:

- I am at peace and free of fear. I know God loves me and will perfectly care for me.
- By faith I receive God's love and allow it to fill my heart completely.
- I believe that God is Love. In Christ I am perfectly protected.

JANUARY 16
SEEK SELF AWARENESS

What weakness can hold you back in the face of this promise? Do you think you are too old, young, unskilled, over-qualified, or shy? Imagine God noticing you and saying, "Oh no, I forgot about that college education (or age requirement or experience) and now the eternal destiny that I had planned, before the foundation of the earth, can't happen. I blew it!" Don't think so. There is nothing about you that can stop what God has planned from the beginning of time. So change your mind about your "limitations" and let the power of Christ carry you through to the finish line. Never forget our God is able!

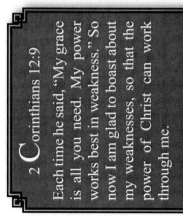

2 Corinthians 12:9

Each time he said, "My grace is all you need. My power works best in weakness." So now I am glad to boast about my weaknesses, so that the power of Christ can work through me.

DECLARE THIS:

- I am not limited by my weaknesses. Christ is more than enough.
- I know that the God who made me will lead me to victory.
- By faith I receive from Christ all that I will ever need.

DECEMBER 15
ASK ABOUT YOUR PURPOSE

Philippians 3:10

[For my determined purpose is] that I may know Him [that I may progressively become more deeply and intimately acquainted with Him, perceiving and recognizing and understanding the wonders of His Person more strongly and more clearly], and that I may in that same way come to know the power out-flowing from His resurrection [which it exerts over believers], and that I may so share His sufferings as to be continually transformed [in spirit into His likeness even] to His death, [in the hope] (The Amplified Bible)

The apostle Paul wanted to fully understand Christ and the awesome power that flows from Him. Ultimately, Paul wanted to become like Christ. That was his determined purpose, and nothing was going to get in the way of it. That's the perspective we need to adopt. Yes, we need to be employed and contribute our skills and talents in the workplace. There's no question that the world needs our abilities. Certainly, we should enjoy the fruits of our labors when we make our contribution. But when job success becomes our primary goal, when earning an income is viewed as most important, we've become just like the world. That should not be. We have a higher, eternal, and divine purpose for our lives. We're to demonstrate the Kingdom of God. When we understand this, the rest will fall into place.

DECLARE THIS:

- I desire to know Christ and to become like Him.
- I receive revelation of the wonder of Christ and His resurrection power.
- I am transformed by the power of Christ who dwells in me now.

JANUARY 17
SEEK THE DIRECTION OF THE HOLY SPIRIT

Wouldn't the world love to have this? Look at all the things they do to find out about the future. Psychic hot lines, forecasters, analysts.... Imagine what they'd pay to get answers from The Source of all wisdom and knowledge. God offers this to us. Christ himself moved into each of us on the day of our new birth, ready to bring us word from the very throne room of God. We'll be told whatever we need to know. What a deal. God has given Jesus everything He has and Jesus is ready to share it. You won't want to miss this.

John 16:13-15

When the Spirit of truth comes, he will guide you into all truth. He will not speak on his own but will tell you what he has heard. He will tell you about the future. He will bring me glory by telling you whatever he receives from me. All that belongs to the Father is mine; this is why I said, 'The Spirit will tell you whatever he receives from me.'

DECLARE THIS:

- I am not confused. God's Word is my lamp and light.
- I trust the leading of the Spirit and the timing of God.
- I will hear from the Father and follow His lead.

DECEMBER 14
ASK ABOUT YOUR DESIGN

> **Ephesians 4:13-14**
>
> This will continue until we all come to such unity in our faith and knowledge of God's Son that we will be mature in the Lord, measuring up to the full and complete standard of Christ. Then we will no longer be immature like children. We won't be tossed and blown about by every wind of new teaching. We will not be influenced when people try to trick us with lies so clever they sound like the truth.

What would God like to see in us? Maybe He desires mature Kingdom citizens who aren't tossed to and fro all the time? The scripture shows us the way to achieve stability. We will defend ourselves against the emotional roller coaster of doubt and unbelief by "speaking the truth in love." The Word always brings us back to this foundation — we are designed in the image of God who is <u>Love</u>. Our power and authority depends upon our development into Christlikeness. Love is our nature and the source of our strength. So if we want to stay rooted and grounded in times of uncertainty we must allow His love in us to be released.

DECLARE THIS:

- I love with the very love of Christ Jesus.
- By faith I receive my perfection into the stature of Christ.
- I speak the truth in love as I grow up into Christ.

JANUARY 18
SEEK DIVINE CONNECTIONS

Ecclesiastes 4:9-12

Two people are better off than one, for they can help each other succeed. If one person falls, the other can reach out and help. But someone who falls alone is in real trouble. Likewise, two people lying close together can keep each other warm. But how can one be warm alone? A person standing alone can be attacked and defeated, but two can stand back-to-back and conquer. Three are even better, for a triple-braided cord is not easily broken.

A job search can really make you feel alone. Everybody goes off to work, school or some routine and there you are all alone. Or so it seems. But God never leaves you and He sends others. Here are some clues to help you recognize them. First, they are committed to your success—looking for leads and talking to others about you. Second, they help you when you fall, reminding you to ask for forgiveness and "let it go." Third, they "keep you warm" and connected to others. Some folks might avoid you while you're unemployed, but these people stand and fight with you. Connect with people like this and become the kind of person God can send to others.

DECLARE THIS:

- I am never alone.
- God has arranged divine connections for me in the body of Christ.
- I am committed to helping others succeed.

DECEMBER 13
ASK ABOUT YOUR GIFTS

1 Corinthians 1:4-7

I thank my God always concerning you for the grace of God which was given to you by Christ Jesus, that you were enriched in everything by Him in all utterance and all knowledge, even as the testimony of Christ was confirmed in you, so that you come short in no gift, eagerly waiting for the revelation of our Lord Jesus Christ (NKJV)

Don't you love that statement "you come short in no gift?" Whenever you're tempted to think that no one wants what you can do, or that your gifts aren't good enough, think again. By Christ Jesus we have been "enriched." God has given you more than enough. You don't lack anything you need. We're not just ordinary workers; we have the spirit of God empowering us from the inside out. Make no mistake — you have good gifts and the world needs what you have to offer. If you don't know what they are or how to activate them, get in touch with your "Manufacturer."

DECLARE THIS:

- I have gifts and they are good ones.
- By faith I receive insight about ways to use my gifts to bless others.
- All that I have I give back to God for His use and my prosperity.

JANUARY 19
SEEK HIDDEN TREASURES

Have you ever wondered why Jesus talked in parables? His disciples did, so they asked Him about it. He said He spoke in parables because He didn't intend for everyone to understand His teaching. We are privileged to receive knowledge that is hidden from others. So what's our part? We need to recognize when God is speaking to us and to watch for His hidden secrets all the time. We are being given insight into an invisible Kingdom and, make no mistake about it, it's the Kingdom that matters. When this world fades away, God's Kingdom will remain. So we need to know its secrets — for abundant life now and for all eternity.

Matthew 13:11

He replied, "You are permitted to understand the secrets of the Kingdom of Heaven, but others are not.

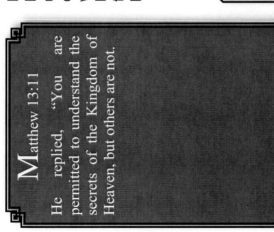

DECLARE THIS:

- I have been given the secrets of the Kingdom.
- I hear from God and I can know His will.
- God desires to fill me with understanding. By faith I receive it.

DECEMBER 12
ASK FOR FIRST THINGS FIRST

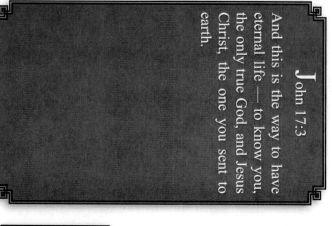

John 17:3
And this is the way to have eternal life — to know you, the only true God, and Jesus Christ, the one you sent to earth.

As we think about the most important things to pray for, this scripture points to a top priority. Ask to know Christ and to know the Father as He did. There is no better request to put before God every day of your job search. This is the foundation for everything! When we draw near to God, just to get to know Him personally, He will draw near to us. When He comes near, His love is so wonderful it will carry you through anything the day might hold in store. We're going to spend eternity with Jesus. We might as well get to know Him now.

DECLARE THIS:

- I know that I belong to God and that Christ has redeemed me from all sin.
- I accept eternal and abundant life, starting this very moment.
- By faith I receive a deep and personal relationship with the living Christ. I can know Him.

JANUARY 20
Seek To Stay Focused On Jesus

Nothing will bring a job seeker down faster or harder than thinking about the wrong things. Turn on a news story about unemployment rates and bam, the wind will go completely out of your sails! What does that tell you? Simply that you need to guard your thoughts. Unemployment rates do not concern you; negative reports do not apply to you. "You have been raised to a new life in Christ." No matter what is going on in the world, you are safe in the Kingdom of God. Fill your mind with His truth and your heart with His love. Don't let anything else in.

Colossians 3:1-2

Since you have been raised to new life with Christ, set your sights on the realities of heaven, where Christ sits in the place of honor at God's right hand. Think about the things of heaven, not the things of earth.

DECLARE THIS:

- I have set my sights on Jesus and Him only.
- I am becoming like Him because I imitate Him.
- My thoughts line up with His thoughts for I have the mind of Christ.

DECEMBER 11
ASK EXPECTING RESULTS

> Mark 10:29-30
>
> "Yes," Jesus replied, "and I assure you that everyone who has given up house or brothers or sisters or mother or father or children or property, for my sake and for the Good News, will receive now in return a hundred times as many houses, brothers, sisters, mothers, children, and property — along with persecution. And in the world to come that person will have eternal life.

Perhaps you know how good it feels to invest a dime and get back a dollar. That's a ten-fold return. Now look at what Jesus tells us to expect — a 100-fold return! He's not talking about a heavenly reward either, but a return "in this present age." Of course, we'll still experience the enemy's persecution, but who cares? When we know that we can expect a 100-fold return for whatever we give up in pursuit of Jesus and His Kingdom, what else matters? So now you know. Expect these results in your life, and receive the prosperity God has stored up for you.

DECLARE THIS:

- I believe that God is an extravagant rewarder of those that follow Him.
- By faith I receive the promised return on my Kingdom investments. I give freely and expect an abundant harvest.
- I do not give in order to get but I know I cannot outgive God!

JANUARY 21
KNOCK WITH BOLDNESS

This is a command, not a suggestion. No head hanging, shoulder drooping, foot dragging for you. No "I can't help feeling down; I'm only human." You are to face every moment of every day knowing that God is with you. He's in the car with you. He's on the phone with you. He's filling out applications with you. More than that His plans for you are awesome and His provision for you is limitless. Focus on His promises. Meditate on them, murmur them under your breath, and keep your eyes on them. Will you obey this command or shrug it off and keep struggling?

DECLARE THIS:

- I have the victory in every situation.
- I have no fear because I trust that God is working His perfect will in my life.
- My God is with me wherever I go so I cannot fail.

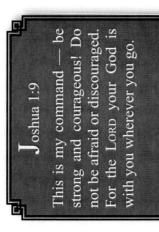

Joshua 1:9

This is my command — be strong and courageous! Do not be afraid or discouraged. For the LORD your God is with you wherever you go.

DECEMBER 10
CHOOSE YOUR BATTLE

> Revelation 12:11
> And they overcame him by the blood of the Lamb and by the word of their testimony, and they did not love their lives to the death. (NKJV)

The strategy for absolute victory every time is His blood and the words of our mouth. So our words become the deciding factor in our ability to overcome and experience victory. In a crisis, words can slip out before we know what we're saying. To guarantee that we will overcome with the word of our testimony we have to fill ourselves with love and Word of God. It's up to us to be sure we're equipped for battle with His Words. He's done the hard part -- now it's up to us to finish the job.

DECLARE THIS:

- I will overcome the condition of unemployment and walk victoriously into a great job.
- Jesus has already paid for my righteousness, my salvation, my forgiveness and my prosperity.
- By faith I apply the Blood of the Lamb and the Word of God to my problems knowing they will be resolved.

JANUARY 22
KNOCK WITH THANKSGIVING

We don't have to be thankful for all circumstances, just thankful in the midst of them. When situations are bad, God isn't the source or the cause. You can be assured He has something else in mind for us. What allows us to give thanks in those circumstances is the absolute confidence that God has already made a way out for us! Our solution is already on its way. Think about what God has promised and how you'll feel when the victory is yours. Now give thanks in all circumstances.

DECLARE THIS:

- I am grateful for my life and all the promise that it holds.
- God has already blessed me with so much that I can't help but thank Him.
- I know God will bring me through to victory.

1 Thessalonians 5:18
Be thankful in all circumstances, for this is God's will for you who belong to Christ Jesus.

DECEMBER 9
CHOOSE YOUR BEHAVIOR

> **John 15:7**
> If you abide in Me, and My words abide in you, you will ask what you desire, and it shall be done for you. (NKJV)

Have you ever puzzled over this verse knowing you've asked God for some desire and it never came to pass? It causes a lot of pain when job seekers ask for jobs and don't get them. But notice what has to be true if our desires are to come to pass. His words have to abide in us. Our desires have to match His desires. It's commonly known that people who live together and love each other tend to become more and more alike. It's the same with us as we dwell in Jesus. When our desires come from Him and our words match what He has said, we can count on them coming to pass. This is one more reason to seek the Kingdom and the King. Then our words will have power and our desires will be satisfied.

DECLARE THIS:

- I will to will the will of God. My desires and words match my King's.
- By faith I claim God's Word over all my circumstances.
- I willingly release my demands and invite God to fill me with His words and desires.

JANUARY 23
KNOCK WITH CONFIDENCE

We get to choose. We can decide to allow the Holy Spirit to give us power or we can choose to struggle, fail, and struggle some more. I think the best choice is rather obvious. The quality of life that God desires for us, can only be obtained by our habitually making the choice to listen to and obey the Spirit in us. Then, with that empowerment, we will put to death evil deeds and the limitations of our worldly nature. It's time to hit the streets in the strength of the Lord and in the confidence that a powerful, God-quality life is already working in us.

DECLARE THIS:

- I have the guarantee of eternal life and nothing can change that.
- The Holy Spirit is working to perfect me and He is faithful to complete that work.
- By faith I receive everything I need.

Romans 8:13

For if you live according to [the dictates of] the flesh, you will surely die. But if through the power of the [Holy] Spirit you are [habitually] putting to death (making extinct, deadening) the [evil] deeds prompted by the body, you shall [really and genuinely] live forever. (The Amplified Bible)

DECEMBER 8
CHOOSE YOUR TRAINING

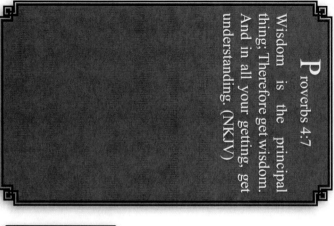

P roverbs 4:7

Wisdom is the principal thing; Therefore get wisdom. And in all your getting, get understanding. (NKJV)

We're in the process of being trained for Kingdom service. Before we go back into a job in the workplace, God wants us to learn a few things about Kingdom life. This scripture is pointing to a top priority for our learning, get Wisdom and understanding. Not worldly understanding or knowledge, but rather the Mind of God Himself. We are to think just like Him, talk just like Him and act just like Him. We're His apprentices and this is our top-priority "search" objective.

DECLARE THIS:

- I seek the wisdom of God and a clear understanding of His ways.
- I believe that God will freely give me wisdom when I ask and by faith I receive it.
- The wisdom of God is my light. He makes my path clear to me.

JANUARY 24
KNOCK AND BRING GIFTS

You are the messenger with good news. Jesus is your Lord and Savior. You have abundant life, wisdom, peace and blessings that are priceless and without number. Imagine what a difference it would make if you demonstrated that message everywhere you went. People expect job seekers to be worried, desperate and down-trodden. What would happen if you showed up radiating the peace of God? Conduct a little test for one week. Walk around like you really have been given good news. See if people ask why you're so happy. When you become a messenger of the gospel people will look forward to your coming and you'll probably be invited back!

> Isaiah 52:7
>
> How beautiful on the mountains are the feet of the messenger who brings good news, the good news of peace and salvation, the news that the God of Israel reigns!

DECLARE THIS:

- I bring life, and light, and truth with me.
- I know the good news of Christ and my life reflects it.
- I am welcomed wherever I go because I bring peace and good news.

DECEMBER 7
CHOOSE YOUR PAY

Deuteronomy 8:18

Remember the LORD your God. He is the one who gives you power to be successful, in order to fulfill the covenant he confirmed to your ancestors with an oath.

There's another translation of this scripture that says God gives us the power to get wealth. We don't realize it's His doing whenever prosperity comes. Like healing, we tend to think wealth and success are only God's doing when they come instantly and miraculously like some lottery jackpot. We forget that it is God who gave us bodies naturally designed to heal and return to wholeness time and time again. He's the One who gives ideas for inventions and guidance for business. He leads us to places where we will prosper. God has faithfully bestowed this wealth-gaining power throughout history. Look at Abraham, Isaac, Jacob, Job, Solomon, David and Joseph. What He has done for one He will do for you because He never changes. Receive your power to succeed.

DECLARE THIS:

- I am equipped to prosper because God has promised it and He is faithful.
- I receive the blessing of Abraham purchased for me by Christ Jesus.
- I have what it takes to succeed because I have the spirit of the living God within me.

JANUARY 25
KNOCK AND EXERCISE YOUR FAITH

What are we going to do with this scripture? Jesus said that anyone who believes in Him will do the same works as He did. We have His love inside us, His mind, His spirit… we're completely equipped. We are on a path to greatness. But we have to absolutely believe that Jesus is who He says He is and that we are who He says we are. We have to decide to believe. Then, by faith, we can go into jobs that are too big and work that is too challenging and accomplish great things for the Kingdom. We can do it. Jesus said so!

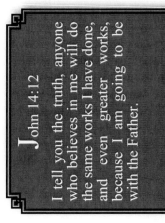

John 14:12

I tell you the truth, anyone who believes in me will do the same works I have done, and even greater works, because I am going to be with the Father.

DECLARE THIS:

- I am on my way to my God-ordained destiny.
- My faith grows and deepens with time and patience.
- I have what it takes to do great works for the Kingdom of God because God is with me and Christ is in me.

DECEMBER 6
CHOOSE YOUR WORK

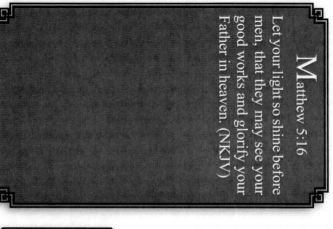

M atthew 5:16

Let your light so shine before men, that they may see your good works and glorify your Father in heaven. (NKJV)

This scripture deserves another look. It reveals the real purpose behind our Kingdom assignments. We are here to bring God glory, not because He needs it, but because He alone deserves it. God, who is perfect Love, has changed our lives and showered us with blessing. He has given us the strategies to turn unemployment into a season of prosperity. He has gone before us to ensure our victory and has stationed angels around us to keep us safe. Who besides our God loves us so perfectly? The more we really understand this God, this Love, the more we will be lit up from the inside out. The world won't be able to miss it! Take that with you into the workplace!

DECLARE THIS:

- I am filled with the love and light of God.
- The good works I do are by the grace of God and I give Him all the glory.
- By faith I accept the direction of the Lord to do the works He has planned just for me.

JANUARY 26

1 Corinthians 10:31

So whether you eat or drink, or whatever you do, do it all for the glory of God.

Do you think you're off the hook because you're unemployed or in a temporary job that "doesn't count?" Well, this word says that even when we're eating or drinking we're supposed bring God glory, so I'd say it's a full time assignment. But that raises some interesting questions. How can we bring God glory when we're unemployed? What can we do to bring our families closer to God when we're not going off to work each day? If you don't know the answer to these questions, ask God. He already has something in mind, I promise.

DECLARE THIS:

- I am an ambassador for Christ and I know the world is watching me.
- I glorify God with my every word and action. I am never "off duty."
- Christ in me brings hope to a dark and frightened world.

DECEMBER 5
CHOOSE YOUR BENEFITS

Psalm 128:1-2

Blessed is every one who fears the LORD, Who walks in His ways. When you eat the labor of your hands, You shall be happy, and it shall be well with you. (NKJV)

Can you see the promises of God here? You're going to get a GREAT job! If you were headed to a lower salary, poor work hours or a terrible commute, you couldn't possibly experience the promise that "it shall be well with you?" So read this scripture again and notice every part. You will eat the labor of your hands. That means you will be employed. What's more, "you shall be happy and it shall be well with you." Now you know how your story turns out. So fear the Lord. Stand in awe and wonder at His great and perfect love for you. Then walk in His ways and behave like a citizen of His Kingdom. Your great job awaits you!

DECLARE THIS:

- I am happy because I know how everything turns out. I land a great job!
- By faith I put my trust in God and walk in the way of Love.
- I expect to enjoy my labor and to be well satisfied.

JANUARY 27
KNOCK AND OVERCOME

This is an intriguing idea, isn't it? Could it really mean that the Lord commits Himself to make some things happen; that our job search isn't all up to us? Absolutely! I find that very comforting. But we have to know what He has said He'll do. He promises to give us the right words to say, to make a way where there is none, and protect us from harm. Search for His promises and expect Him to make things happen. We can count on it. That's good news, if I ever heard any.

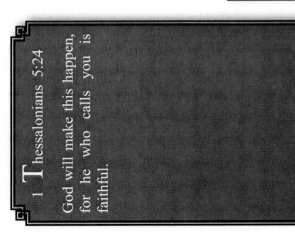

1 Thessalonians 5:24

God will make this happen, for he who calls you is faithful.

DECLARE THIS:

- I will always overcome because God brings the victory.
- I know God is willing and able to care for me.
- My trust is in the Lord and in the power and authority of His name.

DECEMBER 4
CHOOSE YOUR BOSS

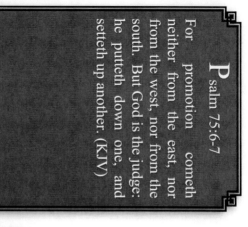

Psalm 75:6-7

For promotion cometh neither from the east, nor from the west, nor from the south. But God is the judge: he putteth down one, and setteth up another. (KJV)

There is no need to resent an earthly boss for letting you go, or worry about someone else being selected for the job you want. God is the one who places you in assignments and promotes you. He decides when you're ready. This is true when you are in the workforce and also when you're finding your re-entry point. Our mission is to be excellent in His sight. Serve each of your employers as if they were Christ Himself. Approach every prospective employer as God's highly trusted servant sent to bring His blessing. Then watch as your promotions come.

DECLARE THIS:

- I know my promotion is in the hands of God who loves me perfectly.
- By faith I accept the perfect timing of God and trust His plans for me.
- I am open to God's assignment and expect promotion wherever I go.

JANUARY 28
Knock And Faint Not!

> ## 1 Peter 5:7
> Give all your worries and cares to God, for he cares about you.

This just doesn't seem right to many of us. How can we be adults and not worry? We need to "worry things in for a landing" if we really want them to happen, don't we? When we get anxious about the future, we excuse ourselves saying "After all, I'm only human." But that's not how God sees it. His Word is clear — give your concerns to Him and fear not. God views worry, fear and anxiety as a vote of "no confidence" in His Word. Either you believe He cares for you and He is able to handle everything that concerns you or you don't. Which is it? I think the right answer is pretty obvious. Give God all your cares and get on with other things.

DECLARE THIS:

- I have no cares. I have a good and faithful Shepherd to watch over me.
- God will handle perfectly everything that concerns me.
- I rise up and lie down in peace and without the burden of care.

DECEMBER 3
CHOOSE YOUR FUTURE

You might have been a great worker but you still lost your job. It hurts when you feel unappreciated or devalued, doesn't it? Well, isn't that what the disciples experienced? Imagine going from town to town to proclaim the best news ever — "the Kingdom of God is near" and it's available to everyone. And many would not receive their message. You know the feeling, don't you? Most likely you're having a hard time getting people to see your worth, understand your value, or receive what you have to offer. So take the advice offered here. Just wipe the job search dust from your feet and move on. You're on a mission for God. He has something wonderful in mind for you. Keep your attention on that.

Luke 10:9-11

Heal the sick, and tell them, 'The Kingdom of God is near you now.' But if a town refuses to welcome you, go out into its streets and say, 'We wipe even the dust of your town from our feet to show that we have abandoned you to your fate. And know this — the Kingdom of God is near!'

DECLARE THIS:

- I work for God and He has something great in mind for me.
- By faith I trust in the leading of the Holy Spirit and I release the past.
- I bless every place that I have worked and I look forward to being a blessing in my next job.

JANUARY 29
Knock And Be Encouraged

Take heart and be encouraged. You are eternally connected to Jesus Christ and nothing can change that. You have been adopted into the royal household of God Almighty and there is an inheritance there with your name on it! God chose you, before you ever set foot on earth, and He is working everything out according to the plan He has for you. That's not all. Jeremiah 29:11 says His plan is a good one and you're going to like it. So relax, God's got you and He'll never let you go. Just keep on — knocking on doors, doing the good works He gives you to do, and loving others. The rest is up to Him and He's faithful to do what He has promised.

Ephesians 1:9-11

God has now revealed to us His mysterious plan regarding Christ, a plan to fulfill His own good pleasure. And this is the plan: At the right time he will bring everything together under the authority of Christ — everything in heaven and on earth. Furthermore, because we are united with Christ, we have received an inheritance from God, for he chose us in advance, and he makes everything work out according to His plan.

DECLARE THIS:

- I have peace and joy because I know how everything turns out.
- I am so glad that I am on the winning side and my victory is guaranteed in Christ.
- By faith, I receive my inheritance from Christ now, in this life.

DECEMBER 2
CHOOSE YOUR THOUGHTS

D euteronomy 30:19

"Today I have given you the choice between life and death, between blessings and curses. Now I call on heaven and earth to witness the choice you make. Oh, that you would choose life, so that you and your descendants might live!"

Isn't it amazing that God has to suggest to us which choice to make? Who wouldn't choose life? But when we have to decide between God's way of responding in love or the more common way of looking out for ourselves and responding in anger, do we always choose life? Consider the choice we face as job seekers. Ask yourself, am I living my life as God's royal heir and an ambassador for Christ? Or am I behaving like a beggar, hoping someone will have pity on me and give me any old job before I lose everything? It's up to each of us to choose life and stand on the Word until we see it come to pass. God's blessing isn't ours automatically — we have to choose it with every thought, every action and every word, every day.

DECLARE THIS:

- I choose life. The blessing of Abraham is manifesting in my life.
- My choice brings blessing to my children and I receive that gift by faith.
- I declare that I am a child of God and Jesus is my King and Master.

JANUARY 30
Knock And Keep Knocking

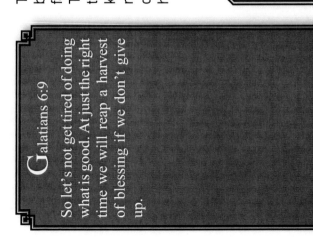

Galatians 6:9

So let's not get tired of doing what is good. At just the right time we will reap a harvest of blessing if we don't give up.

This is a perfect "job search scripture"! It's a guarantee that we will reap a harvest of blessing right when we need it. That's exactly what we've been praying for. The deciding factor is "if we don't give up." It's so easy to run out of ideas and contacts and energy. Then what? Find a way to "seed" your talents somewhere. Where can you volunteer your time and talents? Where can you use your skills and talents to make a difference for the kingdom? Don't say you don't have time. You can't afford not to because there can be no harvest where there has been no planting. Ask God where you can make a kingdom difference. Then watch for God to open up new opportunities for you and help you to harvest the assignment he has in mind for you.

DECLARE THIS:

- I will never quit. By faith I claim my harvest.
- I trust in God's word about seed time and harvest. I give liberally and I reap bountifully.
- I have good seed in the ground and I plant continuously.

DECEMBER 1
CHOOSE YOUR KINGDOM

Acts 17:26-28

"The God who made the world and everything in it, this Master of sky and land, doesn't live in custom-made shrines or need the human race to run errands for him, as if he couldn't take care of himself. He makes the creatures; the creatures don't make him... He doesn't play hide-and-seek with us. He's not remote; he's near. We live and move in him, can't get away from him! (Message)

Consider that first line of scripture. What is your picture of "the God who made the world and everything in it?" Do you understand the size and power of our God? Do you think that any of your needs could possibly be too big for Him to handle? He makes people, for goodness sake. If He can do that and then care for every one of us without ceasing, we may safely assume that He is not confounded by our problems. Your job loss did not catch Him unaware and it poses no great challenge for Him. It's time to stop telling God how big your problems are and start telling your problems how big your God is. He's here and He's ready to get involved in your situation. Just remember.... He's the Creator and He the best One to decide how things should go. Let Him!

DECLARE THIS:

- I trust my Creator with my life.
- I know that God is ever near me and I feel His presence.
- My heart is to seek and follow God, who is all powerful, all sufficient and perfect Love.

JANUARY 31
KNOCK AND BE AT PEACE

The Lord has gifts in mind for believers who are going through the experience of unemployment and job search. He wants to permanently change your life for the better. One of His key objectives is to give His children continuous and unshakable peace. Not just peace during the time of unemployment but for the rest of our lives. If we can experience His peace during a job search when everything looks shaky and out of control, it is not hard to imagine that we will be able to stay in peace for the rest of our lives, right? So where will peace like this come from? How can we experience peace in these uncertain and chaotic times? His Word says that we have to listen to Him. We have to hear His word and pay attention to only what He tells us. Isn't peace worth the effort to do that?

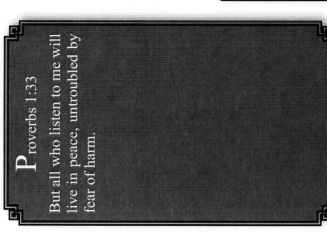

DECLARE THIS:

- I have unshakable peace.
- I listen to God because He is my shepherd and my Lord.
- I will not be harmed no matter what. I am safe and at peace.

Proverbs 1:33

But all who listen to me will live in peace, untroubled by fear of harm.

DECEMBER

GOOD NEWS

FEBRUARY

GOOD NEWS

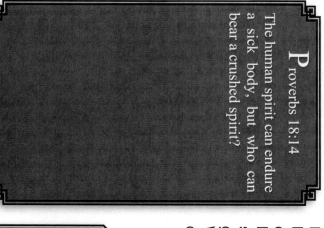

Proverbs 18:14
The human spirit can endure a sick body, but who can bear a crushed spirit?

No one likes to be sick, but most of us would prefer it to being crushed, depressed and heartbroken. The enemy knows this. That's why he keeps the pressure directed against our thoughts. The battlefield really is in the mind, and the enemy's objective is to crush us by using our own thoughts against us. The good news is that we can prevent a crushed spirit. We can keep the enemy from getting close to our hearts. But we cannot let our guard down for a minute. That's why the Word says to guard our hearts with all diligence. We cannot be crushed when our hearts are filled with the Word and our minds are focused on God's promises. Keep your guard up!

DECLARE THIS:

- I am strong in the Lord and in the power of His might.
- By faith I guard my spirit, soul and body with the Word of God.
- My defense is sure. I will not be crushed, depressed or in despair, ever!

FEBRUARY 1
CHOOSE YOUR KINGDOM

Notice the wording in this scripture. We are "permitted to understand," not we are "given understanding." That suggests that there is effort involved. Whenever we are given permission it simply means that the door has been unlocked for us. It's up to us to make the investment in reading the Word, after we have asked for the Holy Spirit's assistance so that we can access the secrets that have been given to us. This is a key concept – if you don't really seek to learn and understand the way of the Kingdom, you will struggle to find meaning in it for you.

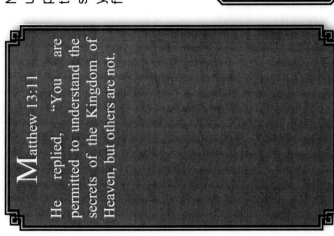

Matthew 13:11

He replied, "You are permitted to understand the secrets of the Kingdom of Heaven, but others are not.

DECLARE THIS:

- By faith I receive understanding of the word whenever I read it.
- I expect to understand secrets from God that the world does not know.
- I am God's child, a citizen of the Kingdom, and God's ways are not a mystery to me.

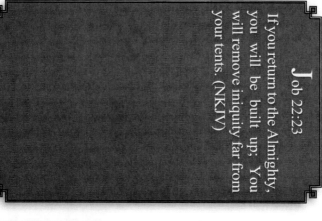

NOVEMBER 29
KNOCK AND BE ENCOURAGED

Job 22:23
If you return to the Almighty, you will be built up; You will remove iniquity far from your tents. (NKJV)

When we turn to focus all our attention and thoughts on the Lord two amazing things happen. We get built up and our sinful habits are driven out of us. The darkness of depression and discouragement must yield to the light of God. Sin cannot stay where Jesus dwells so your bad habits and shortcomings have to flee. A beautiful song reminds us, "Turn your eyes upon Jesus. Look full in His wonderful face. And the things of this life will grow strangely dim in the light of His glory and grace." You have no shortcomings that can prevent you from getting a job when God is in charge. Let Jesus build you up as you lean on Him. No matter what you're struggling with, if you follow where the Good Shepherd leads He'll keep you in green pastures. Cast your cares on Him and feel the relief.

DECLARE THIS:

- I am a child of God and He builds me up. I am righteous in Christ.
- By faith I receive strength and victory in my job search and my life because I dwell in God and He in me.
- The Lord is my strength and my confidence; I will not be moved.

FEBRUARY 2
CHOOSE YOUR THOUGHTS

What does the world say about the job search process? How do people think about the experience of unemployment? You don't have to look far to find grim predictions and bad news. But that is not the truth for believers. There are circumstances in the world that are tragic but Christ has overcome the world! He is not affected by unemployment, layoffs or economic bad news of any kind. His ability to provide for us is not limited to any company's payroll department. We have been set free from this world's economic system. When we buy into all the negative messages about employment we are playing by the rules of the world. Rather, let's find out what God promises and play by His rules. Fill your heart and mind with the "new rules of the game."

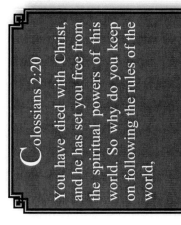

Colossians 2:20

You have died with Christ, and he has set you free from the spiritual powers of this world. So why do you keep on following the rules of the world,

DECLARE THIS:

- I am so glad that I am no longer a citizen of this world.
- I belong to God's economy and there is no lack in Him.
- I obey the Law of Love and the blessing is active in every part of my life.

Psalm 34:17-18

When the righteous cry for help, the Lord hears, and delivers them out of all their distress and troubles. The Lord is close to those who are of a broken heart and saves such as are crushed with sorrow for sin and are humbly and thoroughly penitent. (The Amplified Bible)

This is the truth about God. David knew it but unfortunately many of us do not. God hurts when we hurt and He saves us when we acknowledge our need for Him. We prevent God from doing this if we don't believe the Word or we don't believe we're righteous. What do you believe today? Do you know that God desires to deliver you; that He is almighty, all-powerful and well able to handle all your challenges? Do you believe you are righteous? If not, then you must believe that that the sacrifice of Jesus was not good enough. It's this simple. We are righteous because Jesus is righteous and we are in Him. God delivers the righteous, therefore God delivers us. If you are in distress today, cry out and expect a response from the God who loves you perfectly. That's His promise and He does not lie.

DECLARE THIS:

- I am righteous in Christ and I believe God hears my cries and rescues me.
- By faith I receive my right standing with God.
- I thank God that He cares for me, saves me, heals me, loves me and delivers me from evil.

FEBRUARY 3
CHOOSE YOUR FUTURE

Let's look at yesterday's scripture again. How much do you find yourself dwelling on the past? Are you reliving the things you did or said and wishing that you had behaved differently? If you are spending your thought time like this stop it! The enemy uses the strategy of guilt, shame and condemnation to keep us stuck. We cannot move into our God-designed destiny if we're facing backwards. It's like tying yourself to a tree in your back yard and then wondering why you can't get to the picnic on the front lawn. So don't look back. You are in God's Kingdom where there is no lack and where you are blessed because Christ made you His heir! If you buy into the world's view and act as if it's true, you'll go nowhere. Make the Kingdom your home and keep your focus on the future.

Colossians 2:20

Therefore, if you died with Christ from the basic principles of the world, why, as though living in the world, do you subject yourselves to regulations —— (NKJV)

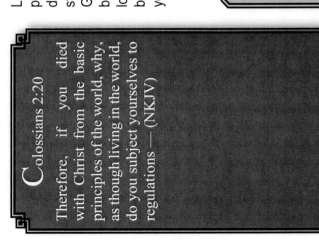

DECLARE THIS:

- The bad news of the world does not apply to me.
- I live by Kingdom rules as set out in the Word of God.
- I know the promises God has made to me and by faith I receive every one!

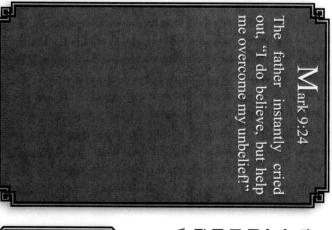

Mark 9:24

The father instantly cried out, "I do believe, but help me overcome my unbelief!"

"Lord, I believe but help me overcome my unbelief!" Isn't it great that this was recorded for all of us to see? Apparently there is no requirement that we be perfect at believing. Jesus pulled Peter out of the water when he stepped out into the waves and then wavered. Jesus was there when Jairus heard the report that his daughter had died and He reminded him, "Fear not. Believe only." Jesus is saying the exact same thing to us, "Fear not! Believe only." He knows we too will experience moments that challenge our faith. Don't let the enemy tell you that you're failing to receive God's promises because your belief isn't perfect enough. Just cast fear far away from you and decide again to believe. Do it whenever you waver and keep your focus on Him. He'll get us the rest of the way there.

DECLARE THIS:

- I believe that God is good and He will help me when I waver.
- By faith I receive the empowerment of the Holy Spirit to overcome thoughts of fear, doubt and unbelief.
- I thank God that Jesus dwells in me.

FEBRUARY 4
Choose Your Boss

Do you wonder why God didn't protect you from this experience of unemployment? It could be because He doesn't think you're "jobless." In God's mind, you work for Him. After all, He is your provider and He has plans for you to accomplish. He doesn't need a payroll department to meet your needs either. Now is the time to discover just how wonderful, powerful and awesome He is. He never takes His eyes off you and He won't let you stumble. He never sleeps. He never takes a break from caring for you. Do you really know the God that you belong to? Make time to get to know Him — allow the opportunity for just the two of you to get together and talk.

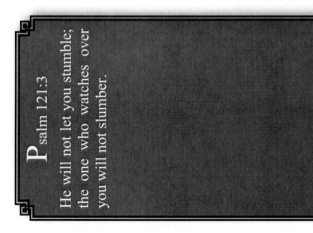

DECLARE THIS:

- My God cares deeply for me and I am glad that I work for Him.
- By faith I accept every blessing God has for me in this time and season.
- I believe that God wants me to really know Him and I am open to a deep personal relationship with Him.

Psalm 121:3

He will not let you stumble; the one who watches over you will not slumber.

NOVEMBER 26
KNOCK AND WITNESS FOR THE KINGDOM

P salm 17:3

You have tested my thoughts and examined my heart in the night. You have scrutinized me and found nothing wrong. I am determined not to sin in what I say.

It's not enough to "try" to watch what comes out of our mouths. We think we'll automatically speak the truth of God when a challenge comes, but without preparation, we're likely to slip up. We can become better witnesses with these three steps. First, ask for God's conviction when your thoughts stray from His thoughts. Next, ask Jesus to come into your heart and find and heal what may be hidden there. Then carefully guard your thoughts and heart to keep them clear. Finally, make a determination not to sin with the words of your mouth. Purpose to keep all your words the words befitting a child of the King.

DECLARE THIS:

- I am determined not to sin in what I say.
- By faith I receive the ability to control my tongue and to speak the Word only.
- I trust in the healing work of Jesus. By faith I receive the complete healing of my heart and the renewing of my mind.

FEBRUARY 5
CHOOSE YOUR BENEFITS

God understands that times get tough and we get weary. God is aware that we cannot see into the future as He can, and that uncertainty can cause us distress. He also knows that our enemy is relentless in his attempts to destroy us. So not only does God protect and defend us, He also shows His amazing love with His comfort. The promise is not that we will be physically comfortable, but He does provide spiritual comfort to protect us when the challenge is great. We don't have to wait until the battle is over either. Go ahead, ask for comfort right in the middle of the trial… then sit still. Allow Him to minister this amazing gift to you. It is a gift of peace the world does not have. Consider it just one more benefit from an employer who loves us with a perfect and unfailing love.

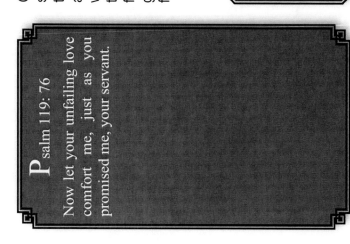

DECLARE THIS:

- I ask for comfort whenever I need it and God is faithful to provide it.
- By faith I receive comfort and peace in the face of unsettling and difficult circumstances.
- I can be comforted even when I am not comfortable!

P salm 119: 76
Now let your unfailing love comfort me, just as you promised me, your servant.

NOVEMBER 25
KNOCK AND EXERCISE YOUR FAITH

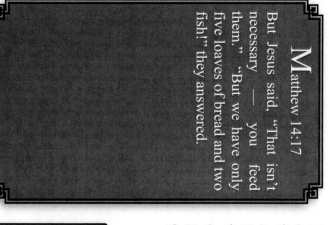

M atthew 14:17

But Jesus said, "That isn't necessary — you feed them." "But we have only five loaves of bread and two fish!" they answered.

Do you argue with God's Word when faced with facts and circumstances that seem to dispute it? The disciples looked at a couple of fish and some loaves of bread and called their situation impossible. That's just like us when we look at the little amount in our bank accounts and all those bills on the table. But Jesus showed the disciples that what they had in their hands was all they needed. He blessed what they had and it became more than enough. We need to declare "In the name of Jesus I bless my current resources and command them to stretch and multiply to meet all my needs." Then we too can expect provision, revelation and miracles. Stand in faith to see what God can do with what you give Him.

DECLARE THIS:

- My confidence is in the Word of God and the work of Jesus.
- By faith I receive all that I need and more because God has promised it.
- I send forth my faith to claim the provision God has for me right now.

FEBRUARY 6
CHOOSE YOUR WORK

Your next job will no doubt come with a job description. God's assignments come with a job description too. Jesus told us that our job is to love as He loved no matter what work we go into. A little-known truth about God's assignment is that we are the most blessed ones when we do it well. As we commit ourselves to love, and to become like Christ, we magnify God's blessing in our own lives. We attract every good thing. We increase in power and authority and we live in peace and joy. Accept the assignment to love, and then experience the overwhelming abundant life that flows out of God's love for us. Feel free to ask your trainer, the Holy Spirit, if you need any help.

---

1 Corinthians 13:4-7

Love is patient and kind. Love is not jealous or boastful or proud or rude. It does not demand its own way. It is not irritable, and it keeps no record of being wronged. It does not rejoice about injustice but rejoices whenever the truth wins out. Love never gives up, never loses faith, is always hopeful, and endures through every circumstance.

DECLARE THIS:

- I love because God first loved me. I am filled with His love.
- By faith I receive the power to love as Christ loved.
- I know that perfect love releases God's blessing in my life and casts out every fear.

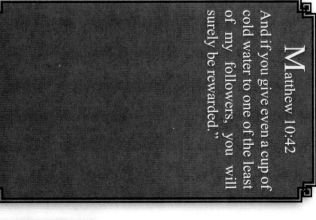

Matthew 10:42

And if you give even a cup of cold water to one of the least of my followers, you will surely be rewarded."

This is such a great scripture to reveal God's view about our giving. It makes the point that we are never unable to give something. Here it's a cup of cold water. For us it might be an extra shirt in the closet. Perhaps we could give an hour or two of house or yard work for an elderly neighbor. We always have something to give. God will even direct us to the ones to whom He wants us to give. God ends this instruction by saying "you will surely be rewarded" when obeying the command to give. Notice that it's a sure reward. So don't stop seeking opportunities to give. Open up the abundant flow in your life by pouring out to others. That's what primes the pump.

DECLARE THIS:

- I am a giver. I love to follow the command of Jesus to feed His sheep.
- I know that God is a rewarder and He will do what He says in His Word.
- I thank God that I am never without something to give!

FEBRUARY 7
CHOOSE YOUR PAY

Do you really understand that you belong to Christ? Most of us know that we were forgiven, redeemed and given eternal life when we accepted Christ. But we may not have thought much about the fact that we also made Him the Lord and Master of our lives. He has the final say about our lives now. Here's the nearly-too-good-to-be-true part. He paid for us with His life, so He could treat us as His joint heirs. We can expect to live as royalty in this life. It's important that we fully comprehend this. We now work for the Lord. God is our source and His greatest desire is to richly bless us. You'll never find a job that will pay you like He can!

DECLARE THIS:

- God has adopted me and He alone is my source and provider.
- By faith I receive the blessing of Abraham and I prosper in all that I do.
- I work for the Lord and walk in His ways so that He is free to bless me fully.

Galatians 3:29

And now that you belong to Christ, you are the true children of Abraham. You are his heirs, and God's promise to Abraham belongs to you.

NOVEMBER 23
KNOCK WITH CONFIDENCE

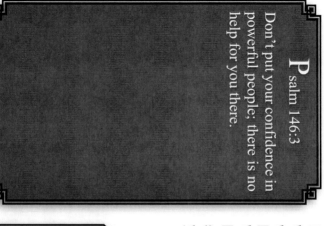

Psalm 146:3

Don't put your confidence in powerful people; there is no help for you there.

It's easy to say we have confidence in God but so very hard to walk that out. One minute we're walking in faith and next moment we're sure we need some manager to hire us and we have to have some specific job or else! We may start out believing that God will provide but panic when we find out that the support we expected from our church is not available. We must stop looking for safety nets. Let's acknowledge that we may not be able to see how He will sustain us but our lack of vision doesn't limit His abilities. Do what this verse says; keep all your confidence in God. People are not and will never be your source or your supply. God is!

DECLARE THIS:

- I place my confidence in God alone.
- By faith I receive all that I can think or imagine through Christ.
- God has already done all that I need and I receive it in faith.

King David understood the real value of a life that follows God's plan, and so should we. The covenant we've been given is even better than David's. We've been given a trainer — the Holy Spirit — Who now dwells within us to teach, guide and empower us. As we follow the path that God has prepared for us we will walk right into our happiness. If we leave that path, we leave our happiness as well. David says something to his trainer in this verse that we might want to say to ours... "Make me walk along God's path. Don't let me leave it for any reason." If we do this, the Holy Spirit will make sure we stay where our happiness can be found.

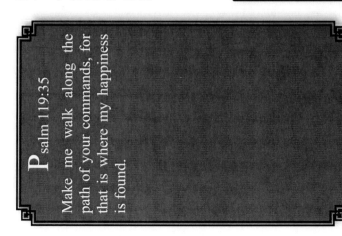

Psalm 119:35

Make me walk along the path of your commands, for that is where my happiness is found.

DECLARE THIS:

- I know that my happiness is found when I walk in the ways of the Lord.
- By faith I receive the ability to hear God's instructions and the power to obey them.
- I invite the Holy Spirit to rule and reign in my life.

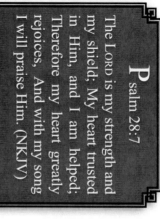

Psalm 28:7

The LORD is my strength and my shield; My heart trusted in Him, and I am helped; Therefore my heart greatly rejoices, And with my song I will praise Him. (NKJV)

If we truly believe that God is behind the scenes, working every moment to give us victory, peace and prosperity, wouldn't we praise Him? If we are fully persuaded that Jesus Christ freed us from our sins forever and guaranteed our victory in this life, wouldn't we be constantly rejoicing? We claim to believe all these things. Now the question is, do our actions line up with what we say we believe? The truth is that the Lord really is ready to help us every day of the job search. He has an excellent conclusion planned for each of us. So let's start now to thank Him and get a head start on the worship that He is due.

DECLARE THIS:

- I know how everything turns out and I thank God now for my new job.
- By faith I receive God's help, strength and protection. All my needs are met in Christ Jesus.
- I rejoice because I serve the God who is good and who loves me perfectly.

FEBRUARY 9
CHOOSE YOUR BEHAVIOR

Consider the job search instructions available to job seekers. There are directions for finding unadvertised positions in the workplace, tactics for contacting people directly, and methods for overcoming objections. Unfortunately very few job seekers ever follow those instructions. The same is true spiritually. Someone once said "Christianity hasn't been tried and found wanting. It has been found difficult and not tried." Our instructions are clear — "Seek the Kingdom." Study, read, meditate on and learn the Word. Speak only the Word. Guard your heart and mind from anything else. Why? Simple — if we listen to the instructions and do what we are taught, we prosper. It's time for all of us to become "doers of the Word" and put God's instructions to good use!

DECLARE THIS:

- I am open to instruction and committed to being the best I can be.
- By faith I practice the best job search practices of the world and follow the guidance of the Holy Spirit to make me more and more excellent.
- I am learning and growing continuously.

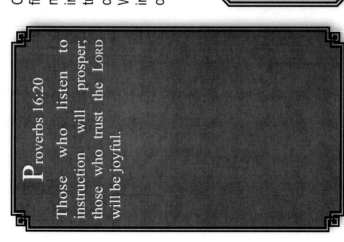

Proverbs 16:20

Those who listen to instruction will prosper; those who trust the LORD will be joyful.

NOVEMBER 21
KNOCK WITH BOLDNESS

1 John 4:17

Love has been perfected among us in this: that we may have boldness in the day of judgment; because as He is, so are we in this world. (NKJV)

Why do we need boldness? Because as Christ is, so are we right now in this world and we're supposed to act like it. No one can judge us to be overqualified, under-qualified, too old, too uneducated, or lacking in any way. God has judged us and declared us blessed. Let that work in your spirit until boldness and confidence rises up in you! Know that He has a place and a purpose that only you can fulfill. Jesus dwells in us to release perfect love through us into the world. Go out today knowing that He is working through you to accomplish something marvelous and eternal. Keep your eyes on Jesus as your role model and your confidence in the Creator of all who made you.

DECLARE THIS:

- I am a creation of God and I am designed for greatness.
- By faith I receive my identity in Christ and boldness to accomplish great things in His name.
- I will not believe what the world says about me. I will believe the report of the Lord

FEBRUARY 10
CHOOSE YOUR BATTLE

Most of the enemy's best strongholds are right between our ears! When our minds are filled with human reasoning, false beliefs, and arguments against the Word of faith, we need to clean house. It's the enemy's dirty tactic to plant lies in our minds, but if he's effective in doing so he won't have to spend any more energy trying to defeat us. We'll take ourselves out of the game by worrying, scheming, fretting and striving. So recognize his tactics and knock down the strongholds. The Word of God in your mouth and the empowerment of the Holy Spirit are all that you'll need.

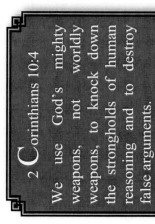

2 Corinthians 10:4

We use God's mighty weapons, not worldly weapons, to knock down the strongholds of human reasoning and to destroy false arguments.

DECLARE THIS:

- I will not help the enemy to defeat me with my own wrong thinking.
- By faith I receive God's revelation light to show me the errors in my thinking and the false beliefs I have been holding.
- My mind is renewed by the Word and my life is transformed.

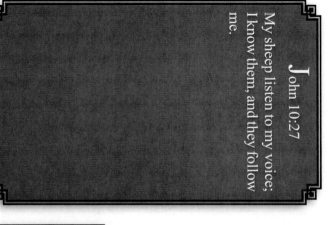

John 10:27
My sheep listen to my voice;
I know them, and they follow
me.

Many job seekers complain that they can't hear from God, that He doesn't talk to them. Really the problem is that they never get quiet enough to listen. Have you noticed that LISTEN is an anagram of SILENT? Too often we use all our prayer time making our requests and then expect revelation knowledge and insight in the last few minutes. It's kind of like being in a thirty minute interview and then being asked, with only thirty seconds of time left, "Do you have any questions?" If we could grasp how much richer our lives would be if we stopped to listen to our shepherd, we'd get really quiet every day to make sure not to miss anything.

DECLARE THIS:

- I am intent on hearing from the Lord.
- By faith I receive the ability to recognize the voice of God when He speaks to me.
- I trust that Jesus is my shepherd and that He will always take care of me.

FEBRUARY 11
ASK EXPECTING RESULTS

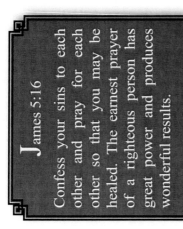

James 5:16

Confess your sins to each other and pray for each other so that you may be healed. The earnest prayer of a righteous person has great power and produces wonderful results.

The earnest prayer of a righteous person produces wonderful results... not sometimes, but all the time. Do you honestly expect to see results every time you pray? When you don't see results, do you just let it go or do you get on your face before the Lord to find out why not? We've been made righteous in Christ, so the issue can't be our righteousness. Or can it? If we're praying and thinking we have to be righteous through our own doing there will be no power in our prayers. We must fully comprehend that we stand in Christ's righteousness. If we aren't seeing results we have to examine ourselves to find out why not. So start with this — expect results. And when they're not there, don't ask God why He didn't answer; ask "Where have I missed it, Lord?"

DECLARE THIS:

- I know my prayers have great power because I have the righteousness of Christ backing them up.
- By faith I believe that God answers prayers when we follow His rules.
- I trust the Holy Spirit to teach me how to pray in a way that consistently gets results.

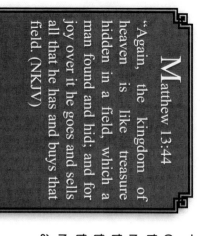

Matthew 13:44

"Again, the kingdom of heaven is like treasure hidden in a field, which a man found and hid; and for joy over it he goes and sells all that he has and buys that field. (NKJV)

The Kingdom of God is indeed a hidden treasure. When He was with them, Jesus told his disciples that the Kingdom was there in their midst but they did not understand because they didn't see any kingdom. The government He was talking about was invisible to the natural eye, but very real. We cannot see the Kingdom of God, yet we are citizens in that Kingdom right now. We cannot see our King, but we can have complete confidence that He is real. In fact, as we comprehend this revelation we will realize that this hidden treasure is truly worth all that we have to give. As we go about our job search, let's remember that we already hold the greatest position we'll ever hold — the place of kings and priests in the Kingdom of God.

DECLARE THIS:

- I rule and reign with Jesus Christ in the Kingdom of God.
- By faith I receive my inheritance as a joint heir with Jesus.
- I thank God for the gift of Kingdom citizenship and for the authority I have in the name of Jesus.

FEBRUARY 12
ASK FOR FIRST THINGS FIRST

Many believers know they need to read the Word, but they don't seem to be able to make Bible-reading a daily habit. Even in a crisis they just don't think to pick it up and seek their solution there. Reading God's Word is just one more thing on the "ought to do" list. So what's the solution? Ask God for a hunger and thirst for the Word. Ask for a desire that can't be satisfied any other way. Then put yourself in a position to hear the Word — on the radio, on CDs, on television — and get "hooked." Ask the Holy Spirit to give you understanding as you read. It only takes a few times of experiencing a personal word — the very thing you needed at the very moment you needed it — and you'll be back for more. Ask for that!

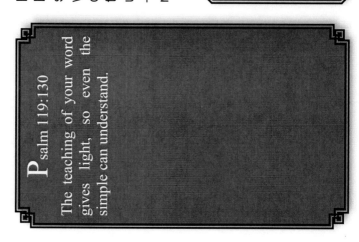

DECLARE THIS:

- By faith I receive a hunger and thirst for God's Word.
- I believe that God talks to me personally in his Word and I will find my answers there.
- By faith I receive an ability to understand the Word and to recognize when God is speaking to me.

Psalm 119:130

The teaching of your word gives light, so even the simple can understand.

NOVEMBER 18
SEEK DIVINE CONNECTIONS

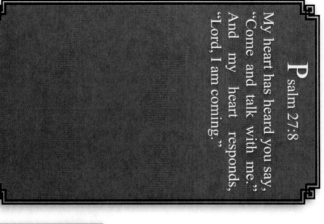

P salm 27:8

My heart has heard you say,
"Come and talk with me."
And my heart responds,
"Lord, I am coming."

When we think about making divine connections it probably doesn't occur to us to connect with our own hearts. Yet that connection is essential to our well-being and our spiritual health. We have to be able to hear from our hearts. This is the seat of the Holy Spirit in us. We must be able to recognize His voice. So make a decision to connect with your heart. Invite Jesus in for a cleansing. Get your heart empty of all the past garbage so God will have plenty of room to work within you. Then your heart will be able to lead you into abundant life.

DECLARE THIS:

- I open every part of my heart to the Lord and invite His healing power to fix all the broken places.
- By faith I release the Holy Spirit within me and I listen for His voice.
- I seek God with my whole heart because I have heard His call to me.

FEBRUARY 13
ASK ABOUT YOUR GIFTS

No other person can do what God has designed you to do. Each of us has been given different gifts by God's grace. It doesn't appear that there are any better gifts or lesser ones — they're just different. So our goal isn't to determine the value of our gifts or compare our gifts to those others have received. The point is to use our gifts! What comes easy to you? What do you thoroughly enjoy doing? What would you do with your life if you weren't thinking about earning an income? Look to those answers to see what your gifts might be. Once you find them and the Spirit confirms what you discover, give the gifts that you alone can give to God's Kingdom.

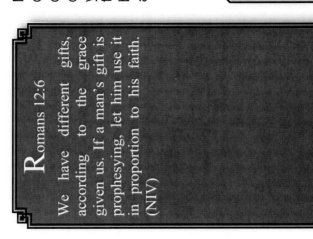

DECLARE THIS:

- I am gifted and I use my gifts to serve the Kingdom.
- By faith I receive understanding of my gifts and direction for their use so that God might be glorified.
- I am fearfully and wonderfully made to accomplish great things.

NOVEMBER 17

SEEK THE DIRECTION OF THE HOLY SPIRIT

Isaiah 8:19

Someone may say to you, "Let's ask the mediums and those who consult the spirits of the dead. With their whisperings and mutterings, they will tell us what to do." But shouldn't people ask God for guidance? Should the living seek guidance from the dead?

Why shouldn't you read your horoscope or ask a psychic about your job search? Most likely the more time you spend unemployed, the more likely you will feel the tug to seek some way to look into the future in order to find a way out of your circumstances. Don't do it. You don't have to find your own way out and you certainly don't need any occult methods to give you guidance. God Himself has put the Holy Spirit, with all the answers you'll ever need, right inside you. It's His voice you need to learn to hear! There is no other God and no other source of answers. He is Almighty God and He dwells within you. Look for Him there, in your heart.

DECLARE THIS:

- I look to my God alone for all my answers. There is no other source of guidance for my life.
- God has all I need and more that I could imagine or ask for.
- By faith I place my complete trust in Him and I wait on His leading.

FEBRUARY 14
ASK ABOUT YOUR DESIGN

We are a habitation for God. The moment we are born again we become His dwelling place — Christ in us! That realization alone should spark a change in us. How will you present yourself in an interview or on the phone when you know that Christ Himself is with you to lend His power and authority to all you do? Keep this in mind as you go out to face the day. Jesus walked in victory wherever He went and now that He goes with you, so will you!

DECLARE THIS:

- I am the dwelling place for the very Spirit of God Himself.
- By faith I receive the mind and nature of Jesus Christ who lives in me.
- Wherever I go and whatever I do Jesus is with me.

---

1 Corinthians 3:16

Don't you realize that all of you together are the temple of God and that the Spirit of God lives in you?

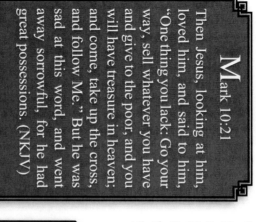

Mark 10:21

Then Jesus, looking at him, loved him, and said to him, "One thing you lack: Go your way, sell whatever you have and give to the poor, and you will have treasure in heaven; and come, take up the cross, and follow Me." But he was sad at this word, and went away sorrowful, for he had great possessions. (NKJV)

What stands between you and the promises of God? A bad habit? A hidden sin? A little resentment, unwillingness to forgive, or offense? Are you still procrastinating on some direction He's given you? What are you waiting for? Throw down whatever is in the way! Now is the time to really surrender all... let God have His way with you. He designed you and He has a perfect plan of blessing in mind for you. If you are clinging to anything He wants you to release, let it go. Abundant life is within your reach, in this life, and nothing you're holding onto can compare to it!

DECLARE THIS:

- I receive whatever God has for me and know that it is good and only good.

- By faith I receive my inheritance in Christ and expect the blessing to manifest in my life.

- My treasure is in heaven and God's promise is that I will receive abundant life now.

FEBRUARY 15
ASK ABOUT YOUR PURPOSE

Believers often fear that they might miss God's purpose by choosing the wrong job. Well, guess what? We can do nearly every kind of occupation and still honor God's purpose for our lives. We're called to bring God glory in whatever we do and to demonstrate how a life following God is radically better than a life without Him. So we can now stop waiting for some big light bulb to go on and direct us to a particular line of work. We can choose our work based on our interests, passions and gifts, and commit to serving God wherever we go. Let's just live in such a way that those who know us but do not know God will come to know God because they know us. There's our purpose!

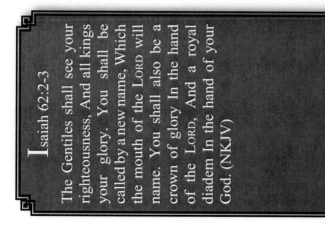

Isaiah 62:2-3

The Gentiles shall see your righteousness, And all kings your glory. You shall be called by a new name, Which the mouth of the LORD will name. You shall also be a crown of glory In the hand of glory In the hand of the LORD, And a royal diadem In the hand of your God. (NKJV)

DECLARE THIS:

- I am an ambassador for Christ who makes His appeal to unbelievers through me.
- By faith I receive guidance and approval from God as I put my gifts to work for His glory.
- I intend to live my life in such a way that unbelievers will be attracted to what I have.

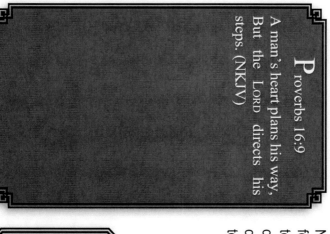

Proverbs 16:9

A man's heart plans his way,
But the LORD directs his
steps. (NKJV)

Now that's a great partnership. We tell God the plans of our hearts we would like to fulfill for the Kingdom, and God shows us the path to our desired destinations. We are designed to co-create with God Almighty! That means that as we surrender to God, He will listen to our desires and dreams and show us the way to accomplish them. Verse 3 in this same chapter of Proverbs spells out the result of this divine partnership. "Commit your actions to the Lord and your plans will succeed." What a great way to handle a job search.

DECLARE THIS:

- I am in a partnership with God.
- By faith I receive the ability to hear and to follow the direction of the Lord.
- I commit all my actions to the Lord and my plans all succeed.

FEBRUARY 16
SEEK SELF AWARENESS

Let's take a good look at ourselves to see where we may be missing it in our walk with God. Many believers know God is there and they know He loves them, but they put no demand on His Word. They still think they can handle the things of life on their own. They don't ask him for help or search the Word for direction. Is this true of you? Jesus stands ready to meet all our needs. He promises the very things we thirst for right now! So if you're still trying to win the battle on your own, it's time to come to the realization that you can't. As soon as we understand that we really need Him and turn to Him, He will fill us up. It's free and it's everything we need. Receive it.

DECLARE THIS:

- I believe that I am complete in Christ and all my needs are met.
- By faith I accept that Jesus has taken care of all that I need in life and I receive His provisions.
- I receive the water of life and expect to be fully satisfied.

Revelation 21:6

And he also said, "It is finished! I am the Alpha and the Omega — the Beginning and the End. To all who are thirsty I will give freely from the springs of the water of life.

John 14:12

"I tell you the truth, anyone who believes in me will do the same works I have done, and even greater works, because I am going to be with the Father.

The spirit of Christ Himself has been poured out on all flesh. We collectively can do much more than Jesus could do in His short time on earth. Each one of us has been designed to do the same works that Jesus did — and now there are millions of us! Imagine the impact we can have. He has already done the "heavy lifting." He conquered sin and death and destroyed the works of the enemy. Now He invites us to walk in the authority and power He paid for at Calvary. This is our real work and our primary assignment. While we're looking for jobs, let's not forget what we have been designed to accomplish for the Kingdom.

DECLARE THIS:

- I am filled with the love and life of Christ Jesus Himself.
- By faith I receive my assignment to do the works of Jesus alongside all the rest of the body of Christ.
- I believe in the power of Jesus and release His Spirit to work through

FEBRUARY 17

SEEK THE DIRECTION OF THE HOLY SPIRIT

Do you believe that you're supposed to be good to make God happy? God isn't trying to have His way just because He's God. Many still think God is constantly measuring us and is ever-ready to zap us if we miss the mark. That is so very far from the truth. The truth is, God has set before us a clean, clear path, covered it with His protection, and He's provided a Guide to ensure our safety. It's only when we step off that path or fail to follow our Guide that we get into trouble. It's never for God's sake that we are called to obey. It's for our sake. The greatest joy in life's magnificent journey is experienced by following our "owner's manual", the Word of God. Take some time to study this manual for life. You will need it to get you through unharmed.

DECLARE THIS:

- I choose to obey God at all times.
- By faith I receive guidance and direction from the Word and I am kept in safety.
- God's instructions are for my sake and in His Word I find all that I need for daily life.

Psalm 119:133

Guide my steps by your word, so I will not be overcome by evil.

NOVEMBER 13
ASK ABOUT YOUR GIFTS

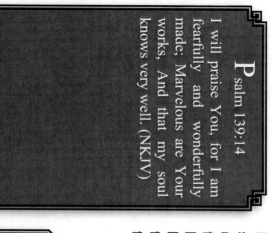

Psalm 139:14
I will praise You, for I am fearfully and wonderfully made; Marvelous are Your works, And that my soul knows very well. (NKJV)

It's important for job seekers to ask God about their gifts because many of us aren't even sure we have any. Beyond that we need to know He has a plan to put our design to good use. Imagine our Heavenly Father creating us in His very image and likeness, giving us talent, passion, energy and life, only to have the whole design sit unnoticed on a shelf. Nonsense! It isn't humble to think less of ourselves than we ought. And it isn't okay to keep our gifts hidden. It's wasteful. We are created to make important contributions for the Kingdom. Don't let another day go by without finding out what your gifts are and how to put them to use.

DECLARE THIS:

- I know that God has made me and given me gifts to bring to the workplace.
- By faith I activate my gifts to bless others and to build the body of Christ.
- I will use my gifts to create and to bring glory to God.

FEBRUARY 18
SEEK DIVINE CONNECTIONS

Do you know how angels figure into God's divine plan? Many of us were never even taught that they were real. But make no mistake, they do figure into the plan. When you read Psalm 91 you quickly see that God has given angels an assignment to protect us and to guard all our ways. Psalm 103 tells us that they excel at doing the Word of God, so we must be in very good hands. However, they can't do their job if we won't recognize them and release them to work for us. Ask God for the ability to recognize the angels He has sent and to invite them to cover you in your job search. They are just one more wonderful provision from the Lord and they are waiting to serve you.

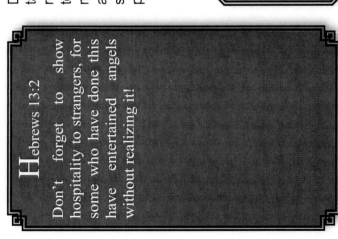

DECLARE THIS:

- I believe the Word of God and ask that angels be released on my behalf.
- By faith I believe in the reality and truth of God's Kingdom.
- I invite the care and ministrations of angels and accept their protection over all my ways.

Hebrews 13:2

Don't forget to show hospitality to strangers, for some who have done this have entertained angels without realizing it!

NOVEMBER 12
ASK FOR FIRST THINGS FIRST

P salm 19:14

Let the words of my mouth, and the meditation of my heart, be acceptable in thy sight, O Lord, my strength, and my redeemer. (KJV)

We are created in the image of God. He creates with the words of His mouth. We create with our words too. So here's a worthy prayer — "Lord, help me to control my tongue and keep the things I say in line with your Word." We'd better get help with the "meditation of our hearts", too. David knew of his need in this area. He was well aware of the power of the tongue and the impossibility of taming it on his own. He sought God and asked for help. The Holy Spirit in us offers that same help. Quit struggling on your own and ask for some supernatural, Holy Spirit, Christ-in-you assistance with your mouth! Then you'll be able to create with your Words just like your Father.

DECLARE THIS:

- My heart and my mouth belong to the Lord and He will make them pure and acceptable in His sight.
- I am unable to help myself but I belong to the One who saves me. I am redeemed.
- By faith I receive God's power to control my mouth and line up my words with the Word of God.

FEBRUARY 19
SEEK HIDDEN TREASURES

God loves treasure hunts. We have our focus fixed in one direction, looking for a particular answer and then God points us to treasure after treasure that He has hidden away in some other direction just to surprise us. Sometimes we don't like what He gives because it's not exactly what we asked for. Let's allow God to surprise us and care for us according to His plan. Knowing that He is intent on caring for us, and perfecting us, let's let Him do it His way. Keep your eyes open for hidden treasures and secret riches. If we want the greater riches let's start with gratitude for the little ways that He demonstrates His care for us. Don't miss what has been hidden in plain sight!

DECLARE THIS:

- I look for God's hidden treasures for my life every day and I am grateful for His gifts.
- By faith I receive eyes to see the demonstration of God's love for me.
- I am precious to God and He will never leave me or forsake me.

Isaiah 45:3

And I will give you treasures hidden in the darkness — secret riches. I will do this so you may know that I am the LORD, the God of Israel, the one who calls you by name.

NOVEMBER 11
ASK EXPECTING RESULTS

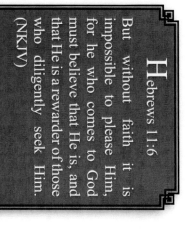

Hebrews 11:6

But without faith it is impossible to please Him, for he who comes to God must believe that He is, and that He is a rewarder of those who diligently seek Him. (NKJV)

You have faith enough to please God and to accomplish His Word in your life. That's not our problem. We have each been given "the measure of faith" that it takes to get started. If you're a parent you might remember how excited you were watching your child's first steps, cheering as if they deserved an Olympic medal. That's God, watching as we put our baby faith to work. For example, His Word says that we will have favor, so we use our faith to believe that our call will be answered by the hiring manager and not blocked by a secretary. Lo and behold, the manager answers! That's how it goes, one faith step at a time, always based on the Word. Expect to be rewarded.

DECLARE THIS:

- I have been given the faith required to do great things.
- By faith I believe that my faith will grow as I exercise it.
- I have faith in the name of Jesus and it does all the heavy lifting for me.

FEBRUARY 20
SEEK TO STAY FOCUSED ON JESUS

If we want faith to grow and be strong (and we do!), we need to be focused on Jesus. I'm using the word "focused" on purpose here. The attention so many of us give Jesus is more like a casual glance in His direction from time to time than the concentrated focus of our complete attention on Him. William Barclay had the right idea when he said, "So often we have a kind of vague, wistful longing that the promises of Jesus should be true. The only way really to enter into them is to believe them with the clutching intensity of a drowning man." We cannot afford to be casual about this. Our lives depend upon strong faith and the ability to walk in the power and authority of Christ. Focus on Jesus. Exercise and build your faith.

DECLARE THIS:

- I am focused on Jesus and my faith is growing.
- By faith I receive strong faith and my place in Christ at the right hand of God.
- Because I am in Christ, I live a victorious life.

Hebrews 12:2

Looking unto Jesus, the author and finisher of our faith, who for the joy that was set before Him endured the cross, despising the shame, and has sat down at the right hand of the throne of God. (NKJV)

NOVEMBER 10
CHOOSE YOUR BATTLE

We already know the outcome of the battle—Jesus returns and His Kingdom is established forever. But while the battle rages, let's never forget that Jesus has already defeated the enemy, conquered death and set us free. He has also given us His power and authority, so we can have dominion over all the earth right now. He has overcome every strategy of the enemy, and now He invites us to become one with Him to enjoy the peace He has already won. Do we dare to do what He suggests and "be of good cheer"? Absolutely. A season of unemployment is nothing to the One who has already conquered both hell and death!

John 16:33

These things I have spoken to you, that in Me you may have peace. In the world you will have tribulation; but be of good cheer, I have overcome the world." (NKJV)

DECLARE THIS:

- I choose to be of good cheer and at peace because I am in Christ.
- By faith I receive His overcoming power in the face of every challenge and trial.
- I have the overcoming power of Christ for His spirit lives in me.

FEBRUARY 21
KNOCK WITH BOLDNESS

Ephesians 3:20

Now all glory to God, who is able, through his mighty power at work within us, to accomplish infinitely more than we might ask or think.

This great promise also carries with it the message of personal responsibility. We see here that work will get done, but not by God. It will be His power working in us. The wonderful thing is that He will carry us far beyond what we asked for, far beyond what we thought possible. So the only question to be answered is "What is the power of God that will produce such awesome results?" It is the power of Love working in and through us. We can be bold and walk in confidence when we know that our motives are unselfish and our goal is to be of service. That's love in action. As we go through the job search process let's stay mindful that we are "powered by love" and as Willa Cather has said, "Where there is great love there are always miracles."

DECLARE THIS:

- I have God's mighty power at work in me.
- By faith I receive this promise that God will enable me to accomplish more than I ever dreamed.
- I thank God that He is able and I give Him all the glory for the accomplishments of my life.

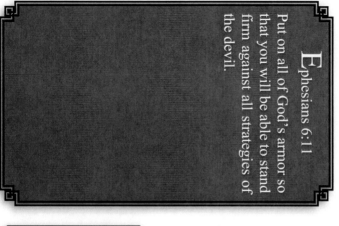

Ephesians 6:11
Put on all of God's armor so that you will be able to stand firm against all strategies of the devil.

We are in the middle of a battle. This means, unfortunately, that we need to adopt some wartime behaviors. No smart soldier runs onto the battlefield unarmed. We can't afford to launch into our day without our armor either. Just because our enemy is invisible to the natural eye doesn't mean he isn't working to steal from you and destroy your life every chance he gets. His best strategy is to convince believers that he isn't real and that there's no need to be vigilant. Don't fall for it. But neither should you forget that the greater army is on your side and the far greater power is within you. That's the key — don't forget, and don't go out unarmed.

DECLARE THIS:

- I am in the Lord's army and I am well equipped for battle.
- By faith I go out in the full armor of God and I am completely protected and able to withstand all enemy attacks.
- I am not moved by what I see for I know that "He who is in me is greater than he who is in the world."

FEBRUARY 22
Knock With Thanksgiving

For many of us the idea of praying about all the good things that happen in the day is a new one. We tend to take good things for granted. They may even go by unnoticed. But we're quick to cry "foul" if something happens that we don't like. How about trying an experiment? Spend one whole day thanking God for every good thing big and small. Just reverse the habit of a quick thank-you and a long laundry list of needs and disappointments. Instead, spend all your time thanking God for all he has already done, with a quick mention of the needs you're still waiting on in faith. As we cultivate an attitude of gratitude the entire world will seem lighter and brighter. We may even realize how wonderful our lives are despite the challenges.

Philippians 4:6

Don't worry about anything; instead, pray about everything. Tell God what you need, and thank him for all he has done.

DECLARE THIS:

- I am so thankful for the gift of eternal life and freedom from sin.
- By faith I believe that my needs are met according to God's riches.
- I thank God for Jesus, the most precious gift of love that the world has ever received.

NOVEMBER 8
CHOOSE YOUR TRAINING

Psalm 139: 23-24

Search me, O God, and know my heart; test me and know my anxious thoughts. Point out anything in me that offends you, and lead me along the path of everlasting life.

Most of us dislike getting feedback, especially the corrective kind. How many of us say to God, "Please show me anything I'm thinking, believing or doing that doesn't line up with your Word." Yet in the workplace, in the job search, and in the Kingdom, nothing is likely to be more beneficial than hearing the straight truth. This scripture provides a great model for us. Let's develop the courage to ask God to point out the sin, strongholds, and errors in our thinking and to lead us to His way of doing and being right. Then with the confidence of a clean heart and mind, let's ask for feedback about our performance in the workplace as well. For most of us, there's room for improvement!

DECLARE THIS:

- I ask for feedback because I desire to be excellent in all that I do.
- By faith I receive God's correction and the power to make the necessary changes.
- I receive feedback as a gift and bless the giver for helping me to get better.

FEBRUARY 23
KNOCK WITH CONFIDENCE

Many Christian job seekers are afraid they might move in the wrong direction. But look again at this scripture. God puts seed and resources into our hands and works through us to produce something. He knows what He has given us and He knows what He wants to accomplish both in and through us. We need to trust in His ability to do it. Determine where your passion is and where you want to make a Kingdom difference. Tell God what you'd like to do and ask Him to lead you to a place to make that impact. Then move with confidence knowing that He "who began a good work in you is faithful to complete it." Expect God's provisions and supernatural support. That's how love works and confidence is built.

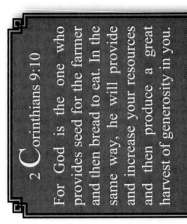

2 Corinthians 9:10

For God is the one who provides seed for the farmer and then bread to eat. In the same way, he will provide and increase your resources and then produce a great harvest of generosity in you.

DECLARE THIS:

- I am a co-laborer with God.
- By faith I move into the workplace in confidence knowing that God goes with me.
- I surrender all my selfish motives at the feet of Jesus and choose to work for the Kingdom of God in whatever I do.

NOVEMBER 7
CHOOSE YOUR PAY

Malachi 3:10

Bring all the tithes into the storehouse so there will be enough food in my Temple. If you do," says the LORD of Heaven's Armies, "I will open the windows of heaven for you. I will pour out a blessing so great you won't have enough room to take it in! Try it! Put me to the test!

If you don't already tithe, now is the time to begin. That ten percent you've been withholding isn't yours; it belongs to God. And face it, you probably aren't covering all your bills right now with 100% of your income. Ten percent less won't make much difference in the natural realm. But in the spiritual realm, it's all you need to take God up on His promise to pour out a blessing upon you that is so great you won't be able to contain it. You need that blessing, don't you? Well, put God to the test. If you have no money coming in, commit to being a tither and find a way to give His church a tenth of your time. If your heart is in it, he'll receive it. This is a bonus plan that is simply too good to pass up.

DECLARE THIS:

- I am a tither because God commands it.
- By faith I return ten percent of my income to God to free Him to release a covenant blessing on me.
- I know that as I return His tithe in obedience God leads me into prosperity.

FEBRUARY 24
KNOCK AND BRING GIFTS

This may seem an unusual choice of scripture for those who are looking for work. But let's remember that unemployment is a temporary condition. That's why it's important to plan for the way you'll behave when you start working again. Take a moment and examine your motive for working. Do you still think you're working for a living, or have you come to realize that you are working in order to give? This Word makes it clear — we work in order to give generously to others. John Wesley put it this way, "Do all the good you can, By all the means you can, In all the ways you can, In all the places you can, At all the times you can, To all the people you can, As long as ever you can." Let's practice that mind-set now and let it carry us into our next position in the workplace.

Ephesians 4:28
If you are a thief, quit stealing. Instead, use your hands for good hard work, and then give generously to others in need.

DECLARE THIS:

- I live to give and know that my Father does the same!
- By faith I focus on giving to others.
- I work hard in order to bless others and show God's love to them.

NOVEMBER 6
CHOOSE YOUR WORK

> 2 Corinthians 5:20
>
> So we are Christ's ambassadors, God making His appeal as it were through us. We [as Christ's personal representatives] beg you for His sake to lay hold of the divine favor [now offered you] and be reconciled to God. (The Amplified Bible)

We have been hired to serve as ambassadors in a foreign land. Did you know that? We represent Christ in the earth now. Unfortunately, many of us still behave so much like non-believers that it is hard to identify us as special people representing Almighty God. No wonder the apostle Paul begs us to "lay hold of" the truth of our identity in Christ and start acting like we know who we truly are. If we really understood this truth it would change the way we walk into an interview, the way we talk about our circumstances, and the way we interact with everyone we meet. Above all, knowing that Christ makes His appeal to a lost people though us would change how we go about our business. We're all He's got on this planet. Whether we're employed or jobless, we will always be His ambassadors.

DECLARE THIS:

- I accept my assignment as an ambassador for Christ. I want to bring His appeal to a hurting and hungry world.
- By faith I receive all that I need to represent Jesus and the Kingdom of God.
- My life is a testimony to the God I serve.

FEBRUARY 25

KNOCK AND EXERCISE YOUR FAITH

Are we really making every effort to respond to God's promises? Peter goes on to explain that we can do our very best to be morally excellent. We can work at increasing our knowledge of the Kingdom and we can work at developing self control. It's our responsibility to develop patient endurance — something few of us truly aspire to. We'd rather receive everything immediately, microwave style. And then we are called to brotherly affection and love for everyone. Notice that not one of these things requires us to be employed. These are all characteristics we can work on every day of the job search. This will build our Christ likeness and grow our faith, so we need to give our energy to the effort.

> ## 2 Peter 1:5-7
>
> In view of all this, make every effort to respond to God's promises. Supplement your faith with a generous provision of moral excellence, and moral excellence with knowledge, and knowledge with self-control, and self-control with patient endurance, and patient endurance with godliness, and godliness with brotherly affection, and brotherly affection with love for everyone.

DECLARE THIS:

- I am willing to grow in character and the likeness of Jesus.
- By faith I receive the empowerment of the Holy Spirit to help me to develop day-by-day.
- With the Holy Spirit I become the person I was designed to be.

NOVEMBER 5
CHOOSE YOUR BENEFITS

Matthew 7:24-25

"Therefore whoever hears these sayings of Mine, and does them, I will liken him to a wise man who built his house on the rock: and the rain descended, the floods came, and the winds blew and beat on that house; and it did not fall, for it was founded on the rock.

How many people wish they could find some proven, solid foundation on which to base their trust? The shifting sands of the world provide no firm footing. But we are not citizens of this world. Our foundation is secure. We stand on The Rock and we cannot be moved. Notice in this scripture that the wise man went through the same storm as the foolish one. He experienced the rain, the flood and the strong wind. Obviously, he hadn't been promised that storms, trials and testing wouldn't come… and neither have we. But for those who have made Jesus their Lord, and His Father their God, the outcome has been decided. Our houses stand. We will endure the storms and emerge unharmed. There is no insurance policy on this planet that can provide that benefit!

DECLARE THIS:

- My house is built on the Rock and I am secure.
- I hear the Word of the Lord and I do it. I know that the Word keeps me safe from harm.
- By faith I trust in God through every storm and I listen for His voice to direct my steps.

FEBRUARY 26

KNOCK AND WITNESS FOR THE KINGDOM

Matthew 5:16

In the same way, let your good deeds shine out for all to see, so that everyone will praise your heavenly Father.

This scripture gives us clear direction. We work for God and we are always on duty. Since God is the One who is paying us, we need to be excellent in carrying out the assignment He gives us. Whether we are sending out resumes, going to interviews, working on a temporary assignment, or just scouting for leads, we need to be in the business of continuously doing good deeds. It works like this: You, as a representative of the Kingdom of God, bring excellence everywhere you go and look for opportunities to perform good deeds. Then the people you encounter are glad they've met you and wonder at the kind of God you serve. Now you're in line for a blessing overflow, a harvest beyond your wildest imagination. That's God's promise to those who work for Him.

DECLARE THIS:

- I work for God and my good deeds bring Him glory.
- By faith I receive direction from the Holy Spirit and I am led to opportunities for service.
- I am in the good-deed-doing business everywhere I go and I plant good seed for a supernatural harvest.

> ### Daniel 4:17
>
> For this has been decreed by the messengers; it is commanded by the holy ones, so that everyone may know that the Most High rules over the kingdoms of the world. He gives them to anyone he chooses—even to the lowliest of people."

Some believers think that after accepting Jesus as their Lord and King, God starts watching them to decide if they're worthy of His continued blessing. But the truth is, while we were sinners Christ died for us. When we accepted Him, both Jesus and His Father committed to giving blessing and inheritance to us. We don't have to earn this day by day; we just have to accept it. God will give the kingdoms of this earth to anyone He chooses and He has chosen us! Dwell on that... let it sink in. You might see yourself as "the lowliest of people" but it doesn't matter. He has declared that we are kings and priests. Let's act like God's elect and expect to find great positions in the kingdom of the workplace.

DECLARE THIS:

- I know that I am chosen by God and richly blessed.
- By faith I accept the training of the Lord that I might be made ready for my next Kingdom assignment.
- I do not work for a living; I work for God Who meets all my needs.

FEBRUARY 27
KNOCK AND OVERCOME

Does it sometimes it seems like everyone is judging and criticizing your job search performance? Plenty of people seem more than ready to offer that "there's no reason for your job search to take this long." But then there's God! Our Father tells us that we are exactly right and that He is perfectly pleased with us. So how are we to decide which report to believe? Vincent Van Gogh once said, "If you hear a voice within you saying, 'You are not a painter,' then by all means paint and that voice will be silenced." Press on in faith and stand on God's Word. If you hear voices saying you're failing and will never get a good job, just keep going. When the Lord walks you into a wonderful new position those voices will fall silent.

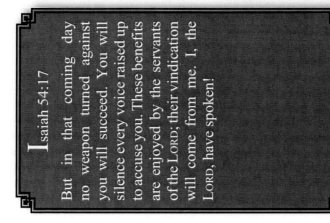

Isaiah 54:17

But in that coming day no weapon turned against you will succeed. You will silence every voice raised up to accuse you. These benefits are enjoyed by the servants of the LORD; their vindication will come from me. I, the LORD, have spoken!

DECLARE THIS:

- I trust that the Good Shepherd will lead me to a beautiful, green pasture.
- By faith I stand on God's promise that He will supply all my needs, including a good job and income.
- I claim the benefits of servants of the Lord.

NOVEMBER 3
CHOOSE YOUR FUTURE

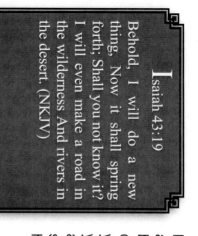

Isaiah 43:19

Behold, I will do a new thing; Now it shall spring forth; Shall you not know it? I will even make a road in the wilderness And rivers in the desert. (NKJV)

No matter where you are in your job search process, seize this promise. God is doing a new thing with you. You are not unemployed because tragedy struck or without a job because God wasn't paying attention. Your situation is not an indication that He didn't care enough to save you. He is doing a new thing! Don't make the mistake of viewing your situation the way non-believers view it. You are a child of the King. No matter what your job search has been like, His Word says "I will even make a road in the wilderness and rivers in the desert" for you. He can do it. You can count on Him to handle your job search. Look for the new thing to spring forth before you. Keep your eyes open and your heart expecting. He will not disappoint you.

DECLARE THIS:

- My eyes are open to see the goodness of the Lord and the new thing He is doing in my life.
- I know God is well able to handle every situation that I face.
- I see God acting in my life and have the willingness to follow His lead.

FEBRUARY 28
Knock And Faint Not!

If you've been looking for work a long time and you feel like you're running out of gas, this scripture is for you. Receive it as a personal word. There is a truth that you can count on — God never runs out of love for us. He is our Source and supply. He never looks away and He never loses interest in us. Every morning we receive a fresh supply of love, mercy and provision. So when you feel like you can't go on, turn all your thoughts towards the God who loves you and remember these words of Emily Dickinson, "I know not where His islands lift their fronded palms in air, I only know I cannot drift beyond His love and care."

Lamentations 3:22

It is of the Lord's mercies that we are not consumed, because his compassions fail not. They are new every morning: great is thy faithfulness. The LORD is my portion, saith my soul; therefore will I hope in him. (KJV)

DECLARE THIS:

- I am safe in the love and mercy of God.
- By faith I receive my provisions from God and I know that my supply will never run out.
- I thank God for His faithfulness and I place all my hope in Him alone.

NOVEMBER 2
CHOOSE YOUR THOUGHTS

E phesians 1:18-23

the eyes of your understanding being enlightened; that you may know what is the hope of His calling, what are the riches of the glory of His inheritance in the saints, and what is the exceeding greatness of His power toward us who believe, according to the working of His mighty power which He worked in Christ when He raised Him from the dead and seated Him at His right hand in the heavenly places, far above all principality and power and might and dominion, and every name that is named, not only in this age but also in that which is to come. And He put all things under His feet, and gave Him to be head over all things to the church, which is His body, the fullness of Him who fills all in all. (NKJV)

We are God's feet and hands on this planet. We are the manifestation of God on earth. God needs us! We are His body with Christ as the head. The two were designed to function as one. Don't think of yourself as separate from God any longer. Don't think that you can choose to do your own thing. Hands don't decide what to do. Feet don't walk away of their own accord. We need to receive our way of thinking from the mind of Christ. When we get into our right position in Him we will experience the thrill of having the enemy under our feet and the power and authority of God in our lives. That bit of knowledge opens up boundless possibilities for job seekers, doesn't it?

DECLARE THIS:

- I have hope in God and by faith I receive understanding about His plans for me.
- I am ready to be used by God for His purposes on earth.
- I am His body and He is my head and all power and authority has been given to me in Him.

FEBRUARY 29
KNOCK AND BE ENCOURAGED

The vast majority of comments you'll see on the news or hear from others are likely to be negative. If you spend much time absorbing these you'll be defeated before your day even starts! The only source of consistently positive news is the Word of God for new covenant believers. Here's a tip — encourage yourself. Expect exactly what today's scripture says. God has plans for us that far exceed our best daydreams, so go ahead, take the time to envision your life in the fullness of God's blessing. See yourself strong and prosperous. Plan how you'll be a blessing to others. That's our truth, so hold fast to it and be encouraged.

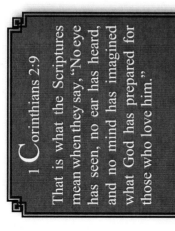

1 Corinthians 2:9

That is what the Scriptures mean when they say, "No eye has seen, no ear has heard, and no mind has imagined what God has prepared for those who love him."

DECLARE THIS:

- I am encouraged because I know God has wonderful plans to prosper me in all my ways.
- By faith I receive the fullness of the blessing that Jesus died to give me.
- I thank God for His promises and His enduring faithfulness. I trust Him to care for me.

NOVEMBER 1
CHOOSE YOUR KINGDOM

Ezekiel 33:30-31

"Son of man, your people talk about you in their houses and whisper about you at the doors. They say to each other, 'Come on, let's go hear the prophet tell us what the Lord is saying!' So my people come pretending to be sincere and sit before you. They listen to your words, but they have no intention of doing what you say. Their mouths are full of lustful words, and their hearts seek only after money. You are very entertaining to them, like someone who sings love songs with a beautiful voice or plays fine music on an instrument. They hear what you say, but they don't act on it!

Is this true of us? Do we show up in church, in small groups, and in bible studies to hear what the Lord is saying from someone else? Then do we walk out and promptly forget what we've heard. Do we say we want to find the Kingdom and serve the King when really we just want to find a job and to get the money we need to pay our bills? God isn't fooled. He knows our hearts. If we want the benefits of His Kingdom we have to pay the price of surrender and submission. We have to "do it His way" and in His order. There are no shortcuts and no dual citizenship in this Kingdom.

DECLARE THIS:

- By faith I seek the Kingdom and surrender everything I have to the King of Kings.
- I reaffirm the choice I made when I was saved; Jesus, I give you my life.
- By the power of the Holy Spirit I will act on what God tells me to do.

MARCH

GOOD NEWS

GOOD NEWS

NOVEMBER

MARCH 1
CHOOSE YOUR KINGDOM

Sometimes we think that the good that comes to us is dependent upon our good behavior, actions or worthiness. Let's never forget that the blessing we receive is all because of what Christ did for us. His blood purchased our salvation and made us kings and priests. Because of what Jesus did we get to reign as kings over the earth. When we think we have to earn our position with God we get into trouble. It's because of who He is that we can reign and be victorious.

Revelation 5:9-10

And [now] they sing a new song, saying, You are worthy to take the scroll and to break the seals that are on it, for You were slain (sacrificed), and with Your blood You purchased men unto God from every tribe and language and people and nation. And You have made them a kingdom (royal race) and priests to our God, and they shall reign [as kings] over the earth! (The Amplified Bible)

DECLARE THIS:

- I am confident in the finished work of Jesus Christ.
- My faith and trust are in Him alone.
- Jesus is more than enough for everything that I face and that I need.

God knows everything about us. He sees us just the way we are and He heals and blesses us anyway! Don't you love it? God causes us to praise Him because of the wonderful things He does for us. So if you've been thinking that God is withholding your new job, or that God is punishing you for some reason, change your mind! Invite Him into your heart to heal you and accept His promise of peace. In this challenging time, take this opportunity to get all the healing you need and enter into the abundant peace that God offers.

I saiah 57:18-19

I have seen what they do, but I will heal them anyway! I will lead them. I will comfort those who mourn, bringing words of praise to their lips. May they have abundant peace, both near and far," says the LORD, who heals them.

DECLARE THIS:

- I accept the comfort of the Holy Spirit whenever I am disappointed or discouraged.
- With all my heart I praise God and worship Him for who He is and all He has done for me.
- By faith I receive God's blessing purchased for me by Christ, despite my failures and shortcomings.

MARCH 2
CHOOSE YOUR THOUGHTS

God's will for us is good and pleasing and perfect. Isn't that great news? Yet many of us don't believe it. We think we know what we really need, so we focus our energies on trying to persuade God to deliver on our demands. But in this scripture we see that God has a perfect plan for us. That's worth considering, isn't it? We are even told the way to experience what God has in mind. Let God transform us into new people by using His Word to change the way we think. Now that sounds like a really good idea.

R omans 12:2

Don't copy the behavior and customs of this world, but let God transform you into a new person by changing the way you think. Then you will learn to know God's will for you, which is good and pleasing and perfect.

DECLARE THIS:

- I trust that God's will for me is better than anything I could come up with on my own.
- By faith I receive God's transforming power in my life and thoughts.
- I choose to think in line with the Word of God only.

Philippians 2:5

Let this same attitude and purpose and [humble] mind be in you which was in Christ Jesus (The Amplified Bible)

The word "let" means you permit or allow it to be. Just as importantly, it also means you don't have to struggle with all your thoughts and plans and solutions. Just "let" the mind of Christ, his attitude and his purpose, be realized in you. Our natural tendency, of course is to seek our own way out of our problems. But our challenge is to let the "same mind which was in Christ" be also in us. Jesus was rooted and grounded in His Father. He did and said exactly as He was told. He wasn't trying to do His own thing. Now He is in us. We just have to let His mind do our thinking for us. "Let" it be.

DECLARE THIS:

- I choose the will of my Father and my Lord.
- By faith I receive the mind of Christ and seek to be led by His spirit.
- As I allow His mind to work in me I expect to see His promises fulfilled.

MARCH 3
CHOOSE YOUR FUTURE

This scripture has been used to give God such a bad reputation! Every painful and difficult thing believers experience gets attributed to God, who must be punishing them for some mistake they have made. That's not God's way of doing things. God does convict us, but it's between Him and us — not a public event. It may be painful to submit to correction, but, with God, it is never humiliating or devastating. Sanctification requires our cooperation and self discipline as we wait on the Lord to heal and change us. It can be tough to wait patiently as we mature too. But "punishing and scourging" results from a decision to knowingly go against God's will. When we intentionally step outside His commands, we open ourselves to the enemy and destruction. So, if your current situation is the consequence of conscious rebellion, repent, receive forgiveness, and let God lead you back to safety.

DECLARE THIS:

- I trust the Love of God. I am safe with my Father.
- I welcome God's correction and discipline for it leads me to freedom.
- By faith I receive the ability to hear and to obey God's voice.

Hebrews 12:6

For the Lord corrects and disciplines everyone whom He loves, and He punishes, even scourges, every son whom He accepts and welcomes to His heart and cherishes. (The Amplified Bible)

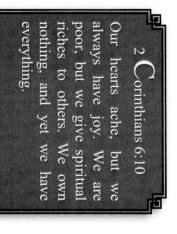

2 Corinthians 6:10

Our hearts ache, but we always have joy. We are poor, but we give spiritual riches to others. We own nothing, and yet we have everything.

Nothing says we have to enjoy being out of the workforce. We have been designed for community and for creating, so it's no wonder that we miss being part of the workplace. But in the midst of our sorrow "we have joy" for we are complete in Christ. This season will pass and you will come through it in victory if you obey God's instructions. Along the way you can bring love, peace, joy and blessing to all those that you encounter. Give your spiritual riches to others and keep looking for the harvest that has been prepared for you in return for the seed you plant. We are always able to bring God glory through the way we live our lives and we can always bring the gift of Jesus Christ to others.

DECLARE THIS:

- I have the joy of the Lord and eternal life in Him.
- By faith I receive encouragement and strength to share with others and to bring God glory.
- I thank God that my purpose is higher than a daily job; that I am blessed to be a blessing.

MARCH 4
CHOOSE YOUR BOSS

This is such an interesting combination of statements. On one hand we are to understand that God is both our Father and our Lord. On the other hand we are to think of Him as a creator who has the ability and the right to take us apart and start all over if He is displeased with what we have become. I am so glad He embodies both of these characteristics. He formed me, but He will not destroy me if I fail, sin or make mistakes. He knows exactly what I need to become like Christ. It's also wonderful to be reminded about our right standing with God. He's not a buddy, or a good fairy sent to grant our wishes. He is God, Lord and Master, Abba, Daddy, the One who completely loves us. He is our Creator, always working to turn us into Kingdom masterpieces.

DECLARE THIS:

- I yield to my Creator to help me be willing to be changed into His likeness.
- By faith I receive God's love and Lordship.
- Because I have been formed by the hand of God I know I am wonderfully made and designed for glory.

Isaiah 64:8

And yet, O LORD, you are our Father. We are the clay, and you are the potter. We all are formed by your hand.

OCTOBER 28
KNOCK AND FAINT NOT!

H ebrews 10:36

Patient endurance is what you need now, so that you will continue to do God's will. Then you will receive all that he has promised.

Francis Fenelon once said, "A life of faith enables us to see God in everything and it holds the mind in a state of readiness for whatever may be His will." That state of readiness enables us to receive God's promises. If we stop expecting the promises, we will waver in our obedience to God's instruction. The choice is ours. We can decide to keep our eyes focused on God's blessings in our lives and the promises in His Word. We can decide to listen for His voice and live in that state of readiness that gives God room to work in our lives. The path to success is clearly spelled out. Patiently endure the process and allow the time required to complete it. Live ready to do whatever God tells you and "you will receive all that He has promised." Not might receive, but will receive!

DECLARE THIS:

- I know how everything turns out. In my obedience I receive all that God has promised.
- By faith I receive the strength to stay in the will of God.
- I thank God that His will for me is good and that He is faithful to lead me into it.

MARCH 5
CHOOSE YOUR BENEFITS

The psalmist wrote this request before the time of Jesus. He was concerned that God might abandon him. He knew that he wasn't equipped to deal with life on his own, so he begged God to stay with him. And he was given a wonderful promise that is ours as well! The One who knows you best, the One who designed and created you, is going to stick with you throughout your life journey. So never think that you're in the job search alone or that God will only re-enter your life once you find a job. He's with you now. You will not miss His destiny for you, because God Himself is working out His plans with you. See yourself putting your hand into the Master's hand. Then get into His Word and listen as He tells you how He sees this all working out.

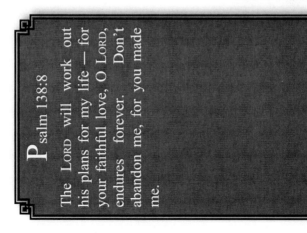

DECLARE THIS:

- I trust the plans God has for me — that they will be good and only good.
- I believe that God's love towards me will never fail and I will never be left on my own.
- By faith I know that I hear God's voice and will follow when He leads me.

P salm 138:8

The LORD will work out his plans for my life — for your faithful love, O LORD, endures forever. Don't abandon me, for you made me.

OCTOBER 27
KNOCK AND OVERCOME

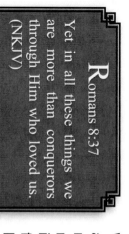

R omans 8:37

Yet in all these things we are more than conquerors through Him who loved us. (NKJV)

What does it mean to be more than a conqueror? Isn't conquest enough? Perhaps the answer is found in the promise in the next verse "that neither death nor life, nor angels nor principalities nor powers, nor things present nor things to come, nor height nor depth, nor any other created thing, shall be able to separate us from the love of God which is in Christ Jesus our Lord." We been given victory over "trouble, hardship, persecution, famine, nakedness, danger and sword" in this life, and we have the assurance of eternal life in the love and presence of God. We walk in the overwhelming victory that Jesus paid for at Calvary and now we need to claim it so we can demonstrate God's mighty power for the entire world to see.

DECLARE THIS:

- I have victory over my circumstances now and eternal life in the love of God.
- By faith I take the authority to rebuke trouble, hardship, persecution and danger in the name of Jesus right now!
- I thank God that I can never be separated from the love and power of God.

MARCH 6
CHOOSE YOUR WORK

Remember that despite what the world may say, you are not unemployed! You work for Almighty God and He will never lay you off or end His relationship with you. Your assignment is to fulfill your Kingdom job description to love. Whether you have a job today or not, you are still called to pray, and to love. Love your enemies. Pray for them, not at them! If you want your Kingdom wages — prosperity, abundance, peace, all the promises — then you have to do your Kingdom work. Ask God to pour His love through you. It's already in you so yield to the Holy Spirit and allow the love in you to grow and flow out to this hurting world. That will give God the room He needs to work in your heart, and manifest His blessing in your life.

DECLARE THIS:

- I pray for my enemies because it frees me to move forward in love.
- By faith I release all past hurts and forgive everyone who has done me harm.
- The love of Christ in me makes it possible for me to pray for my enemies.

Matthew 5:44

But I say, love your enemies! Pray for those who persecute you!

Whenever we make any claim we'll probably be asked to prove it. It's the same with Kingdom life. If God is at the center of our lives and we are walking in His ways, then our lives ought to show it. Here's that assignment again. Do good work. Be excellent at all you do because you represent God. Let your wisdom, your calm and confident demeanor and your lifestyle all demonstrate that you are a citizen of God's higher and more excellent Kingdom. Don't just say that you're a believer who walks in the ways of the Lord. Prove it.

James 3:13

If you are wise and understand God's ways, prove it by living an honorable life, doing good works with the humility that comes from wisdom.

DECLARE THIS:

- I know who I am in the Lord. I walk in confidence and humility.
- By faith I ask for and receive God's wisdom for every decision I make.
- My life demonstrates that I am led by a higher and more excellent power.

MARCH 7
CHOOSE YOUR PAY

Imagine how you'll feel when you have everything you need, whenever you need it. You'll be able to go out and do every good work you've ever wanted to do. That sounds too good to be true, and yet it must be true because His Word says so. What's holding you back? Maybe you were never taught that prosperity is the true heart of God for you. Perhaps some other belief has constrained you. Whatever might be standing against this truth has got to go. Meditate on this verse. Speak it over and over until it comes bubbling up out of your heart all by itself. Accept that abundant life is yours and expect to receive it. Then get ready to abound to every good work that God has designed you to do.

DECLARE THIS:

- I have everything I need to accomplish every good work because God supplies it from His infinite grace.
- I receive this promise — that I always have all sufficiency in all things.
- I receive abundance so that I might be blessed to be a blessing.

---

2 Corinthians 9:8

And God is able to make all grace abound toward you, that you, always having all sufficiency in all things, may have an abundance for every good work. (NKJV)

Ephesians 4:29

Let no foul or polluting language, nor evil word nor unwholesome or worthless talk [ever] come out of your mouth, but only such [speech] as is good and beneficial to the spiritual progress of others, as is fitting to the need and the occasion, that it may be a blessing and give grace (God's favor) to those who hear it. (The Amplified Bible)

When you speak discouragement and frustration and give voice to hopelessness, what effect do you have on family and others? More importantly, what are you exercising—faith or doubt? What gets exercised gets stronger. Listening to the horror stories of others will hurt you. So keep your focus on stories of people who kept their faith, stood and won the victory — the three Hebrew children in the fiery furnace, Daniel in the lion's den, Paul rejoicing in prison. Talk about the victory that's been promised. Tell about the times when God came through for you. As you speak it faith will bring it to pass. But it is up to you to release faith, and only faith, through the words of your mouth.

DECLARE THIS:

- I declare that God is good and only good. I trust in Him.
- My mouth is filled with the Word of God and praise for His marvelous ways.
- By faith I receive the power to control my tongue and speak the Word only.

MARCH 8
CHOOSE YOUR TRAINING

No one wants to be overcome by evil, but there is only one way to avoid it. We have to be led by God. He has to be the One guiding our steps. Are you still developing your own plans and strategies and begging God to bless them? That puts you in a position of not knowing if God approves of your plans.... an unsettling place to be. God doesn't want us to wonder where we stand with Him. He wants us to search the Word for our answers, standing fast until we find them. Only then will we have the assurance that we are being guided by God and completely protected from evil.

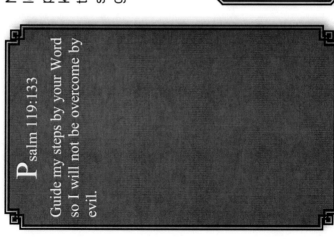

Psalm 119:133
Guide my steps by your Word so I will not be overcome by evil.

DECLARE THIS:

- I have God's Word so I will never be lost.
- By faith I receive the ability to be led by the Holy Spirit in confidence.
- I cannot be overcome by evil or life circumstances because God cares for me.

OCTOBER 24
KNOCK AND BRING GIFTS

Luke 18:22

So when Jesus heard these things, He said to him, "You still lack one thing. Sell all that you have and distribute to the poor, and you will have treasure in heaven; and come, follow Me."

What can we give while we're unemployed and our resources seem scarce? Or to be more precise, let's look at what we might need to give up. Our progress can be held back when we hang on to things that God wants us to release. Many of us have kept a hobby or habit that has pulled our lives out of balance and harmed our relationships. So let's all take some time to check and see if there's anything on the throne of our life other than God. Be ready to give God everything He wants to take away. He only asks for it in order to make room for something so much better.

DECLARE THIS:

- I am willing to release anything the Lord calls for. I know He will give back far better gifts.
- By faith I receive a multiplied return for everything I give up for Christ's sake.
- I thank God that He is after my greatest good and will save me from traps the enemy has set for me.

MARCH 9
Choose Your Behavior

We make a mistake by looking for natural signs to tell us where to look for a job, when to invest in a business venture, or how to grow our own business in troubling economic conditions. There is a much better way to ensure success called seed time and harvest. We just have to plant the seed of the Word of God and He will deliver the harvest. We can go into today's shaky job market confident that we'll secure great jobs because of the seed we've planted. Look at the second verse of this scripture. We are directed to do this every day. Speak the Word, stay busy in all the right actions, and don't try to guess what activity will ultimately produce the job you seek. God's pattern has been established and this principle will not fail!

DECLARE THIS:

- I know God labors with me in my job search and I expect great success.
- By faith I receive the promise of a good reward for my actions.
- I listen to God because He is my shepherd and my Lord.

Ecclesiastes 11:4,6
Farmers who wait for perfect weather never plant. If they watch every cloud, they never harvest... Plant your seed in the morning and keep busy all afternoon, for you don't know if profit will come from one activity or another — or maybe both.

> Hebrews 10:22
>
> Let us draw near to God with a sincere heart in full assurance of faith, having our hearts sprinkled to cleanse us from a guilty conscience and having our bodies washed with pure water. (NIV)

Here are two great clues to finding confidence in this Word. For starters, "Let us draw near to God." When life crashes in and starts to overwhelm us, that's the time to turn our focus back to God and get near to him. Like sheep sensing danger we need to run to the Shepherd. The second clue is that we are reminded that we have been washed clean by our baptism. All guilt and condemnation has been removed from us. Right now, in the middle of our job search, we can be fully assured that Jesus has made us righteous. If we need help, guidance, provision and healing we can put it on our "Master's Card." As we walk in love and grow in our faith in Him, we will receive His promises. Remember who you are in Christ.

DECLARE THIS:

- I am fully persuaded that Jesus is more than enough for all I need.
- By faith I receive confidence and assurance that I am approved by God in Christ and that His promises are mine to claim.
- I thank God that He is both able and willing to meet all my needs.

MARCH 10
CHOOSE YOUR BATTLE

We've heard that the devil will flee if we resist him. But many of us have experienced defeat as a result of those encounters. Why didn't this promise work? The answer is in the opening line of this scriptural reference: "So humble yourselves before God." Our victory is not our doing. It comes from Jesus and His anointing. Faith in His name and in the completed work He accomplished — the destruction of the works of the devil — is what we need. When we understand what He did for us and how He has positioned us, we will rise up in power and authority. Then our resistance of the enemy will send him packing.

James 4:7

So humble yourselves before God. Resist the devil, and he will flee from you.

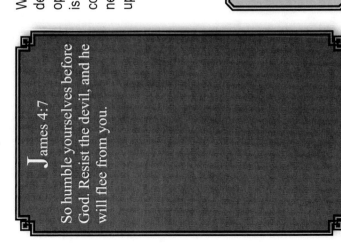

DECLARE THIS:

- I have full confidence in the finished work of Christ Jesus.
- I place my faith in the name and blood of Jesus and I experience victory.
- I am complete in Christ. I have the authority to defeat the devil.

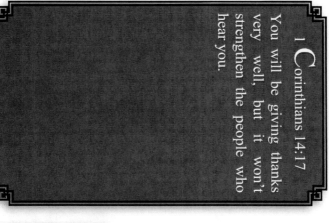

1 Corinthians 14:17

You will be giving thanks very well, but it won't strengthen the people who hear you.

In this scripture the apostle Paul was discussing the appropriate time and place to pray in the Spirit and in our natural language. Look at the reason he gives for praying so others can understand — to "strengthen the people who hear you." Everyone who has ever been unemployed realizes that many people are affected by the situation — spouses, children, relatives and friends. This time can be especially stressful for family members. So imagine the impact you can have if you will pray with your family. As you thank God for His promises and praise Him for meeting all your needs, your prayers will give them strength and confidence. Don't let another day go by without your family members hearing you praise God for your guaranteed victory!

DECLARE THIS:

- I thank God publicly for I know He will meet all our needs.
- I receive confidence in the Word and boldness to pray before others.
- I accept my assignment to strengthen others with my prayers.

MARCH 11
ASK EXPECTING RESULTS

Many people experience great pain and confusion because of this scripture. They have asked God for jobs, for interviews, for money and other things, and they've been disappointed. Let's see if we can find the problem. Do you think this promise means you can ask to marry someone else's spouse, or request a job held by a neighbor? Of course not. You can't ask for things "in Jesus' name" that don't agree with the character of Jesus. Jesus does what we request "so that the Son can bring glory to the Father." Only when we align with the Holy Spirit and step out in faith, can we count on the name of Jesus for supernatural support. This Word guarantees that our prayers will be effective when all the Kingdom conditions have been met.

J ohn 14:13

You can ask for anything in my name, and I will do it, so that the Son can bring glory to the Father.

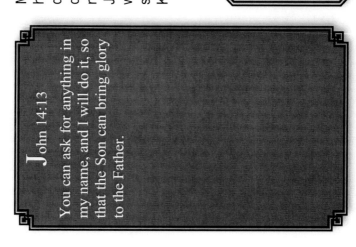

DECLARE THIS:

- I have unshakable faith in the name of Jesus when I use it as God directs.
- I live to bring God glory with my words, actions and life.
- I expect to see God's intervention in my life when I pray His will and exercise my faith in Jesus' name.

OCTOBER 21
KNOCK WITH BOLDNESS

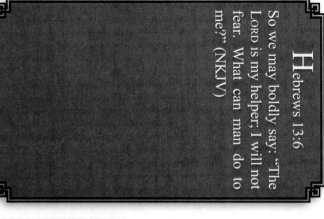

Hebrews 13:6
So we may boldly say: "The LORD is my helper; I will not fear. What can man do to me?" (NKJV)

Faith declares that God is love and he desires to bless us! He is our Helper, our Provider, our Protector and our Guide. Fear, on the other hand, is confidence in the enemy. Fear in any form — from worry to downright panic — gives Satan the legal right to interfere in our lives. That's why these two thoughts appear together in this scripture. We have to declare that the Lord is our Helper and flatly reject all fear. Satan cannot prevail against Christ. Man cannot interfere with the will and plan of God for our lives. We have to believe that, and we cannot be moved by anything we see or hear to the contrary. It's time to make an unshakable decision to believe the Word of God <u>only</u>! Once that decision is made and settled, boldness and confidence are not far behind.

DECLARE THIS:

- I am a child of God. Eternal life and overcoming victory in this life are my inheritance in Him.
- By faith I have decided to reject fear totally.
- I thank God that man cannot harm me and that nothing on earth can keep my good from me.

MARCH 12

Do you want to be wise? Do you want to be revived (made alive again)? Obey the instructions of the Lord. Keep in mind that our most important instruction is the command to love God and to love others as ourselves. This scripture tells us that when we follow His perfect instructions we'll be made wise and our souls will be revived. So ask for the ability to recognize and obey His instructions. The thirteenth chapter of First Corinthians might be a good place to start with this one.

P salm 19:7

The instructions of the Lord are perfect, reviving the soul. The decrees of the Lord are trustworthy, making wise the simple.

DECLARE THIS:

- I trust the instruction of the Lord as my daily guide.
- I know that my God is eternal, all knowing and perfect in wisdom.
- By faith I receive open access to the wisdom of God through His word.

If we want the revelation promised here we have to spend some of our job search time studying His teaching. The Word is there for all those who will take the time to look into it. There are teachers available everywhere, and wonderful CDs and books. But we have to position ourselves to learn. Keep your eyes on him and your ears attuned to his voice. If you do, you'll receive more teaching, more revelation, and an abundance of knowledge and wisdom. Couldn't you use that in your interviews, in your telephone calls, and in your search for openings?

> Matthew 13:12
>
> To those who listen to my teaching, more understanding will be given, and they will have an abundance of knowledge. But for those who are not listening, even what little understanding they have will be taken away from them.

DECLARE THIS:

- I listen to the teaching of the Lord and grow in understanding.
- By faith I receive an abundance of knowledge to guide me in all I do.
- I thank God that He is always pouring new knowledge and understanding into me as I need it.

MARCH 13
Ask About Your Gifts

> **P**roverbs 22:29
>
> Do you see a man skilled in his work? He will serve before kings; he will not serve before obscure men. (NIV)

Do you really excel in the workplace? An excellent worker is always on time, respects authority, doesn't gripe or grumble, and shows respect for everyone. This is the employee who can be completely trusted. Everyone knows that no earthly king would employ anyone except the very best of servants. Well, we serve the King of Kings... there is none higher. So we need to be the best of the best. Now is the time to make a personal commitment to excellence. Start by mastering the job search process. Go after the hidden job market even though it's a challenge. Take the time to practice your interview responses. Work to excel at this process, and become an excellent witness for the Kingdom. You will not end up in obscurity; you'll end up in a palace.

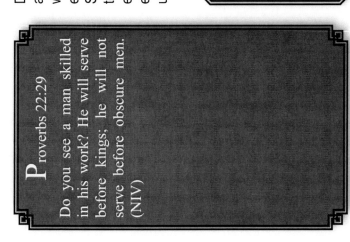

DECLARE THIS:

- I am excellent in all that I do because I represent the King of Kings.
- By faith I accept God's promise that I will be noticed and will find a great place of employment.
- I receive the leading and the correction of the Holy Spirit to make me an excellent and skillful worker.

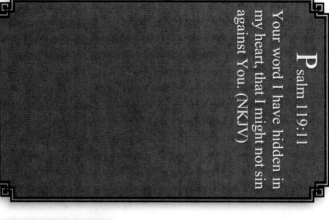

Psalm 119:11
Your word I have hidden in my heart, that I might not sin against You. (NKJV)

The Word of God has the power to bring itself to pass. When a situation looms that appears devastating or overwhelming you can experience the Word that you have hidden in your heart rising up to do battle for you! The Word commands the enemy to flee, and keeps us from turning the wrong way. All we have to do is fill our hearts with it. God's Word will do all the rest of the work for us — freeing us from sin, enabling us to resist temptation, and giving us strength and boldness when we need it! It's time to get busy and get stocked up in the Word.

DECLARE THIS:

- I have the Word of God in my heart and I am complete in Christ.
- By faith I receive the power of the Word to handle every situation I face.
- I thank God for the Word that gives me the victory over sin and temptation.

MARCH 14
Ask About Your Design

While you're looking for a job and it seems that no one is choosing you, remember that you have already been chosen! You are God's very own possession, and He treats His possessions very well indeed. Our eternal future is secure, our past has been washed away and abundant life is racing towards us this very day. Get this revelation into your heart. Knowing who you really are in Christ will affect everything about your job search and your future. When you go forth as a highly favored child of the Most High God, people will treat you differently. You'll find a welcoming reception unlike anything you've ever experienced. Let God reveal your true identity to you and see how life can change, from the inside out.

DECLARE THIS:

- I am a chosen and beloved child of God Almighty.
- The goodness that God showers upon me is evident to all I meet.
- By faith I accept that I have been called into the light of God so that I may lead others out of the darkness.

1 Peter 2:9

But you are not like that, for you are a chosen people. You are royal priests, a holy nation, God's very own possession. As a result, you can show others the goodness of God, for he called you out of the darkness into his wonderful light.

> Ephesians 2:19-21
>
> So now you Gentiles are no longer strangers and foreigners. You are citizens along with all of God's holy people. You are members of God's family. Together, we are his house, built on the foundation of the apostles and the prophets. And the cornerstone is Christ Jesus himself. We are carefully joined together in him, becoming a holy temple for the Lord.

You may come from a small family, so the experience of being surrounded by many aunts, uncles and cousins is unfamiliar to you. Then again, you may come from a large extended family and feel like you're somehow related to everyone you meet. Well, your true family is far bigger than you could ever imagine! You are related to every believer across the globe, and to every saint that has ever lived! Start looking for your "family members." Wherever you find them, connect with them, pray for their needs, and receive their prayers and love for you. It's time for us to rise up in unity and demonstrate our love for one another. Be ready to recognize and to bless the believers you encounter in your job search. Remember — there's tremendous power in our unity in Christ!

DECLARE THIS:

- I am adopted by God into His family and a vital part of His body.
- I stand in unity with all other believers and I am known by my love for them.
- I participate in the love and the oneness of the body in Christ.

MARCH 15
ASK ABOUT YOUR PURPOSE

Don't you wish that people could see what you can do, what you know, the contribution you could make, and the character you bring to the workplace? Then they'd know what a good hire you would be. Instead they use a 30-minute conversation to decide your fate... or so it might seem. But God has seen your entire life from beginning to end and He has a plan for you that will not be thwarted. Your life purpose is not in the hands of a recruiter or employment manager. You are in the hands of God. He is the one who knows what you have been uniquely designed to do, so spend time finding out what He has in mind. As soon as you hear from God you can take it to the bank. If God said it to you, it will come to pass.

DECLARE THIS:

- I hear from God. He desires to speak to me personally.
- Because He is my shepherd I recognize His voice.
- By faith I know that God has a purpose for my life and I receive revelation of it.

Ecclesiastes 3:11

Yet God has made everything beautiful for its own time. He has planted eternity in the human heart, but even so, people cannot see the whole scope of God's work from beginning to end.

OCTOBER 17
SEEK THE DIRECTION OF THE HOLY SPIRIT

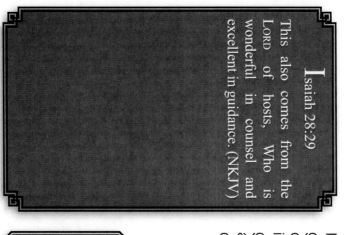

Isaiah 28:29

This also comes from the LORD of hosts, Who is wonderful in counsel and excellent in guidance. (NKJV)

If you read this entire scripture in context (and I hope you will), you will see how God gave farmers instructions about the smallest details of farming. There you will see the character of our God. His Word says He delights in every detail of our lives. He's actively interested and involved in everything that concerns us. He is a wonderful counselor who gives excellent advice. We can trust His instructions and His practical day-to-day guidance about how to conduct our lives. But we can't be led if we don't know His Word. God's counsel is there but we have to go after it.

DECLARE THIS:

- I am hungry to hear God's counsel and eagerly seek His guidance.
- By faith I accept that God cares about every detail of my life and has planned only wonderful things for me.
- My God is good and only good and He is my greatest Counselor.

MARCH 16
SEEK SELF AWARENESS

Many of us have a problem with how God responds to our needs at times. We always want immediate, total healing but most of the time we get better slowly, day by day. It can be the same with growth and change. We want God to fix us and get it over with. Instead, He changes us so slowly that sometimes we aren't even aware of it. We would never choose unemployment as a pathway to prosperity or blessing. Yet we have to admit that God has a habit of doing some unusual things with people. Naaman was enraged at what he was told to do, and yet it healed him of leprosy. Wasn't his restoration worth what he went through? So let God have His way with you now. After all, what wouldn't you do for abundant life?

DECLARE THIS:

- I turn my job search over to God and expect great results.
- By faith I receive blessing and great good from this time of unemployment.
- I know God wants only good for me and I trust the way He leads me.

---

2 Kings 5:11-12

But Naaman became angry and stalked away. "I thought he would certainly come out to meet me!" he said. "I expected him to wave his hand over the leprosy and call on the name of the LORD his God and heal me! Aren't the rivers of Damascus, the Abana and the Pharpar, better than any of the rivers of Israel? Why shouldn't I wash in them and be healed?"

M̲ark 12:17

"Well, then," Jesus said, "give to Caesar what belongs to Caesar, and give to God what belongs to God." His reply completely amazed them.

Some believers think they can do as they please at work and save their "really good service" for God. But Jesus tells us to give to Caesar what belongs to him. The same thing goes for our employers. They are paying our salary so they deserve our best performance. Unfortunately, I've heard many job seekers talk about poor pay or mistreatment in their last job as their justification for giving less than their best. Then they wonder why they were invited to leave. If this sounds like you, it's time to rethink your attitude. When we accept a position, we are making a commitment to give it our very best. As a representative of Christ, you need to be excellent. Don't take a job if you won't make that commitment.

DECLARE THIS:

- I represent the Kingdom of God and always perform with excellence.
- My employers are blessed with my best service at all times.
- By faith I receive forgiveness for all my past shortcomings and move forward free of all condemnation.

MARCH 17

Proverbs 3:5-6

Trust in the LORD with all your heart; do not depend on your own understanding. Seek his will in all you do, and he will show you which path to take.

Obviously there is a difference between trusting God and depending on our own understanding. We have to make the decision to trust God's way, no matter what. The way of the world is to look for any available job and try to talk our way into it. We're supposed to accept that we'll have to take a pay cut and probably move to some place we don't want to live. We're expected to be grateful for the "crumbs that fall from the table." But does any of that sound like abundant life, the promise of the Lord? No, the world's perception is fear-based and desperate. We have to be sure we're standing on God's Word. Trusting God is our way out of the jobless wilderness and into the promised land of employment.

DECLARE THIS:

- I am not unemployed; I work for the Lord.
- By faith I take actions in line with God's Word and the leading of the Spirit.
- I will not move in fear or desperation. The Lord orders my steps.

OCTOBER 15
ASK ABOUT YOUR PURPOSE

Matthew 25:21

"The master was full of praise. 'Well done, my good and faithful servant. You have been faithful in handling this small amount, so now I will give you many more responsibilities. Let's celebrate together!'

This verse tells us a master's response to a servant who successfully fulfilled his purpose. Did you notice that the servant was faithful in handling a small amount? We also have an assignment — to demonstrate God's love. We don't need to be great evangelists or preachers to do this. We just have to be faithful with what we've been given. What does this have to do with a job search? Everything! We can take the little we have, while we're unemployed, and use it for the Kingdom. We can share love and support and encouragement with others right now. In so doing, we can be assured that our Master will reward us with a place in the workplace where we can have an even greater impact.

DECLARE THIS:

- I invest my gifts and talents in others for the sake of the Kingdom.
- By faith I receive wisdom and direction in order to use my gifts as God has designed.
- Each day I will bring God a return on the love He has invested in me.

MARCH 18
SEEK DIVINE CONNECTIONS

Imagine a branch trying to bear fruit without being connected to the vine or its roots. That's us when we try to succeed on our own. His word is clear: "Without Me you can do nothing." Yet we keep running off without Him. Are you praying in the Spirit as you ask for insights about possible employers and new networking connections? Are you tithing your income and your time? Have you stopped to examine exactly how connected you really are to the Vine that gives you life? Sometimes we get so frantic about looking for a job that we forget to live a quality, connected life on a daily basis. Don't let anything distract you from those things that keep you connected to Jesus, the source of abundant life.

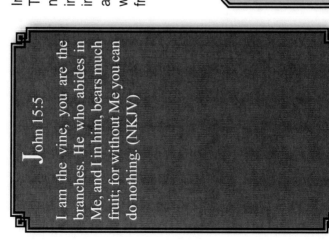

DECLARE THIS:

- I live in Christ and He lives in me.
- By faith I receive the life of God in my body and I am renewed.
- I expect to bear fruit in my job search and in my daily activities because I dwell in the vine.

John 15:5

I am the vine, you are the branches. He who abides in Me, and I in him, bears much fruit; for without Me you can do nothing. (NKJV)

OCTOBER 14
ASK ABOUT YOUR DESIGN

Ephesians 3:19-20 to know the love of Christ which passes knowledge; that you may be filled with all the fullness of God. Now to Him who is able to do exceedingly abundantly above all that we ask or think, according to the power that works in us, (NKJV)

We are designed for greatness — the fullness of God in us. We have the capacity to be filled with all the fullness of God and to receive all that God has planned for us. But notice that God is actually constrained by us and can only do His part in accordance with "the power that works in us." In Galatians 5:6 we see that this power would be "faith working by love." The only limit upon us, then, is that we must access our power by faith and through love if we want to release God to act.

DECLARE THIS:

- I receive the fullness of God in me now.
- By faith I receive a full revelation of the love of Christ for me.
- I release the power of God in me by faith in the love of Christ in me.

MARCH 19
SEEK HIDDEN TREASURES

We are accountable for the treasures and secrets God has revealed to us. Our children are depending on us to share revelation with them so that they too might walk in truth and possess God's promises. Clearly His Word is there for us to access. The Holy Spirit is ready to speak to us and instruct each one of us individually and personally. Teachers, pastors and spiritual leaders have been provided to guide us as well. So there's no excuse for us to walk in darkness. God doesn't want to bless your job search only — He wants to bless every aspect of your life. The guidance you are seeking and the answers you need are right there for you. Make time for Him to whisper His secrets to you.

Deuteronomy 29:29

The LORD our God has secrets known to no one. We are not accountable for them, but we and our children are accountable forever for all that he has revealed to us, so that we may obey all the terms of these instructions.

DECLARE THIS:

- I expect to receive the wisdom I need as I read the living Word of God.
- I ask the Holy Spirit to teach me to recognize the secrets and revelation that I need.
- By faith I receive the mind of Christ, wisdom and understanding of the ways of God.

OCTOBER 13
ASK ABOUT YOUR GIFTS

2 Kings 5:15

And he returned to the man of God, he and all his aides, and came and stood before him; and he said, "Indeed, now I know that there is no God in all the earth, except in Israel; now therefore, please take a gift from your servant." (NKJV)

Think about the poor widow Jesus spoke about, "But she out of her poverty put in the entire livelihood that she had." It doesn't matter if we're out of work, money is tight, and we may not know where the next dollar is coming from. May we never take God's blessing and our Kingdom inheritance for granted. Just because it has been freely given to us doesn't mean it isn't priceless. When we truly realize what we've been given, we'll respond to God with whatever we can find to give — our time, our money, our fellowship, and our talents.

DECLARE THIS:

- I am grateful to God for His priceless gifts to me and I look for ways to bring Him gifts of thanksgiving.
- By faith I take my gifts and invest them in the Kingdom so that I might produce a great harvest for the Lord.
- I am ever mindful of what the Lord has done for me.

MARCH 20

SEEK TO STAY FOCUSED ON JESUS

It's easy to have peace when our situation is stable and calm, or when we find the answer to a question that's been puzzling us. We feel better because our immediate need has been addressed. But that's not perfect peace. True peace, perfect peace, is a constant state of being and it's only possible when we keep our gaze fixed on Jesus. To have our thoughts fixed on Him requires that we have our hearts filled with His Word and our minds made up about where we stand. Until we make a quality decision to trust God completely, we will get distressed and shaken. As soon as we establish our complete trust and our determined focus on Jesus, we'll experience the promise of perfect peace.

> Isaiah 26:3
> You will keep in perfect peace all who trust in you, all whose thoughts are fixed on you!

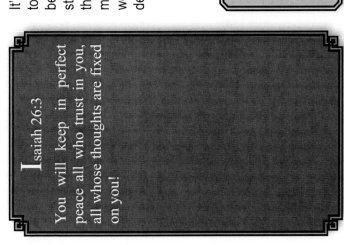

DECLARE THIS:

- I have peace because I keep my mind on Christ.
- My trust is in the Lord and I will not be moved.
- By faith I receive an awareness of God's Spirit within me and I am calm.

Once again it's time to focus on first things first. And here comes the foundational message one more time — Jesus is our starting place. Indeed, a true revelation of God is really all we will ever need, and it's freely available. God wants to give us the spirit of wisdom and revelation. How will this wisdom and revelation come to us? "In the knowledge of Him." No wonder God says to seek the Kingdom (and the King!) first. Every good thing is waiting for you in Him. Go ahead and ask for your eyes to be opened to see Him and to fully comprehend what He has already done for you. In these uncertain times, wouldn't a solid understanding and confidence in God be valuable?

Ephesians 1:17-19

That the God of our Lord Jesus Christ, the Father of glory, may give unto you the spirit of wisdom and revelation in the knowledge of him: The eyes of your understanding being enlightened; that ye may know what is the hope of his calling, and what the riches of the glory of his inheritance in the saints, And what is the exceeding greatness of his power to us-ward who believe, according to the working of his mighty power, (NKJV)

DECLARE THIS:

- I rule and reign in Jesus, the Anointed One.
- I receive enlightened eyes and the revelation of all that I have in Christ.
- There is no power on earth equal to the power I have in Christ Jesus.

MARCH 21
KNOCK WITH BOLDNESS

Who wouldn't choose to walk in confidence and speak with boldness? But that gets really difficult when you've been without a job for a while. People start to comment on your inability to find work. They question your efforts, your persistence, your commitment, and maybe even your qualifications. In the face of the accusations and condemnation, it's tough to be bold. That's when this verse helps. The disciples were uneducated and untrained men, with no skills and no training. But they were bold, because they had been with Jesus. That's our solution too. Get with Jesus. Spend time with Him. Bask in His love before you go anywhere or do anything. You need an infusion of Christ every day of the job search if you intend to stay bold and confident. Go ahead, let people marvel at you too!

Acts 4:13

Now when they saw the boldness of Peter and John, and perceived that they were uneducated and untrained men, they marveled. And they realized that they had been with Jesus.

DECLARE THIS:

- I have been with Jesus and my confidence is unshakable.
- By faith I receive revelation of Christ in me and I am bold.
- I will not be discouraged by what others say; my God has equipped me for success.

Matthew 11:18-20

For John didn't spend his time eating and drinking, and you say, 'He's possessed by a demon.' The Son of Man, on the other hand, feasts and drinks, and you say, 'He's a glutton and a drunkard, and a friend of tax collectors and other sinners!' But wisdom is shown to be right by its results."

No one will believe that God desires to prosper His children if they see you living in lack. No one will want to follow our God if He can't help His children find job or get their bills paid. If we want anyone to believe that the one true God is perfect love, we're going to have to prove it. Jesus says that "wisdom is shown to be right by its results." We're supposed to be followed by signs and wonders. Tell God that's what you want. And be assured that God doesn't want us showing no results either! So ask Him to use you as a poster child for the Kingdom and to show Himself strong in your life.

DECLARE THIS:

- I reveal the power of the God I serve by manifesting His blessing in my life.
- By faith I receive God's wisdom, and the results show in my life.
- God's reputation rests with me. I cannot fail.

MARCH 22
KNOCK WITH THANKSGIVING

If God never did another thing for us, wouldn't we still be blessed? There are more than a hundred promises that come with our inheritance in Christ. We have life, health, opportunities, and the ability to think and to perform. We have love, eternal life, forgiveness from sin, hope, and the promises in God's Word. We have The Blessing of Abraham — an eternal covenant of God's love — and faith to receive it. We are seated in Christ at the right hand of God. All of the authority and power of God has been given to us, in the name of Jesus. We live in the light while the rest of the world suffers darkness. Doesn't all this merit our thanks and praise? Before you head out today, stop and give thanks, remembering that Jesus paid with His life to give you this inheritance.

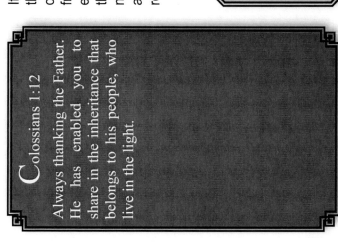

Colossians 1:12

Always thanking the Father. He has enabled you to share in the inheritance that belongs to his people, who live in the light.

DECLARE THIS:

- I give continuous thanks to God for blessing me.
- By faith I receive my inheritance in Christ and call forth every blessing in the name of Jesus.
- I thank God that I am in His Kingdom and I live in the Light.

OCTOBER 10
CHOOSE YOUR BATTLE

P salm 91:4-7

...His truth shall be your shield and buckler. You shall not be afraid of the terror by night, Nor of the arrow that flies by day Nor of the pestilence that walks in darkness, Nor of the destruction that lays waste at noonday. A thousand may fall at your side, And ten thousand at your right hand; But it shall not come near you. (NKJV)

This scripture gives us insight into the enemy's tactics. He attacks in the night with terror, waiting until we're alone in the dark to start with every fearful thought he can bring. In the day, when we're out with others, he sees to it that negative and condemning comments fly at us like arrows. When we can't see him, he arranges for diseases to come into us through toxic emotions and stress. In the middle of the day, on every news broadcast, he publishes reports of widespread destruction. Those are his tactics. "But it will not come near you." Why? Because we have God's shield all around us. We are hidden under the shadow of His wings and Satan cannot reach us there.

DECLARE THIS:

- I am not moved by what I see or by what I hear. I believe what God says about the matter.

- The things that are happening to others do not apply to me. I am Christ's ambassador and subject only to the rules of His Kingdom.

- My God is good and only good. Because He is perfect love He keeps me from all harm.

MARCH 23
KNOCK WITH CONFIDENCE

Whenever something big or overwhelming comes against us, we simply have to read this scripture. It's hard not to experience comfort and assurance by reading miracle stories in the bible — how God split the Red Sea, held back the river Jordan, caused the Sun to stand still for a day. Remember the walls of Jericho crumbling; the blinding of an entire enemy army so the prophet could lead them into the city of Samaria without force? The message is simple — God is capable of whatever we need. Settle this in your mind once and for all. When asking the question, "Is anything too hard for the Lord?" the answer will always be "No, nothing." Then have faith to believe that God will do something this wonderful for you.

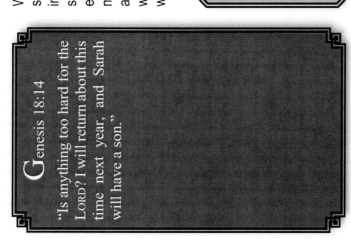

DECLARE THIS:

- I have unshakable faith that God is able to do all things. Nothing is too hard for Him.
- By faith I receive what God has promised me.
- I know that God has a work assignment for me and nothing can hold it back from me.

Genesis 18:14
"Is anything too hard for the LORD? I will return about this time next year, and Sarah will have a son."

OCTOBER 9
CHOOSE YOUR BEHAVIOR

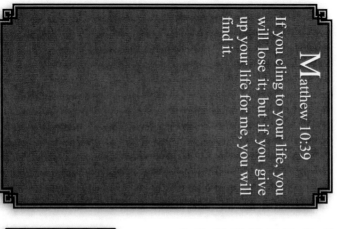

Matthew 10:39

If you cling to your life, you will lose it; but if you give up your life for me, you will find it.

William Sloan once said, "God loves you totally, unconditionally, just as you are right now... and He loves you too much to leave you there." That's a difficult concept. How can God possibly love us completely when there is still so much wrong with us? Maybe it's a bit like Jell-O. We know it is fine in its powdered form, but it isn't edible yet. It is going to take time, hot water and continuous stirring to produce the finished product. Somewhere along the way it has to be molded. We too have the raw ingredients God needs to make us into the image of Christ, and He's delighted to go through the process. We simply need to give up our hold on our little life plans and allow the Master to mold us. When we cooperate we end up with so much more than we could have ever imagined!

DECLARE THIS:

- I let go of my plans for my life to receive the much better plan of God.
- I know that God has plans to prosper me and never harm me.
- God gives me a future and a hope that I can't find anywhere else.

MARCH 24
KNOCK AND BRING GIFTS

This world is in a mess, and every day it becomes more evident that government leaders aren't going to be able to fix it. The scriptures tell us that world systems will fail. Built on greed, selfishness and pride, they cannot produce long-term prosperity, peace or security. But God has given us all those things for free, in abundance, in a Kingdom that has no end. He has given us the power to get wealth. He has met all our needs and given us all things richly to enjoy. We may not have the manifestation of these promises in our lives yet, but they are still the truth. We will, by faith, see the abundant life God has procured for us, in this lifetime. So shine like the city on the hill. Don't wait until God's Word is fully manifest to start talking about His goodness. Get on fire for the Lord now, and as you go about your job search, let your light shine.

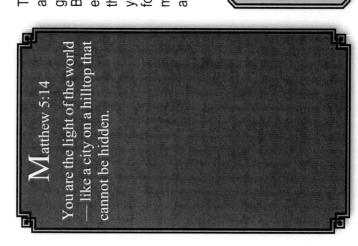

Matthew 5:14

You are the light of the world — like a city on a hilltop that cannot be hidden.

DECLARE THIS:

- I belong to an unshakable Kingdom.
- The Holy Spirit in me reveals ways that I can be a light in this dark world.
- I declare the truth of God's goodness and I expect to see abundance manifest in my life.

OCTOBER 8
CHOOSE YOUR TRAINING

1 Corinthians 2:10-13

The Spirit, not content to flit around on the surface, dives into the depths of God, and brings out what God planned all along. Who ever knows what you're thinking and planning except you yourself? The same with God — except that he not only knows what he's thinking, but he lets us in on it. God offers a full report on the gifts of life and salvation that he is giving us. We don't have to rely on the world's guesses and opinions. We didn't learn this by reading books or going to school; we learned it from God, who taught us person-to-person through Jesus, and we're passing it on to you in the same firsthand, personal way. (Message)

The Message Bible just hits the nail on the head with this scripture. Study the picture presented here. God is standing in eternity, seeing everything from beginning to end. He has, from that perspective, already provided every gift we're going to need for an abundant life and the path that will lead us to it. Now He turns to us and says, through the Spirit living inside us, "Let me tell you what I have arranged for you — life, salvation, understanding, prosperity, every good and perfect thing." Many job seekers worry that they'll take the wrong job, say the wrong thing, or make the wrong decision. Not to worry! In a first-hand, personal way the Holy Spirit will tell us things directly from the heart of God. Our part is to focus our full attention on Him... and wait to act until we hear His voice!

DECLARE THIS:

- I am so grateful that God wants to share His heart with me.
- I make space in my life to hear what God has for me.
- By faith I receive the full revelation of His plans for my life.

MARCH 25
KNOCK AND EXERCISE YOUR FAITH

Faith is the key... faith in God alone. This is the deciding factor for success. Many people believe in God, but so what? The Word says even the demons believe in Him. Belief is not enough. We have to take the full measure of faith that we've been given and put it into action. Stake your faith on God's promises and do not move. If you have the faith to spend eternity with God, you ought to be able to put your faith and complete trust in Him now, right? So stand your ground and watch what happens.

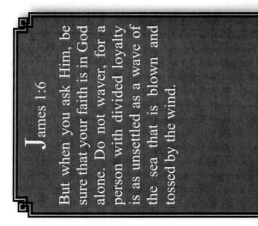

James 1:6

But when you ask Him, be sure that your faith is in God alone. Do not waver, for a person with divided loyalty is as unsettled as a wave of the sea that is blown and tossed by the wind.

DECLARE THIS:

- I know that my security and confidence is in God alone.
- My loyalty is not divided and my mind is made up. I trust in God.
- By faith I choose to ignore the circumstances that surround me and keep my gaze fixed on "things above", the Word of God.

OCTOBER 7
CHOOSE YOUR PAY

Philippians 4:19

And this same God who takes care of me will supply all your needs from his glorious riches, which have been given to us in Christ Jesus.

No doubt about it, God took care of Paul. The man was shipwrecked repeatedly but always rescued. He was bitten by a poisonous viper but not harmed. He was even stoned and left for dead, then was raised up to preach again! Don't think God caused Paul's suffering. Paul was being persecuted by the enemy for preaching the gospel. Paul understood that it was God alone who continued to save and deliver him. He saw himself as indestructible because of the God he served. The God that cared for Paul is the same God that is supplying all your needs. He isn't the cause of your distress but He is the One who is more than able to take you through to victory.

DECLARE THIS:

- I believe that God is willing and able to meet all my needs from His supply of glorious riches.
- I receive everything Jesus died to give me. He is more than enough.
- By faith I declare that all my needs are met.

MARCH 26

KNOCK AND WITNESS FOR THE KINGDOM

> Isaiah 6:8
>
> Then I heard the Lord asking, "Whom should I send as a messenger to this people? Who will go for us?" I said, "Here I am. Send me."

After all this time, God is still asking the question, "Who will be my messenger? Who can I send?" He's hoping that we will jump up and say, "Me! Please send me!" This has nothing to do with being employed, talented, or successful. It has to do with willingness. Are we willing to forget our needs and remember that there is a world of hurting people out there in desperate need of Jesus? Are you willing to be God's messenger today? No matter where you go or how you plan to spend your time today, you can be His spokesperson. That's what this life is all about. We're here to practice for our eternal role. Work that into your job search and bring the light of God wherever you go.

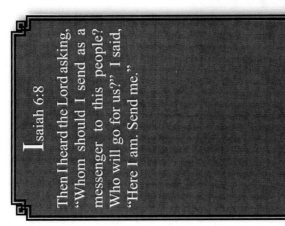

DECLARE THIS:

- I am a messenger for God in this dark and hurting world.
- Wherever I go today I ask the Holy Spirit to reveal opportunities to share the good news with the people I meet.
- By faith I accept my assignment to represent the Kingdom of God and to walk in His favor.

OCTOBER 6
CHOOSE YOUR WORK

Matthew 22:37

And He replied to him, You shall love the Lord your God with all your heart and with all your soul and with all your mind (intellect). This is the great (most important, principal) and first commandment. And a second is like it: You shall love your neighbor as [you do] yourself. (The Amplified Bible)

Our God is a jealous God, we've been told. He isn't willing to share any part of you with any other God and He's not willing to be lower than our top priority. He wants our thoughts and our will to align with His, our emotions to be in obedience to His Word, and our hearts filled with His presence. But this is not to meet His needs. It's so we can receive the fullness of His blessing. When we come all the way into His Kingdom we will experience days of heaven on earth. Our entire job description for Kingdom life has been designed to position us for victory and prosperity. When we give all we've got to Him, He has room to work and He'll respond with all we'll ever want or need.

DECLARE THIS:

- I keep God at the center of my life. He is my greatest priority.
- By faith I turn my mind, will and emotions toward God and bring Him all my love.
- I trust that the Holy Spirit will increase my ability to love so that I can better worship the Lord and obey this command.

MARCH 27
KNOCK AND OVERCOME

When we're in a job search and nothing seems to be happening, it's easy to think God has forgotten us. We hear there are no openings, or they just filled the position, or they would never hire anyone without certain skills, and we lose heart. But God's Word assures us that if He ever did something for one of His children, He will do it for you. He doesn't play favorites and He never changes, so this scripture is as true for us today as it was for the people of Judah. He even promises to deal with those who cause you harm. You can count on Him to do it too! So stand on your faith and resist doubt, fatigue, confusion and frustration. God is not unaware of your situation. He has made a way back into the workplace for you and He will reveal it. Keep your ears open and your eyes on His Word.

DECLARE THIS:

- I cannot fail. I belong to the Most High God.
- By faith I trust that God will deal with my enemies and restore me.
- God is more angry at those who try to do me harm than I am. He is my daddy and He isn't going to allow His child to be harmed.

Joel 3:5-7

You have taken my silver and gold and all my precious treasures, and have carried them off to your pagan temples. You have sold the people of Judah and Jerusalem to the Greeks, so they could take them far from their homeland. "But I will bring them back from all the places to which you sold them, and I will pay you back for everything you have done."

OCTOBER 5
CHOOSE YOUR BENEFITS

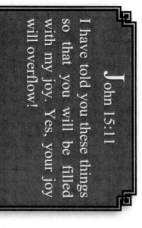

John 15:11

I have told you these things so that you will be filled with my joy. Yes, your joy will overflow!

Imagine looking at the employee benefits of a prospective employer and finding "joy" on the list! Would that be a great place to work? This is precisely what God offers us in Christ Jesus. In fact, He wants us to be so joy-filled that it pours out and splashes on everyone around us! If you don't know that joy is on God's "benefits list," you might not look for or expect it. But it's there, and you can! The joy Jesus felt, the complete joy that comes from God's overwhelming and perfect love, can be yours! Right now, in this season of unemployment ask Jesus to release it in your life. There's no reason you can't be filled with joy during your job search. The world can't do this, but believers can, by God's grace.

DECLARE THIS:

- I experience the joy of the Lord. My happiness is not based on my circumstances.
- By faith I release worry, concern and sadness as I go through my job search.
- I receive the Word of God, the things Jesus has told me, and I have joy unspeakable!

MARCH 28
KNOCK AND FAINT NOT!

Luke 12:32

"So don't be afraid, little flock. For it gives your Father great happiness to give you the Kingdom.

The scriptures refer to us continually as "sheep." At first I didn't care for that comparison. There's nothing appealing about smelly, stupid followers. But there's no more powerful or enduring image than a loving shepherd keeping watch over his well-cared-for flock. It might serve us "sheep" well to know a few things. One: we're in a war zone and we can't see the enemy. Two: we don't have His understanding of the situation. Three: compared to the supernatural power made available to us by Christ, our worldly skills and abilities are nothing. So now I know — being a sheep is fine, just as long as we stay very close to the Good Shepherd who is vigilant over us. Don't forget that for even one moment of your job search.

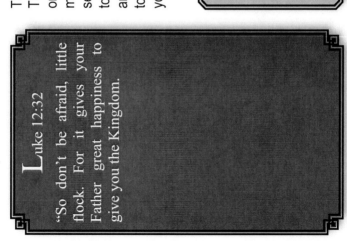

DECLARE THIS:

- I believe that it gives God happiness to bless me with every good thing.
- I refuse to receive a spirit of fear. I recognize fear as a strategy of the enemy and I rebuke it.
- By faith I receive the blessing of Abraham because Jesus bought it for me at Calvary.

OCTOBER 4
CHOOSE YOUR BOSS

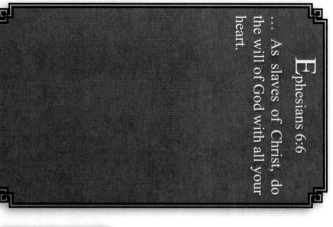

E_{phesians} 6:6
... As slaves of Christ, do the will of God with all your heart.

"Slaves of Christ" — I'd say that makes our employment situation pretty clear. The term slave or bondservant is important here. We don't really understand what it means to be a slave, to be another person's property. Yet we are not our own — Christ became our Master when we accepted our salvation. He owns us and we need to be "sold out" to Him. Just wait until we really discover that our Master is the richest, most powerful, and most awesome Master ever, and He bought us simply because He wants to shower us with blessings. What could be better than that?

DECLARE THIS:

- I am completely sold out to the One who gave His life to purchase mine.
- By faith I accept that God's will for me is far better and far beyond what I could imagine for myself.
- I will to will the will of God.

MARCH 29
Knock And Be Encouraged

You might not find this encouraging, but you need to know that the systems of this world are failing. Perhaps news of the crumbling economy and dismal employment statistics is already keeping you up at night. But you don't have to feel that way. In fact, you don't have to give the world's situation a second thought, because you are not a citizen of this world. Read this scripture again and ask the Holy Spirit to give you its full revelation. The uncertain riches of this world are not to be trusted. You have something so much better. You serve a living God, and He gives everything to you so you can have a great life. Rest in that.

DECLARE THIS:

- My God is the Ruler over all and He loves to give me wonderful gifts.
- By faith I receive all the things that God gives me to enjoy. I expect to live abundantly.
- My confidence is in God as my provider. I don't place any trust in the systems of this world.

---

1 Timothy 6:17

Command those who are rich in this present age not to be haughty, nor to trust in uncertain riches but in the living God, who gives us richly all things to enjoy. (NKJV)

> P salm 68:6
>
> God sets the solitary in families; He brings out those who are bound into prosperity; But the rebellious dwell in a dry land. (NKJV)

This scripture states that God "brings out those who are bound" so that He can get them into prosperity. Consider that, in the context of why you might be unemployed right now. If you were in a job that was going nowhere, or if you were in a bad situation, God might have actually set you free. We are not to be captives, not in the workplace or in life. God wants you to use your gifts to the fullest, to serve His purposes. When that isn't happening in one work environment, He can easily take you to another. If God can lead thousands of Israelites through a sea to freedom, He can certainly take you from one job to another. But don't miss His intention. He is leading you into prosperity... nothing missing, nothing broken, anywhere in your life. That's God's plan and desire for you.

DECLARE THIS:

- I believe that God is leading me into prosperity.
- By faith I receive direction from the Holy Spirit to lead me to my rightful place in the workforce.
- I trust that God is good and His plans for me are better than anything I could imagine.

MARCH 30
KNOCK AND KEEP KNOCKING

The job search process can certainly make us feel powerless. We can't make people call when we want them to. We can't make openings happen. We can't even figure out where to look for our next job. It's obvious that we're not in control of anything. But the truth is, we have never been in control and we never will be. Each of us is standing in the future we were facing a few years ago. Our future never changed. We just didn't know it would look like this, did we? In this world nothing is secure, but in the Kingdom of God everything is secure. This would be a great time to surrender the reins completely to God, and let Him give us the power and strength we've always wanted.

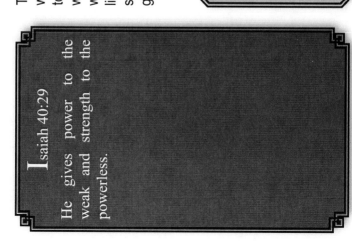

DECLARE THIS:

- I am connected to the Power Source for the whole universe and He makes me strong.
- By faith I receive God's power to carry me where I am weak. I am complete in Christ, lacking nothing.
- I receive God's strength and power in every aspect of my life.

Isaiah 40:29

He gives power to the weak and strength to the powerless.

M̄ark 2:22

"And no one puts new wine into old wineskins. For the wine would burst the wineskins, and the wine and the skins would both be lost. New wine calls for new wineskins."

Have you ever tried to get your head around a radical new thought? Well, there are few thoughts as radical as the mindset that will switch us from the world system into the Kingdom way of life. But sometimes God apprehends us and insists on "new wine and new wineskins." It will take all your effort to keep your thoughts centered on the Word. It will require huge energy to control the words you say and the actions you take. But it is so worth it! You are a new creation in Christ; you have been given the gift of new and abundant life. Allow the Holy Spirit to lead you into new behaviors, new relationships and new thoughts, so that you are able to contain the "new wine" of your life as a believer.

DECLARE THIS:

- I am ready for change and I trust God to make me new.
- I receive the wisdom of God and understanding of my Kingdom purpose.
- I know that God is good and His plans for me are good and only good.

MARCH 31
KNOCK AND BE AT PEACE

Righteousness will bring peace! And here's the really good news. We don't have to come up with the righteousness. If it was up to us to get righteous, we'd never make it. But it isn't up to us. Jesus has already made us righteous. We simply have to receive His righteousness by faith. What Jesus did at Calvary was more than enough. Nothing else needs to be done. Just let that sink all the way into your heart. Then allow peace and quietness and confidence to fill you.

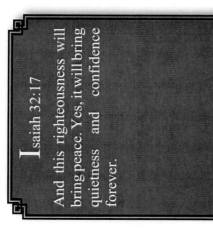

Isaiah 32:17

And this righteousness will bring peace. Yes, it will bring quietness and confidence forever.

DECLARE THIS:

- I am righteous because Christ made me righteous.
- By faith I receive the full inheritance of the righteous.
- I am peaceful, calm and confident.

OCTOBER 1
CHOOSE YOUR KINGDOM

M atthew 6:33
But seek first his kingdom and his righteousness, and all these things will be given to you as well. (NIV)

Let's revisit a scripture we've looked at before. There's a point here that too many of us miss. We are directed to seek God and His righteousness. We are NOT directed to try and make ourselves righteous. That's a good thing, too, because it would be impossible. We cannot clean ourselves up to become acceptable to God and He has not asked us to sanctify ourselves. The direction for Kingdom seekers is to go after God, get to know Him personally, and then seek His righteousness. It is Christ's righteousness, not ours, that opens the Kingdom to us! Place your faith in the completed work of Christ and His promise to make us new in Him.

DECLARE THIS:

- I accept that I have been made righteous in Christ.
- I am a citizen of God's Kingdom and His child and that is all I need for success.
- My needs are met because I am a joint heir with Jesus and God is my Father.

APRIL

GOOD NEWS

GOOD NEWS

OCTOBER

APRIL 1
CHOOSE YOUR KINGDOM

When I first started my job search, I had an image that God was distant from me, and I was chasing him. Imagine my relief when I discovered that God was actually pursuing me! God is also pursuing you. He loves you, values you and wants a relationship with you. This makes your task easier. All you have to do is seek the Kingdom and make time in your life to get to know the King. Don't take the first step to find a job today without spending time with your Father in Heaven. Nothing will be more important for the success of your job search than assuring that you have placed your full confidence in God before you head out the door.

DECLARE THIS:

- My mind is made up. I belong to God alone.
- I am forgiven and cleansed.
- By faith I receive you, Lord. You are my King and I choose to follow you.

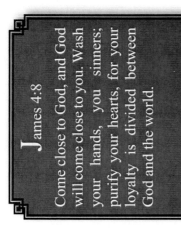

James 4:8

Come close to God, and God will come close to you. Wash your hands, you sinners; purify your hearts, for your loyalty is divided between God and the world.

SEPTEMBER 30
KNOCK AND KEEP KNOCKING

Psalm 138:3

In the day when I called, You answered me; and You strengthened me with strength (might and inflexibility to temptation) in my inner self. (The Amplified Bible)

After all the victories God handed him, you might think King David would have been totally confident, maybe even a bit cocky. Yet David always had the good sense to involve God in everything he was doing. His pattern was always to call on God, expecting His response to be favorable, and then go out with the expectation of a conquest. So often in a job search we become exhausted and frustrated, and we allow fatigue to overwhelm us. If that's you, stop! Don't run yourself out of gas. Call on God. Ask for strength to go through another day of searching. Expect to be strengthened, and expect to receive the might and the power you need to conquer the employment market.

DECLARE THIS:

- I call on the Lord for help and He strengthens me.
- By faith I know that God will always hear me and He will always help. He never fails.
- I expect to receive the strength and might that I need every day.

APRIL 2
CHOOSE YOUR THOUGHTS

God is not focused on our past, our heritage, or our behaviors. What matters to God is whether we will allow Him to turn us into new creations. If we allow God to have His way, we'll realize that we've been adopted by God and we are now royalty. We'll feel securely grafted into the Vine of life with God's very spirit ever-present in us. Can you see how this truth would change the way we behave in our everyday lives? How would you act in an interview with a prospective employer if you fully understood the work God has done in you? Let God renew your mind with his Word and allow His truth to transform you into the new creation He has in mind.

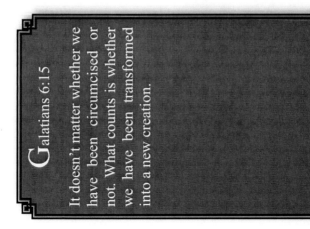

DECLARE THIS:

- By faith I accept that God has made me a new creation—perfect and blameless in His sight.

- I know that God does not judge me by my past behaviors. He sees me through the blood of Christ.

- Because I have been transformed, my behaviors are changing to line up with the Word.

Galatians 6:15

It doesn't matter whether we have been circumcised or not. What counts is whether we have been transformed into a new creation.

SEPTEMBER 29
KNOCK AND BE ENCOURAGED

John 16:13-14

When the Spirit of truth comes, he will guide you into all truth. He will not speak on his own but will tell you what he has heard. He will tell you about the future. He will bring me glory by telling you whatever he receives from me.

Christ dwells in each of us. The indwelling Spirit of God will lead us in the way we should go and will tell us everything we need to know to experience the fullness of life and joy that He desires for us. Our greatest encouragement comes from the realization that with the assistance of the Holy Spirit we cannot "miss it" as we search for a job. If we listen we will hear from God and be led in the way of truth and abundant life. Be encouraged because He has promised that He will be found by those who diligently seek Him. Don't wander in the dark any longer. Run to the Light!

DECLARE THIS:

- I have the power of the Holy Spirit in me and I am strengthened and guided by Him.
- By faith I receive my daily guidance, instructions and confidence from the Lord of my life.
- I thank God that I am led by the One who has already seen the future and made a great plan for me in it.

APRIL 3
CHOOSE YOUR FUTURE

Here is an essential piece of advice for job seekers — forget the past! Wherever you focus your thoughts is where you will stay anchored. Don't become stuck in the past. Whether your past was great and you miss it or it was horrible and it haunts you, it's over. You cannot go back to it, so let it go. Anchor your thoughts to the Word of God and the wonderful promises you'll find there. Let them pull you into the future God has for you... an abundant life filled with every good thing.

DECLARE THIS:

- The past has no hold on me. I am free.
- I joyfully look forward to my future and expect great good.
- I know Who holds my future. My confidence is in Christ alone.

Philippians 3:13

No, dear brothers and sisters, I have not achieved it, but I focus on this one thing: Forgetting the past and looking forward to what lies ahead

SEPTEMBER 28
KNOCK AND FAINT NOT!

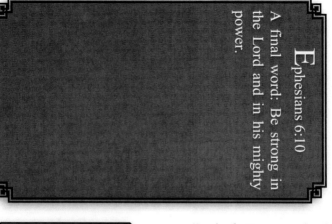

Ephesians 6:10
A final word: Be strong in the Lord and in his mighty power.

What does it mean to be "strong in the Lord?" And what is this mighty power that we are to walk in? The answer can be found in this simple statement — God is love. God Himself is love and love is God. So if we want victory in our life, we must be powered by love. Brother Lawrence had the right idea when he said, "All things are possible to those who believe; still more to those who hope; still more to those who love; and most of all to those who practice all three". Our power is found in faith, hope and love and the greatest of these is love. So as we go through our job search today let's go out in the love of God and share it with everyone we meet.

DECLARE THIS:

- I have the love of Jesus in me and it gives me power.
- By faith I receive the strength of the Lord and the power of His might to accomplish His will for my life.
- I thank God that I don't have to rely on my own strength or wisdom or power.

APRIL 4
CHOOSE YOUR BOSS

There is no other God and no other Rock to stand on. As we read His Word we have to be awestruck at the good He has in mind for us. He reaches out to us to rescue us, lead us, love us and bless us. He tells us not to be afraid because He has us in His hand. We are a significant part of His almighty purposes. He has plans for us to be His witnesses and to bring Him glory. He has to preserve us and care for us because we represent Him! So keep that in mind if you start to become concerned about your situation. God's reputation rests upon you. He will not allow you to fail.

DECLARE THIS:

- I will not fear because I belong to the one true God and He never fails.
- By faith I believe that I am part of God's plan and Kingdom purposes, and He will lead me in the way I am to go.
- I stand on a solid Rock. I will not be moved by evil reports.

Isaiah 44:8

Do not tremble; do not be afraid. Did I not proclaim my purposes for you long ago? You are my witnesses — is there any other God? No! There is no other Rock — not one!

SEPTEMBER 27
KNOCK AND OVERCOME

John 16:33

I have told you all this so that you may have peace in me. Here on earth you will have many trials and sorrows. But take heart, because I have overcome the world.

We don't have to be reminded that we'll have trials and sorrows in this world. We're in the midst of them right now. But our trials and sorrows don't need to have power over us. Jesus has peace and victory for us right now. He tells us, in this verse, how our situation is going to turn out. We win! He has overcome unemployment, poverty, and economic uncertainty. He has overcome this world and taken you into victory with Him. See yourself as an over comer in Christ. Remember, God needs us back in the workplace so we can be a blessing. So claim your victory and go out like someone who expects to be hired into a great job, doing work you really love. Be a demonstration of what God in Christ does for those who love Him!

DECLARE THIS:

- I am an over comer in Jesus Christ. I expect victory in my job search.
- By faith I receive the peace of God in my current circumstances because Jesus has overcome the world.
- I have power and authority in the name of Jesus and I use it to accomplish the work of the Kingdom.

APRIL 5
CHOOSE YOUR BENEFITS

While the rest of the world is reeling in panic and suffering an epidemic of fear, God's people have been given the great "benefit package" of power, love and self-discipline. This scripture tells us that any fear or timidity we experience does not come from within us. It's an enemy attack and we don't have to buy into it. But to fully receive our benefits, we have to walk in love, discipline our minds and bodies, and exercise the power we've been given. Now that we know we can live without fear, this makes walking in love all the more important, doesn't it?

DECLARE THIS:

- I am powerful, loving and self disciplined by the grace of God.
- Fear has no hold on me for it is not my nature. I am bold in the Lord.
- By faith I receive the wisdom to recognize an enemy attack and to stand in love against it.

---

2 Timothy 1:7

For God has not given us a spirit of fear and timidity, but of power, love, and self-discipline.

Titus 2:7

And you yourself must be an example to them by doing good works of every kind. Let everything you do reflect the integrity and seriousness of your teaching.

How can we do good works when we're not working and money is tight? Consider the phrase "good works of every kind." We can always behave with integrity. We can consistently act like someone who has been taught God's way of doing things. There are plenty of opportunities to do things badly in the job search — failing to call when we say we will, failing to be truthful on our resumes, and failing to show up prepared for the interview. We don't have to be like that. We have the golden opportunity to be excellent at things that most job seekers do badly. Take the challenge to "be an example" and show how Kingdom people handle unemployment!

DECLARE THIS:

- I accept the assignment to be an example to others and to behave with excellence and integrity.
- I recognize the good works God has given me to do and I do them.
- I receive the guidance and the power of the Holy Ghost to show me how to be an excellent job seeker.

APRIL 6
CHOOSE YOUR WORK

First and foremost, we work for God. This scripture is His most basic instruction for doing our work. It tells us to be nice to others and to treat them respectfully, but there's more here that can directly benefit you as you look for a job. What would you really like for others to do for you right now while you're unemployed — share leads, tell you about open positions, offer encouragement? Well, if that's the harvest you want, plant those seeds when you interact with others. Find ways to bless those who are also looking for jobs. "Give and it will be given to you" is an infallible Kingdom law. Follow these golden rules and watch how your job search is blessed by sudden sources of support and divine coincidences.

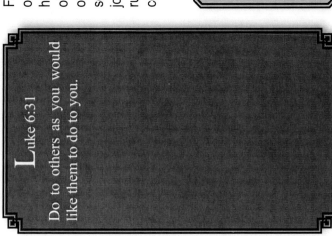

DECLARE THIS:

- I actively seek ways to bless others in their job searches. I know I'll receive a harvest of blessing in return.

- I represent the Kingdom of God and I am blessed to be a blessing.

- By faith I follow the Holy Spirit who shows me what God would have me do for others.

Luke 6:31
Do to others as you would like them to do to you.

SEPTEMBER 25
KNOCK AND EXERCISE YOUR FAITH

James 1:12

Anyone who meets a testing challenge head-on and manages to stick it out is mighty fortunate. For such persons loyally in love with God, the reward is life and more life. (Message)

There are some promises that you cannot have until you meet testing challenge head-on and stick it out. The Amplified Bible says it like this: "Blessed (happy, to be envied) is the man who is patient under trial and stands up under temptation, for when he has stood the test and been approved, he will receive [the victor's] crown of life which God has promised to those who love Him." The crown of life sounds like a pretty decent reward for hanging in there, doesn't it? But notice one other thing — it will take being "loyally in love with God" to stay the course through to the end. So spend time with God and allow your love to grow for Him as you exercise your faith. Then you can confidently expect to receive the reward.

DECLARE THIS:

- I lean into tests and challenges to exercise my faith.
- I trust that God will honor His promise to me, as one who loves Him.
- By faith I receive the patience and strength to meet my challenges head on without being shaken.

APRIL 7
CHOOSE YOUR PAY

We should check ourselves periodically to make sure we haven't become proud of our accomplishments and our possessions. We had so very little to do with acquiring them. The lives we have, the talents we have, the minds we have, the bodies we have — these are all gifts from God. We may have worked hard to earn things, but God made it all possible. Without His enablement we would have nothing. But the last part of this scripture is the best part. There are uncertain riches and certain riches. As God's children our riches are certain! Our needs will be met and, beyond that, we will receive all things richly to enjoy. How many employers offer that?

DECLARE THIS:

- I claim the wealthy place that God created for me before the foundation of the earth.
- By faith I accept and expect everything God has promised me.
- God gives me all things richly to enjoy for I am His royal child.

1 Tim 6:17

Teach those who are rich in this world not to be proud and not to trust in their money, which is so unreliable. Their trust should be in God, who richly gives us all we need for our enjoyment.

SEPTEMBER 24
KNOCK AND BRING GIFTS

We can give our way out of debt, poverty and lack. God's law works every time, but we might be tempted to give up on it because we don't think as farmers do. We forget that there's a period of time between the planting and the harvest. So plant your resources, talents and time in every area where you need a harvest. Give sacrificially into ministries where God's anointing is evident, and don't forget to name the harvest that you are calling forth. Then don't quit. Water your prayer crop with the Word of God every day. Use your mouth to send the Word out and know by faith that the Word will not return to God until it accomplishes the thing it was sent to do.

> ### Luke 6:38
>
> Give, and you will receive. Your gift will return to you in full — pressed down, shaken together to make room for more, running over, and poured into your lap. The amount you give will determine the amount you get back.

DECLARE THIS:

- I am a seed planter. I give and expect to receive a harvest according to the Word of God.
- I raise my prayers to the highest level and line them up with God's plan.
- I thank God for a harvest on His promises.

APRIL 8
CHOOSE YOUR TRAINING

Imagine... the Lord of all creation wants to talk to us every morning. He "opens our ears" so that we are sure to hear His voice. Our part is to decide if we will do what we're told once we hear it. We are not to wait and decide if we like the instructions. If we listen and learn, we will have "the tongue of a disciple", and we will sound just like Jesus. We will be able to say exactly the right thing to lift up someone who is weary. Considering the power and authority Jesus commanded with His words, that's an awesome outcome to our training! During this time of unemployment Jesus might just be saying to us, as He did His other disciples, "Follow me."

DECLARE THIS:

- I choose to be a believer and a disciple. I want to be like Jesus.
- I receive the instruction of the Lord and the ears to recognize His voice.
- I too will use my voice to speak encouraging words of blessing to all who are weary.

Isaiah 50:4-5

[The Servant of God says] The Lord God has given Me the tongue of a disciple and of one who is taught, that I should know how to speak a word in season to him who is weary. He wakens Me morning by morning, He wakens My ear to hear as a disciple [as one who is taught]. The Lord God has opened My ear, and I have not been rebellious or turned backward. (The Amplified Bible)

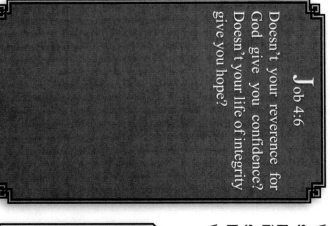

J ob 4:6

Doesn't your reverence for
God give you confidence?
Doesn't your life of integrity
give you hope?

When I put my challenges up against what God has done to keep this planet in orbit and sustaining life, they shrink to insignificance. When I think about the complexity of my problems compared to the structure of one living cell, I am persuaded again that nothing is too hard for our God! This is the very One who loved me enough to give His life for me, so I know He will not leave me unemployed or without provision. His promises will always be good and He will always care for us. As you put all your faith in Him your confidence will abound. Count on it!

DECLARE THIS:

- I am confident that God is able to handle all the challenges that confront me.

- By faith I believe that God desires abundant life and prosperity for me and I open myself to receive it.

- I thank God that my confidence is in His mighty power and perfect love and not in my own abilities.

APRIL 9

CHOOSE YOUR BEHAVIOR

Reflecting on this scripture, how many of us could claim that we "work willingly at whatever we do?" Particularly in times of unemployment, we might think that if there's no employer paying for our work then what we do doesn't matter. That's not how God sees it. He wants us to conduct our job search as if it is a Kingdom assignment, because it is. We need to look at how we're spending our time and the fruit we're producing right now. Are personal and volunteer projects getting completed with excellence? Are our relationships being nurtured? Are we taking care of our bodies to become stronger for the Lord's work? Are we doing all of these activities willingly? We are called to make this entire experience a sacrifice of praise and a gift to God.

> **C**olossians 3:23
>
> Work willingly at whatever you do, as though you were working for the Lord rather than for people.

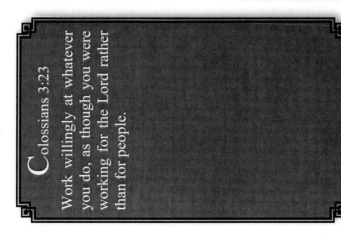

DECLARE THIS:

- I am right where I need to be and I am giving God my very best.
- I receive my five-fold, unemployment blessing that God has for me.
- I work for God alone and I bring a Kingdom blessing wherever I am.

SEPTEMBER 22
KNOCK WITH THANKSGIVING

> 2 Chronicles 5:13
>
> The trumpeters and singers performed together in unison to praise and give thanks to the Lord. Accompanied by trumpets, cymbals, and other instruments, they raised their voices and praised the Lord with these words: "He is good! His faithful love endures forever!" At that moment a thick cloud filled the Temple of the Lord.

Can you picture this? A whole crowd of people all focused on praising God and giving thanks. And when they came into one accord, praising Him in unison, His presence came into their midst as an actual cloud of glory! There's something to be said for corporate praise and thanksgiving. Do you have a place to worship God with other believers? Do you have others who are praying with you and standing in faith for God's promises in your life? This is so important. Take the time in your journey through unemployment to find like-minded, Spirit-filled believers and join them in worship. Invite the glory of God to fill you too. For indeed, "He is good. His faithful love endures forever!"

DECLARE THIS:

- I stand in the midst of countless believers, praising and worshipping God every day.
- By faith I receive the fullness of God's presence and glory in my heart. I know He loves me!
- I thank God that He inhabits the praises of His people for that includes me.

APRIL 10
CHOOSE YOUR BATTLE

It never occurred to me that my life and my livelihood would depend on being "suited up" for battle. But now I know, because I've gone out without God's armor to protect me, and I have the scars to prove it. Our effectiveness and success will require every piece of this spiritual armor — God's truth to fill us, His salvation to deliver us, Christ's righteousness to empower us, our faith to guard us, and His Word and Spirit to mount our defense. Once we recognize that the battle is real and the stakes are high, we'll begin to understand the need for this armor and the great value it holds for us. Thank God He has it all laid out for us — and in our size, too!

DECLARE THIS:

- I have all that I need to win every battle against the enemy.
- By faith I receive the empowerment to use all of God's weapons.
- I stand firm against the enemy because I have been well trained and perfectly equipped.

Ephesians 6:11

Put on all of God's armor so that you will be able to stand firm against all strategies of the devil.

SEPTEMBER 21
KNOCK WITH BOLDNESS

> H ebrews 4:16
> Let us therefore come boldly
> to the throne of grace, that
> we may obtain mercy and
> find grace to help in time of
> need. (NKJV)

This is an open invitation from God Himself to each one of us — "Come into my throne room. I have grace and mercy for you. Whatever you need, I'll help you with it." Unfortunately many believers have been deceived into thinking that God is keeping them unemployed. They believe that God is the author of their confusion and that God punishes the righteous as a way to teach them. That's how effective the enemy has become in getting us to believe his lies. Well, that deceit needs to end right now. God is good and only good. Your Father is just waiting for you to walk into His presence with boldness because of the confidence that you have in His willingness and ability to provide whatever you need.

DECLARE THIS:

- I believe in God's love for me. I trust that He desires to help and to bless me.
- By faith I place my full confidence in the love of God. I know He is willing to lead me to a new job.
- I will serve the Lord with my life and trust that He will place me where I can be of service.

APRIL 11
ASK EXPECTING RESULTS

Let's search for a way of asking that will produce results. As believers that's our goal. We're all agreed that we want to send forth requests, and, of course, receive an immediate and positive response. It's the second part of this verse that poses a problem for many of us. It would appear that we receive what we ask for from God "because we obey Him and we do the things that please Him." It isn't that we must get everything right if we want our prayers answered. We are under a new covenant that doesn't require strict adherence to a rule book, but it does require obedience. We are commanded to love. We are required to forgive. We are directed to seek God in His Word. If we want to see the results of our prayers, we have to do what God tells us to do.

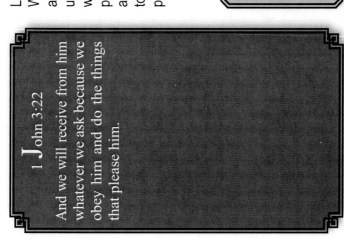

DECLARE THIS:

- I know that God desires to answer our prayers and grant our requests.
- By faith I receive the ability to obey God's Word and activate His promises.
- I obey God and expect to receive what I ask from Him because I always ask in love.

1 John 3:22

And we will receive from him whatever we ask because we obey him and do the things that please him.

SEPTEMBER 20
SEEK TO STAY FOCUSED ON JESUS

Look at the transformation in this man's life. Obviously, Zacchaeus "got it"! He received the revelation that he was loved and accepted by God, and he understood that Jesus was his Lord. Immediately he completely changed his business practices to align with the character of God and the ways of the Kingdom. The same thing is promised to us. When we encounter Jesus at a deep and personal level, all our behaviors will be changed to line up with His Word. A mind renewed and a heart filled with the love of Christ equals a transformed life. Let that be true of us.

> Luke 19:8-9
>
> Meanwhile, Zacchaeus stood before the Lord and said, "I will give half my wealth to the poor, Lord, and if I have cheated people on their taxes, I will give them back four times as much!" Jesus responded, "Salvation has come to this home today, for this man has shown himself to be a true son of Abraham.

DECLARE THIS:

- I am the seed of Abraham and his covenant blessing is mine.
- By faith I receive the transforming presence of Jesus Christ in my life.
- I willingly allow the Word of God to make me a new creation.

APRIL 12

So much of what people call understanding and wisdom really misses the mark by a mile. No wonder smart, supposedly wise people can have lives that are such a mess. They don't know what true wisdom really is. We know that the wisdom spoken of in this verse is the Word of God and His commandments. Cherish His word and prosper — that's the promise. That means if we're not walking in love, we'll miss out on wisdom. Only wisdom and the Word of God will allow us to prosper in every aspect of our lives. His Word provides perfect wisdom for every situation in our lives today. So as we learn to ask for first things first, let's lead off with a request for true wisdom and understanding.

DECLARE THIS:

- I love myself because God loves me and has declared me His child.
- I seek wisdom because it is one of the best gifts I can give myself.
- By faith I receive understanding directly from the throne room of God and I prosper as a result.

Proverbs 19:8

To acquire wisdom is to love oneself; people who cherish understanding will prosper.

SEPTEMBER 19
SEEK HIDDEN TREASURES

M atthew 25:29

To those who use well what they are given, even more will be given, and they will have an abundance. But from those who do nothing, even what little they have will be taken away.

What do you have right now? You may be tempted to say, "Nothing. I don't even have a job." Whether you know it or not, you have the power to get wealth. (Deuteronomy 8:18) It may be invisible but it's definitely there. Just as the wind is unseen but for the effect it has, so is this power to get wealth. But if we don't use it, we'll lose it! So, how do we activate the power to get abundant life and wealth? For starters, we must believe God when He declares that we have this power. Then we have to go to the Source to learn how to use the power well, to find out what we have in our hands that can be used to gain wealth. The Holy Spirit will then show us the talents, skills and timing that will turn what's in our hands into what's in our dreams!

DECLARE THIS:

- I am blessed by God, lacking nothing.
- By faith I receive the abundant life that Jesus died to give me.
- I receive abundance from God because I put His gifts to good use.

APRIL 13
ASK ABOUT YOUR GIFTS

Perhaps you've heard the saying, "Your life is a gift from God. What you do with it is your gift to God!" It's the truth. Take some time to reflect on everything God has already given you. Do you have the gift of sight, speech, hearing and touch? Have you experienced laughter and joy and peace and comfort? Do you have people to love who love you back? All these wonderful gifts came from a Father who loves us perfectly. So now it's our turn. What can we give to Him? Only one thing — our lives in obedience to His will. With our complete surrender we open ourselves to our greatest blessing and a life filled with wonders. We simply cannot out-give God… but it's worth a try!

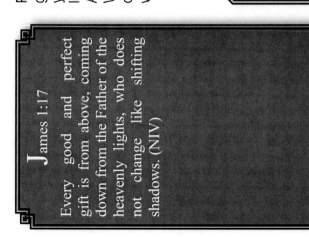

James 1:17

Every good and perfect gift is from above, coming down from the Father of the heavenly lights, who does not change like shifting shadows. (NIV)

DECLARE THIS:

- I thank God for all He has done for me and I offer Him my life.
- By faith I receive the full blessing of God that I might bless others.
- I ask the Holy Spirit to keep me ever mindful of all that God has given me.

SEPTEMBER 18
SEEK DIVINE CONNECTIONS

1 Corinthians 12:28

Here are some of the parts God has appointed for the church: first are apostles, second are prophets, third are teachers, then those who do miracles, those who have the gift of healing, those who can help others, those who have the gift of leadership, those who speak in unknown languages.

When we were working, many of us said we wished we had more time to study the Word and get closer to God. Don't think God missed those comments. He may well be giving you an opportunity to grow your understanding and your faith right now. Teachers are one of the most wonderful gifts God gives us during this time. Thanks to television, radio and the internet, we have access to biblical teachers nearly every hour of the day. Now is the time to enroll in the school of the Word and get the best instruction those teachers offer. You will be amazed at how often they will provide just the answer you are looking for if you put yourself in the position to hear it.

DECLARE THIS:

- I receive insight into the Word through godly teachers who share revelation with me.
- By faith I open myself to the teaching of the Lord and exercise my faith to receive understanding.
- I know that God has provided all the resources I need in the body of Christ.

APRIL 14
Ask About Your Design

The moon is the same moon whether we see it as a tiny crescent or as the entire sphere. We also know that the moon does not make its own light — it is merely reflecting light from another source. That's how it is with us as well. Kingdom leaders are both born and made. We are the very image and likeness of God, designed as rulers on this earth whether we look like it right now or not. We're born leaders when the Spirit of God comes to live inside us but we are not made leaders until we release God's light and power in our lives. His intention is for us to have dominion, so it's time for us to take authority over the workplace and bring it under Kingdom rule.

DECLARE THIS:

- I am designed in the image and likeness of God.
- By faith I receive revelation of the power and authority I have been given by God in Christ.
- I take dominion over the workplace and bring the Kingdom way of life with me as I enter it.

Genesis 1:26

Then God said, "Let Us make man in Our image, according to Our likeness; let them have dominion over the fish of the sea, over the birds of the air, and over the cattle, over all the earth and over every creeping thing that creeps on the earth." (NKJV)

Proverbs 3:5-6

Lean on, trust in, and be confident in the Lord with all your heart and mind and do not rely on your own insight or understanding. In all your ways know, recognize, and acknowledge Him, and He will direct and make straight and plain your paths. (The Amplified Bible)

Do you think it's possible that God would hear us ask Him to show the way, see us put our trust in Him, and then just let us fail? Could He hold our solution and fail to cut through our confusion to make Himself heard? What kind of Father would do that to His children? God never walks us into traps and He will never permit us to make a wrong step if we're listening to Him. If His Word says "He will direct, and make straight and make plain our path," then that's exactly what He will do. Our task is to seek Him and to wait until an answer comes that we understand and can follow with peace in our hearts. When we follow the Word of God we cannot fail.

DECLARE THIS:

- I know that I don't know enough to make my own plans for my life.
- By faith I receive God's help to grow my trust and confidence in Him. He will help me in my unbelief.
- The path the Lord has for me is straight, wide, and plain. He sets my boundaries in pleasant places.

APRIL 15
ASK ABOUT YOUR PURPOSE

Read this scripture out loud, and imagine that David is speaking directly to you about your job search. Go ahead, he says, and be strong, but no matter what, do the work. Don't stop making calls and putting out the word that you're seeking employment. Don't let the circumstances you face discourage or frighten you. Remember that you have the very same God that parted the Red Sea for the Israelites and shook open prison doors for Paul and Silas. He will not fail you nor leave you during this season of unemployment. You just need to work with God to bring yourself in line with His Word and become fully submitted to His will. Put your focus on that and see how your job search unfolds under the power of His mighty hand.

1 Chronicles 28:20

Then David continued, "Be strong and courageous, and do the work. Don't be afraid or discouraged, for the Lord God, my God, is with you. He will not fail you or forsake you. He will see to it that all the work related to the Temple of the Lord is finished correctly.

DECLARE THIS:

- I am strong and courageous in my job search because God is with me and leading me.
- By faith I receive His will for my life and the ability to hear directly from His spirit within me.
- I trust God to perfect me and to prepare me for my next work assignment and my role in His Kingdom.

Galatians 6:7-8

Don't be misled — you cannot mock the justice of God. You will always harvest what you plant. Those who live only to satisfy their own sinful nature will harvest decay and death from that sinful nature. But those who live to please the Spirit will harvest everlasting life from the Spirit.

Do we have God's priorities when it comes to our personal lives? We might not think this is an issue right now. We just want a job, right? But God has something else in mind. God wants us and He wants us perfected. We'll hurt ourselves and stall our progress if we don't pay attention to this. We can't receive a perfect job assignment from God while holding on to disobedience and sin. What is God trying to do in you? Is He calling for temperance in your eating habits, or some other behavior change? Do you need to get out of some bad relationships? We cannot plant seeds of disobedience and expect a harvest of blessing. So drop everything that isn't pleasing to God, then expect a harvest of everlasting and abundant life!

DECLARE THIS:

- I choose to live a Kingdom lifestyle and to give up every sinful behavior.
- I receive by faith the ability to walk in line with God's will for my life.
- I have, in Christ, the ability to break every bad habit and turn away from every wrong behavior.

APRIL 16
SEEK SELF AWARENESS

As we turn our thoughts to self-awareness, it's a good idea to examine our motives... are they set on anything other than God's priorities? Are you thinking you'll be glad when you're back to work because you won't need God so much? Are you like many of us who only seek God diligently when we're in a crisis? Would a nice job with a fat paycheck mean you wouldn't have to spend so much time praying and seeking God? Be honest. Who really occupies the throne in your heart? If it's someone or something other than God and His will, repent and ask God to help you make and keep Him the center of your life from this moment on.

DECLARE THIS:

- I turn my entire life over to God again and ask Him to be my only King.
- By faith I receive God's priorities and will for my life, and I trust Him to lead me in the way I should go.
- I will to will the will of God.

1 Timothy 6:10

For the love of money is the root of all kinds of evil. And some people, craving money, have wandered from the true faith and pierced themselves with many sorrows.

SEPTEMBER 15
ASK ABOUT YOUR PURPOSE

2 Timothy 1:9

For God saved us and called us to live a holy life. He did this, not because we deserved it, but because that was his plan from before the beginning of time — to show us his grace through Christ Jesus.

George MacDonald, a well known Christian writer of the 1800s once said, "This is a sane, wholesome, practical working faith; that it is a man's business to do the will of God; second, that God Himself takes on the care of that man and third, that therefore, that man ought never to be afraid of anything." That pretty much sums up the whole Kingdom lifestyle. God's plan has been to show us His grace and His love. Not one bit of this marvelous plan hinges on our ability to earn His grace. Jesus simply came to show us how deeply and perfectly God loves us. Knowing that, let us now walk in our purpose by allowing Christ to rule and reign in our hearts. As we do the will of God, we'll live holy lives and fear will be banished from our lives.

DECLARE THIS:

- I will to will the will of God. I know His will for me is perfect and wonderful.
- By faith I believe that all my needs are met as I follow God.
- I believe that I am in Christ and filled with the grace and love of God.

APRIL 17
SEEK THE DIRECTION OF THE HOLY SPIRIT

There's a popular bumper sticker that says "God is my co-pilot". If that's true for you, be quick – trade seats! God needs to be the One in charge, the Holy Spirit in us should be calling all the shots. We are not able to plan our own courses, because we can't see around corners and into the future. But He who sees the end from the beginning is more than able to lead us. Let's not miss the first statement here, either. Our lives no longer belong to us. Jesus bought us and we are His. So allow Him His proper place in your life and enjoy the ride.

Jeremiah 10:23
I know, LORD, that our lives are not our own. We are not able to plan our own course.

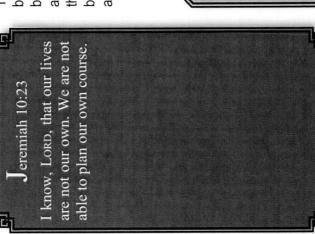

DECLARE THIS:

- I thank God that it is not up to me to plan my own course. Perfect Love leads me.
- By faith I acknowledge that God is good and only good and I trust in Him completely.
- I belong to Jesus and will follow where He leads me.

SEPTEMBER 14
ASK ABOUT YOUR DESIGN

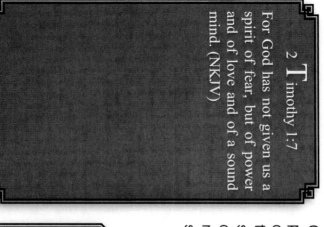

2 Timothy 1:7

For God has not given us a spirit of fear, but of power and of love and of a sound mind. (NKJV)

God did not give us a spirit of fear. That's good to know. Now let's look at the Spirit of power, love and a sound mind that He did give us! The Holy Spirit is an essential part of our born-again identity. We have been made into containers for God Himself! Fear has to flee from the perfect love we hold inside. It cannot exist in the presence of God. Better still, He comes to us as a free gift. We don't have to build up the love of God in us and we don't have to chase after it in order to fill ourselves with it. We are already full! In Him our minds are sound and our thoughts are clear. We just have to realize what we have and step aside to release God's power and light from within.

DECLARE THIS:

- I am free of fear for I am filled with the presence of God Himself.
- By faith I receive a revelation of the Spirit of God that lives in me now.
- I have the power and love and mind of Christ Jesus within me.

APRIL 18
SEEK DIVINE CONNECTIONS

It's important to connect with the body of Christ and to take advantage of a shepherd's covering. Find those who are looking out for you, who will teach you the way of Truth. If you haven't found a local church, add that quest to your job search process. In addition to a local church, get connected with excellent teachers and pastors on television and the radio. Fill yourself with God's Word from all these anointed shepherds and dwell in safety. They will accelerate your understanding and knowledge and light the path before you.

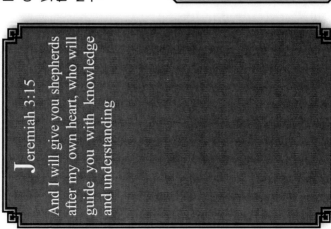

DECLARE THIS:

- I am open to the gift of shepherds in my life. I know that I am a sheep in need of protection.
- By faith I receive direction from God's appointed shepherds. I examine what I am taught against the Word and grow in truth.
- I trust the Holy Spirit in me to guard me from false shepherds who would do me harm.

Jeremiah 3:15

And I will give you shepherds after my own heart, who will guide you with knowledge and understanding

Numbers 18:6

Behold, I Myself have taken your brethren the Levites from among the children of Israel; they are a gift to you, given by the LORD, to do the work of the tabernacle of meeting. (NKJV)

Imagine God introducing you to a group of people and telling them that you are His gift to them! That is precisely His message about you. He designed us for a specific Kingdom purpose and when we operate in our gifts we are a blessing to others. As we come to understand our awesome design and gifts, our approach to the workplace will be different. No longer will we look for a place that is willing to hire us. Instead we'll be looking for the perfect place to put our gifts to work blessing others. So don't undervalue yourself. When a hiring manager asks, "What are you worth?" The most accurate answer would be "You could never afford what I'm worth!" Of course, you won't want to say that out loud, but in your heart you'll know it's true.

DECLARE THIS:

- I am a gift from God to the workplace. I bless everyone I work for.
- I receive guidance from the Holy Spirit about the places to use my gifts.
- I freely give because I have freely received so much from the Lord.

APRIL 19
SEEK HIDDEN TREASURES

Many believers who are currently jobless are painfully aware that they don't have wealth and riches in their houses. So who is this verse talking about? If we go to the beginning of the Psalm we'll see that the answer is "the man who fears the Lord and obeys His commands." We can be assured that when we aren't experiencing the promises of God, the problem is not with God, it's with us. Here's the good news, though. While we're out of the workplace, we have a perfect opportunity to fix our problems once and for all. Now is the time to find disobedience in our lives and ask for help to eliminate it. Then, as we walk in His plan and His will, wealth and riches will flow into our lives.

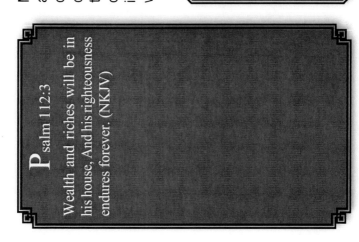

DECLARE THIS:

- I am blessed with all spiritual blessings and prosperous in every way because the Word says so.
- By faith I receive revelation and correction so that my life might come into obedience to God.
- I thank God for the wealth and riches He has already given to me and I believe that I receive them now, in Jesus' name.

Psalm 112:3

Wealth and riches will be in his house, And his righteousness endures forever. (NKJV)

SEPTEMBER 12
ASK FOR FIRST THINGS FIRST

> Matthew 20:20
> Then the mother of Zebedee's children came up to Him with her sons and, kneeling, worshipped Him and asked a favor of Him. (The Amplified Bible)

I can really relate to this scripture! First the mother worshipped Jesus and then she asked a favor. That's pretty much what happens to me. I start out worshipping Him and next thing I know I'm asking for something. Many of us start out with a desire to just love God for a few moments but then our needs break in and we're back in the request business again. The good news is that God is willing to help us. It's okay to come to Him with both praise and requests. If knowing God through Christ is our true, first, and highest motive, that will be more than enough. He'll do the rest for you. Just ask God for the ability to worship Him more perfectly and to love Him more fully, for He is worthy of our praise.

DECLARE THIS:

- I worship the Lord and love Him with my whole heart.
- My faith I accept God's power to cleanse me and to receive my requests with love.
- I know that I deserve nothing on my own but I am not on my own. I accept the righteousness of Christ as mine.

APRIL 20
SEEK TO STAY FOCUSED ON JESUS

Hebrews 12:2

We do this by keeping our eyes on Jesus, the champion who initiates and perfects our faith.

Jesus is the source of our faith, and the One who grows our faith to perfection and completion. The Holy Spirit that dwells in every born-again believer is the Spirit of Christ. But how do we keep our eyes on someone who isn't here? Realize – He is here! The Bible tells us that Jesus is the Word that became flesh. He is still the Word so we can meet Him in the Bible. As He promised, His spirit has been poured out on us. We are closer to Jesus right now than many people were when He was on the earth. Let's seek Him while He may be found, in the Word and in our hearts, that our faith might be perfected. We will need Him to make it through the job search as overcomers.

DECLARE THIS:

- I keep my eyes on Jesus and my faith grows strong.
- I receive the work of Christ in me to perfect my faith.
- I thank God that He will never stop working on me until I look like Jesus.

SEPTEMBER 11
ASK EXPECTING RESULTS

Psalm 34:10

The young lions lack food and suffer hunger, but they who seek (inquire of and require) the Lord [by right of their need and on the authority of His Word], none of them shall lack any beneficial thing. (The Amplified Bible)

God promises a select group of people that none of them shall lack any beneficial thing. Are we in that privileged group? It looks like three things are required — you must seek the Lord, have a need, and rely on the authority of His Word. Without confidence in that authority, without the ability to stand on the Word no matter what, we'll still be in lack. But when we know the Word and we know the character of God, we can command our blessing in the name of Jesus. No matter what the challenge, crisis, or need, God's Word has a promise that will trump that problem. Find it, believe it and call the promise into being on the authority of the Word. What are you waiting for? A new job certainly qualifies as a beneficial thing, doesn't it?

DECLARE THIS:

- God said it, I believe it, and that settles it.
- By faith I believe what God says in His Word and I will not be moved.
- My problems are nothing to the God who created all things. I trust Him to handle my needs for me.

APRIL 21
KNOCK WITH BOLDNESS

For years I was afraid to cry out to God because I feared what He might say. Then I learned that He could only treat me with love because He is completely love. As I began to experience His faithfulness and great love for me, all my fears about Him melted away. That's something every believer needs to comprehend. We have to stop thinking that it was God who made us unemployed, and that God doesn't care about us. We have to believe what the Word tells us about the more excellent covenant we have in Christ. We can rejoice knowing that the God of perfect love will answer us personally every time we call out to Him. That's where our strength and our boldness will be found.

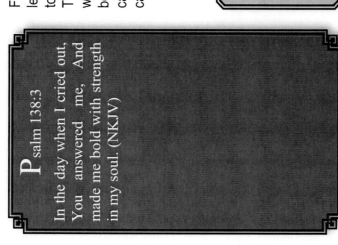

> Psalm 138:3
>
> In the day when I cried out, You answered me, And made me bold with strength in my soul. (NKJV)

DECLARE THIS:

- I know that God hears me when I cry out and He will always answer me.
- By faith I receive that God is good and loving. When He speaks to me it makes me confident and bold.
- I go into the job market in the Lord's strength and powerful might.

Isaiah 43:2

When you pass through the waters, I will be with you; And through the rivers, they shall not overflow you. When you walk through the fire, you shall not be burned, Nor shall the flame scorch you. (NKJV)

This is a bad news/good news scripture. The bad news is that we will have to pass through high waters and walk through fire. Nobody wants to hear that. But the good news is, we won't go under when the floods come. We won't be burned or scorched. Remember that part. If you recall, God has already done this with three Hebrew children in a fiery furnace. That fire was so hot the guards died just getting close enough to throw them into it! Yet the three young men experienced only the burning away of the bonds that had held them. Hold that picture in your mind. With Christ in us we will walk right into whatever circumstances come at us, knowing that we'll emerge on the other side freer than we were when we started.

DECLARE THIS:

- In Christ I am well able to handle any circumstance that comes.
- I expect trials and challenges. My faith grows strong as I overcome them.
- By faith I receive God's promise of deliverance and victory.

APRIL 22
KNOCK WITH THANKSGIVING

A life rooted and grounded in Christ will produce Christians abounding in thanksgiving. Imagine what it will be like to be unshakable, completely established in faith. Can you see yourself in such a deep and personal relationship with God that you confidently follow the direction He gives you with the expectation of good and only good? Just realize that the God of all creation loves us perfectly. The truth is that He has wonderful plans for us that start now and extend into all eternity. That ought to thrill us to the core of our beings. Absolute thanksgiving is the by-product of believers who really understand the magnitude of the gift we've already been given.

DECLARE THIS:

- I am so grateful that I have been chosen by God to reign for all eternity.
- By faith I receive a life rooted and grounded in Jesus and His anointing.
- The gift of the name of Jesus, and the authority to use it, makes me dance with thanksgiving.

Colossians 2:6-7

As you therefore have received Christ Jesus the Lord, so walk in Him, rooted and built up in Him and established in the faith, as you have been taught, abounding in it with thanksgiving (NKJV)

SEPTEMBER 9
CHOOSE YOUR BEHAVIOR

John 15:5
"I am the vine, you are the branches. He who abides in Me, and I in him, bears much fruit; for without Me you can do nothing." (NKJV)

There's a beautiful old hymn that says, "Breathe on me, breath of God. Fill me with life anew. That I may love what Thou dost love, and do what Thou wouldst do." We need His breath to fill us. We need His life to flow into us. Job seekers want phone calls to turn into interviews and interviews to turn into offers. Yet fruit is only guaranteed to those who are being fed by the Word flowing through their minds and hearts. Let the life and love of Christ feed you by staying in constant communion with Him. Just like a branch that receives sap from the vine, we will produce the fruit if we stay firmly connected to Him. Then we will love what Jesus loves and do what Jesus would do.

DECLARE THIS:

- I am connected to the Vine of abundant life and I bear much fruit.
- By faith I accept that all my good comes from Christ as my source.
- I thank God that I have been grafted into Christ and I am firmly rooted in His Kingdom.

APRIL 23
KNOCK WITH CONFIDENCE

You can probably recall times when you were feeling fairly comfortable with your faith and trust in God. Then a crisis happened and you panicked. That's what it is to "fling away your fearless confidence." Whether we do this or not is up to us. Nothing can take our confidence from us. No one can make us afraid. We decide either to stand in faith that God will do what He says He will do, or to put our confidence in the lies of the enemy. God says we are not only to believe that He exists but also to believe that He is a rewarder of those who love and fear Him. Ask the Holy Spirit to reinforce your confidence and your strength and don't let it go for any reason. Keep the confidence that carries the reward. It's your choice.

Hebrews 10:35
Do not, therefore, fling away your fearless confidence, for it carries a great and glorious compensation of reward.
(The Amplified Bible)

DECLARE THIS:

- I have fearless confidence and I will not let it go.
- By faith I build my hope on the promises of God. He cares for me.
- I receive the great and glorious reward that is mine in Christ Jesus.

SEPTEMBER 8
CHOOSE YOUR TRAINING

> ### Romans 12:2
> Don't copy the behavior and customs of this world, but let God transform you into a new person by changing the way you think. Then you will learn to know God's will for you, which is good and pleasing and perfect.

Look at the process to "let God transform you." First God changes the way we think and then God transforms us because of our new way of thinking. Notice who's doing everything — God. He accomplishes this transformation first in our hearts and minds. Many believers have this backwards. They keep trying to change their behaviors and habits so they can be like Jesus. Unfortunately, that never works. This scripture tells us that God has a good, pleasing and perfect plan for each of us and the only way to know it is by changing the way we think. How do we do that? By diving into His Word and staying there until all our thoughts line up with His.

DECLARE THIS:

- I am determined to think only thoughts that line up with God's Word.
- By faith I rebuke the enemy and refuse to accept his lies any more.
- God's will for me is perfect and I am trusting in Him to transform me and lead me into it.

APRIL 24
KNOCK AND BRING GIFTS

Perhaps you are unable to give money to those in need right now because your income has been reduced. But that didn't stop Peter and John from giving, did it? When they spoke the name of Jesus, with power, it blessed this man beyond his wildest dreams. We too can grow our faith in the name of Jesus, and use it to bring healing and blessing. Start praying for others now. Offer your prayers and your faith as gifts to others. There's an old hymn that puts it this way — "Lord, let me live from day to day, In such a self-forgetful way. That, even when I kneel to pray, My prayers shall be for others."

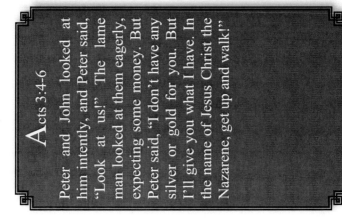

DECLARE THIS:

- I have the power of Jesus' name to use for the benefit of others.
- By faith I receive a full revelation of the power and authority that is mine in Christ.
- I look for opportunities to add my faith and prayers to the prayers of others and release blessings to them.

A cts 3:4-6

Peter and John looked at him intently, and Peter said, "Look at us!" The lame man looked at them eagerly, expecting some money. But Peter said, "I don't have any silver or gold for you. But I'll give you what I have. In the name of Jesus Christ the Nazarene, get up and walk!"

SEPTEMBER 7
CHOOSE YOUR PAY

1 Corinthians 2:9

...no eye has seen, no ear has heard, no mind has conceived what God has prepared for those who love Him.

Our greatest flights of imagination cannot approach what God wants to give us! He has gone beyond our wildest dreams to create a wealthy place for each of us, and He did it before we ever set foot on the earth. There are countless gifts with our names on them in the heavenly realm, but our eyes cannot see them... yet. How do we receive them? Simply by obeying God's commandment to love. Jesus made it clear that by loving others, and by caring for His sheep, we love Him. We're not talking about the fluffy, romantic, emotional love of the movies, but a steadfast and a determined decision to love with the love of Christ in us. It's that simple. Love frees God to bless.

DECLARE THIS:

- Because I love the Lord I obey His commands. I love with the love of Christ.
- By faith I receive God's open heaven blessing in every part of my life and I expect to prosper.
- I know that Christ was more than enough to redeem me and give me a goodly inheritance.

APRIL 25

KNOCK AND EXERCISE YOUR FAITH

Everything we need already exists in the heavenly realm. Just because we can't see it doesn't mean it isn't there. Read the story in 2 Kings 6. Elisha's servant counted thousands of troops amassed against him and his master, and he panicked. But then the prophet prayed and God opened the servant's eyes. Surrounding them on every side were chariots of fire and angelic soldiers ready to defend them. The story ends with the Lord blinding the enemy troops and Elisha leading them inside the walls of Samaria to the King of Israel, without bloodshed. No one could have seen that solution coming! Yet it was right there, waiting in the heavenly realm, until faith called it in. Let this remind you of the truth today. No matter how long it takes, God will deliver your perfect employment opportunity. Put your confidence in that.

H ebrews 11:1

Faith is the confidence that what we hope for will actually happen; it gives us assurance about things we cannot see.

DECLARE THIS:

- I accept by faith that God is real and so are His promises.
- I know that it is safe to put my confidence in the Lord.
- By faith I receive assurance that the things God has promised, and I hope for, will come to pass.

SEPTEMBER 6
CHOOSE YOUR WORK

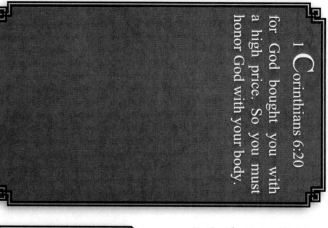

1 Corinthians 6:20

for God bought you with a high price. So you must honor God with your body.

How are you treating your body? This is an important question. Your body no longer belongs to you. It's the container for your spirit and for the Spirit of God. God has plans for that body of yours. We need to feed our minds on the Word of God and we need to honor God with our physical bodies as well. This season of unemployment might be a God-designed opportunity to get your health together. So go ahead, quit smoking, lose weight, and build your strength. Get yourself in shape for the new assignment that's coming. The Holy Spirit can be your physical trainer as surely as He is your employment coach. Give God a good return on His investment in you.

DECLARE THIS:

- My body belongs to God and I will treat it as a temple.
- By faith I receive guidance on how to care for and strengthen my body as I look for a job.
- I will come out of this season stronger, in faith and in my body, than I was when I started.

APRIL 26

The Holy Spirit dwells within you. You may not be able to see into the invisible realm with your natural eyes but you really are walking in God's wonderful light. You really are surrounded by angels. Countless numbers of saints, past and present, are praying for you. It's true! So, don't be moved by what you see or what you feel. You will help yourself grow in His light by determining to show others the goodness of God with your actions. When you tell others how good God is and how glad you are to be in His Kingdom, you will realize more and more that you truly are His chosen one. That revelation will transform your life and you will go into each day in power and authority.

DECLARE THIS:

- I am a chosen child of God, His special and treasured possession.
- I share this nearly-to-good-to-be-true news at every opportunity.
- My life reflects the goodness of God as I walk by faith and not by sight.

1 Peter 2:9

But you are not like that, for you are a chosen people. You are royal priests, a holy nation, and God's very own possession. As a result, you can show others the goodness of God, for he called you out of the darkness into his wonderful light.

SEPTEMBER 5
CHOOSE YOUR BENEFITS

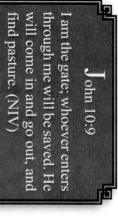

John 10:9

I am the gate; whoever enters through me will be saved. He will come in and go out, and find pasture. (NIV)

This is great news in today's employment market. Jesus is our gate. We are His sheep and the workplace is our pasture. Wherever we are, our shepherd Jesus is right with us. He ensures that when we come out of one workplace He'll be standing at the entrance of another. He will never stop ushering us into new pastures and new provision. He is our protection in the day of layoffs and downsizings. He saves us from our mistakes. He makes a way for us. It makes sense to stay close to the shepherd these days, doesn't it?

DECLARE THIS:

- I have a Good Shepherd and I trust Him to lead me.
- My pasture and my provisions are assured by Jesus Himself.
- By faith I receive my direction and am kept safe because I keep my eyes on the Shepherd and listen for His Word.

APRIL 27
KNOCK AND OVERCOME

Overwhelming victory is ours because Christ loved us. We cannot allow ourselves to forget that Jesus loved each of us so much that He gave His life to save us. If you were the only person in the entire earth, Christ would have died just for you. Now it's up to you to decide God's Word is true. It will take a quality decision on your part to live entirely by faith. You will have to put your trust in the unseen realm of the Kingdom of God and in the powerful name of Jesus. But if you do, then this statement by St. Augustine will be true for you — "Faith is to believe what we do not see, and the reward of faith is to see what we believe." Overwhelming victory is the reward for overcoming faith.

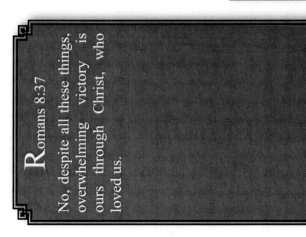

DECLARE THIS:

- I have overwhelming victory in Christ who loves me.
- By faith I receive the promises of the Word. I know the promises are true and they are for me.
- I am so grateful that I am complete in Christ, lacking nothing.

Romans 8:37

No, despite all these things, overwhelming victory is ours through Christ, who loved us.

SEPTEMBER 4
CHOOSE YOUR BOSS

Isaiah 65:13

Therefore, this is what the Sovereign Lord says: "My servants will eat, but you will starve .My servants will drink, but you will be thirsty. My servants will rejoice, but you will be sad and ashamed.

Aren't you glad you made the right choice to be in God's service? Don't think being a servant is a bad thing. As the Pharaoh's servant, Joseph was "second in command" over all Egypt. Highly respected and obedient servants of God always rise to places of great responsibility and prosperity. Look at Abraham, Isaac, Joseph, Solomon and David. God's servants are always extremely well cared for. No wonder His servants will rejoice! That's the promise of this verse. Our Heavenly Boss cares for each one of us and promises to save us from lack as we go through this season of unemployment. Stand in faith and expect it.

DECLARE THIS:

- I am a servant of the Lord and He promises to be my constant and faithful provider.
- By faith I believe that my needs are met and I rejoice in the confidence I have in His Word.
- My God supplies all my needs from His rich storehouse.

APRIL 28
KNOCK AND FAINT NOT!

In 2 Peter 1:4-6 we read that our job is to "add to your faith virtue, to virtue knowledge, to knowledge self-control, to self-control perseverance, to perseverance godliness." We aren't expected to achieve this on our own, but rather to yield to the Holy Spirit who will work these things in us as we listen and obey. This will take strength and courage, but it's the sure path to our reward. This same chapter of Peter tells us that we can expect "exceedingly great and precious promises, that through these you may be partakers of the divine nature, having escaped the corruption that is in the world through lust." If we keep our focus on accomplishing our Kingdom assignment the reward we will experience will surpass our greatest expectations.

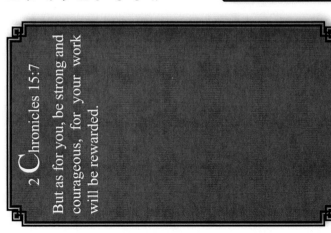

DECLARE THIS:

- I will not quit. I'm in this job search for a promised Kingdom reward.
- By faith I receive the empowerment to grow spiritually and to become prosperous.
- I believe that my work will be rewarded by God if I obey His instructions.

2 Chronicles 15:7

But as for you, be strong and courageous, for your work will be rewarded.

SEPTEMBER 3
CHOOSE YOUR FUTURE

Ephesians 4:31
Get rid of all bitterness, rage, anger, harsh words, and slander, as well as all types of evil behavior.

This scripture appears to be telling us to do the impossible. Who hasn't tried to control themselves, to stop harsh words or anger, only to fail time after time? No amount of will power, personal desire or determination can free us from our bad habits and evil behavior, or give us control over our tongue and our emotions. As soon as we realize that we can't help ourselves, we can turn to the One who has already saved us. This is the perfect time in your life to turn all your shortcomings over to God and allow Him to work His perfection in you. Imagine how wonderful it will be to go into your next job with a set of new behaviors and free of bad habits. Ask God to do that work in you as you journey to your new place of employment!

DECLARE THIS:

- By faith I receive the power to change myself.
- I trust that God has begun a good work in me and He will complete it.
- I willingly release my bad habits and wrong thinking and expect to be transformed into the likeness of Christ.

APRIL 29
KNOCK AND BE ENCOURAGED

It's hard to remember the promises of God when we're in the midst of a trial. It's even harder to recall all the things that the Lord has done for us. That's why it's so important to keep a personal journal and to keep reading about the great miracles performed by God in the Old and New Testament. Be sure you write it down every time God made a way for you when you were backed into a corner. Writing it down helps us to recall the experience when the next tidal wave hits. Read the Bible stories over and over. Reflect on your personal stories until you come to trust that the God who did these things in the past is the very same God who will cover you all the days of your life. He didn't bring you this far to leave you now. Be encouraged!

DECLARE THIS:

- I believe that the Lord is rescuing me from unemployment right now.
- By faith I receive God's promises of rescue, protection and provision.
- I am safe, saved and redeemed. I have the promise of a long and prosperous life.

Psalm 91:14-16

The LORD says, "I will rescue those who love me. I will protect those who trust in my name. When they call on me, I will answer; I will be with them in trouble. I will rescue and honor them. I will reward them with a long life and give them my salvation."

Psalm 119:107

I am sorely afflicted; renew and quicken me [give me life], O Lord, according to Your word! (The Amplified Bible)

Are you brave enough to hear that you may be part of the problem? Many of us have lost jobs without ever understanding what we did wrong or how we contributed to our joblessness. All we know is that we are "sorely afflicted." If we're causing our own troubles we need to know it. One thing is certain — you can't solve a problem with the same level of thinking that produced the problem in the first place. King David acknowledged that he needed to be made new again. Are you willing to say that? Why not go to God in prayer and lay everything before Him? Tell Him how much you're hurting and ask Him to make you new. He will show you things you have to change about yourself. Then He'll give you the ability to change and He'll tell you how. Are you willing?

DECLARE THIS:

- I need God to make me new; I cannot change myself.
- I have the power of the Holy Ghost within me to help me change.
- The Word of God gives me life. I seek it for answers and my direction.

APRIL 30

KNOCK AND KEEP KNOCKING

It's easy to get so caught up in the challenges of the job search that we forget what's really going on. But here's what's really happening: we are being transformed into kings and priests who will reign for all eternity. Each one of us is a critical piece of the awesome spiritual and eternal temple being constructed by God Himself. It's true. We are to rule and reign right now, in our current circumstances, and then for eternity. Now do you understand why the enemy is so intent upon keeping you distracted? Stand in faith for your victory and for the great new position God is leading you to, and allow the job search journey to build your relationship with Jesus. That's what will make this struggle worthwhile.

1 Peter 2:5

And you are living stones that God is building into his spiritual temple. What's more, you are his holy priests. Through the mediation of Jesus Christ, you offer spiritual sacrifices that please God.

DECLARE THIS:

- By faith I receive a revelation of who I am in Christ and what He is working in me.
- I make the quality decision to stand and never waver. I belong to the Kingdom of God.
- I thank God that I am in Christ and pleasing to God.

SEPTEMBER 1
CHOOSE YOUR KINGDOM

1 Chronicles 28:9

And you, Solomon my son, know the God of your father [have personal knowledge of Him, be acquainted with, and understand Him; appreciate, heed, and cherish Him] and serve Him with a blameless heart and a willing mind. For the Lord searches all hearts and minds and understands all the wanderings of the thoughts. If you seek Him [inquiring for and of Him and requiring Him as your first and vital necessity] you will find Him; (The Amplified Bible)

Why am I quoting an Old Testament promise to a New Testament audience? Because our God changes not. If He made this commitment to Solomon, the son of David and descendant of Abraham, then He makes it to us, His adopted sons and daughters in Christ. The only difference is that our "commandments" have been made much simpler. Love God, and love your neighbor as yourself. Indeed, ours is a more excellent covenant. We don't have to provide sacrifices or do works to earn salvation. Jesus has paid the price for us. We simply have to receive, by faith, what He has done. I love this promise — if we seek Him we will find Him. All that matters is that we turn our hearts towards Him and by faith receive what He has purchased for us.

DECLARE THIS:

- I seek you, Lord and believe your Word that I will find you.
- I desire to serve you with my whole heart and mind.
- I am willing for you to search my heart and show me my sins against you.
- I know you are faithful to forgive me and cleanse me when I do.

MAY

GOOD NEWS

SEPTEMBER

GOOD NEWS

MAY 1

CHOOSE YOUR KINGDOM

Job seekers have a tendency to view themselves as beggars — walking around hats-in-hand, hoping for somebody to have pity on them and give them a job. This is not how God views His children! He has something much better in mind. His instruction is simply this — seek Him, because He wants to be found. If we choose to involve God in our daily lives we will see a dramatic difference in everything we do. Can you picture what it will be like when people run to obey you? Can you imagine companies competing to hire you? This is God's Word to us and he cannot lie. Meditate on this scripture and see yourself in your proper role in God's kingdom.... as a ruler! Start practicing now, in this life, to be ready for the day when Jesus returns.

> ### Isaiah 55:5-6
>
> You also will command nations you do not know, and peoples unknown to you will come running to obey, because I, the Lord your God, the Holy One of Israel, have made you glorious. Seek the Lord while you can find Him. Call on Him now while He is near.

DECLARE THIS:

- I thank you Lord for your promises.
- I receive your Word that I am a ruler and that people will run to obey me.
- By faith I know that You will prepare me for the purposes that You designed me to fulfill.

AUGUST 31
KNOCK AND BE AT PEACE

The God of Israel reigns! That's our God. He adopted us as His very own children and has promised us abundant life. That's the truth and that's the good news! Don't let circumstances change your mind about this. Go forth every day and spread this good news. In the midst of chaos and darkness we have the privilege of bringing peace and light. Behave like you know that our God reigns and we are His. He will bring us to victory.

> I saiah 52:7
>
> How beautiful on the mountains are the feet of the messenger who brings good news, the good news of peace and salvation, the news that the God of Israel reigns!

DECLARE THIS:

- I am so glad to be a citizen of the Kingdom of God and I bring joy with me.
- When I speak it is good news only.
- I am welcomed wherever I go because peace comes with me.

MAY 2

CHOOSE YOUR THOUGHTS

As we face yet one more call, show up at one more interview, or try to cheerfully handle one more rejection letter it's easy to think everything depends on us alone. While all this may be normal parts of the search process, it's tough to keep going sometimes. So stop for a few minutes and put this promise to work. Sit still and wait for the Lord to show up for you. Expect to see His hand in your circumstances. Let hope rise up in you as you go back over all His promises. Don't stop doing this until you feel strength and power come back into you. Get help from strong spiritual friends. Sing praises and do whatever you have to do to encourage yourself as you wait for the Lord to renew your strength so you can fly again.

Isaiah 40:31

But those who wait for the Lord [who expect, look for, and hope in Him] shall change and renew their strength and power; they shall lift their wings and mount up [close to God] as eagles [mount up to the sun]; they shall run and not be weary, they shall walk and not faint or become tired. (The Amplified Bible)

DECLARE THIS:

- I am renewed and strengthened day by day because I wait on the Lord.
- I am able to stand and endure because I trust in the Lord.
- My hope is in God alone and every day I look for and expect great good.

Have you ever noticed God's pattern of continuous and repetitive actions? Naaman dipped seven times in the river to be cleansed of leprosy, and the children of Israel circled Jericho repeatedly to take the walls down. God requires the walking of a specified path for a period of time in order to obtain the desired end results. So even if you think you've been around a mountain too many times, don't quit. God is orchestrating things for your benefit. Do you have a clear picture of your desired outcome? Can you see yourself happily and productively employed? Think about the people you'll bless and the joy and peace that will come. Hold the image of yourself working with excellence, representing the Kingdom wherever you go. Keep that in your mind until it comes to pass. The victory will be well worth the price! Don't quit in your actions or your expectations of the promise. The victory will be well worth the price!

2 Kings 5:14

So Naaman went down to the Jordan River and dipped himself seven times, as the man of God had instructed him. And his skin became as healthy as the skin of a young child's, and he was healed!

DECLARE THIS:

- I am not a quitter for my victory is assured.
- I receive the ability to stay the course with my focus on God's promises.
- I search the Word of God and obey what I am directed to do.

MAY 3

CHOOSE YOUR FUTURE

I depend on this promise. God is not keeping a record of our sins, our mistakes, or our failures. In fact, He has declared that He intends to forget our shortcomings as soon as He forgives us. But notice His purpose — "that we might learn to fear (Him)." This isn't the dread-and-terror kind of fear. This is the fear that means "to stand in awe." So here's the plan — we confess our sin, God forgives it and forgets it, and we receive our forgiveness. Immediately we are as blameless as if it had never happened. My hope rests in this scripture. How about you? If you understand this, then there's no need to mention your sins again, right?

DECLARE THIS:

- By faith I receive God's forgiveness once and for all.
- My sins are forgiven and forgotten. I will not mention them again.
- I serve the God of new beginnings and fresh starts.

Psalm 130:3-5

LORD, if You kept a record of our sins, who, O Lord, could ever survive? But You offer forgiveness; that we might learn to fear You. I am counting on the LORD; yes, I am counting on Him. I have put my hope in His Word.

AUGUST 29
KNOCK AND BE ENCOURAGED

> Isaiah 50:10
>
> Who is among you who [reverently] fears the Lord, who obeys the voice of His Servant, yet who walks in darkness and deep trouble and has no shining splendor [in his heart]? Let him rely on, trust in, and be confident in the name of the Lord, and let him lean upon and be supported by his God.
> (The Amplified Bible)

This one simple revelation can make all the difference in the world. When we try to save ourselves and please the Lord in our own strength, we "walk in darkness and deep trouble." Only Jesus can light the way and give the victory. He is all that we need and more than enough! If you aren't experiencing peace and freedom, go back to this verse and examine your heart. Where have you put your trust and confidence? If it's anywhere but in the name of Jesus, you've found the problem and you're on your way to victory. Be encouraged. It's not up to you to solve all your problems and to handle all your challenges. It is up to Christ in you and as you lean on Him you will be supported!

DECLARE THIS:

- I am in Christ and He meets all my needs.
- By faith I rely on, trust in and have confidence in the name of Jesus.
- I thank God that I am covered and empowered by His Spirit working in and through me.

MAY 4
CHOOSE YOUR BOSS

Eagles teach their young to fly by making life so uncomfortable that the young actually fall out of the nest trying to get food. Day after day the parents fly past the nest with food, just beyond the reach of the young eaglets. The baby birds lose weight and develop muscle until they have the strength to support their weight with their wings. When they finally jump from the nest, the parents are there to catch them before they crash, or reward them if they make a successful solo flight. God guides us in the same way. He entices us to take the risk He knows we need to take, while withholding the easy way of comfort and security. He insists that we get the reward He has planned for us. Could that be what He's doing with you? It would be just like Him, you know.

> ## DECLARE THIS:
>
> - I know that God has my highest good in mind as He leads me.
> - By faith I accept the risks and trust in His plan.
> - I expect a wonderful outcome as I journey. He will not let me fail.

> Deuteronomy 32:11-12
>
> As an eagle stirs up its nest, and hovers over its young; as it spreads its wings, takes them up, and bears them aloft on its pinions, the Lord alone guided him.

AUGUST 28
KNOCK AND FAINT NOT!

Isaiah 14:24

The Lord of hosts has sworn, saying, Surely, as I have thought and planned, so shall it come to pass, and as I have purposed, so shall it stand purposed, so shall it stand — (The Amplified Bible)

We're not charging through our job search trying to make it to the other side before we run out of resources. We have our sights set on an extraordinary prize... the five-fold blessing of God. We want a greater relationship with Him, a greater love and understanding of ourselves, more loving relationships, freedom from fear and the snares of the enemy, and a place in the workplace where we can usher in the Kingdom of God. Remember that you are not out of a job. You are on assignment for the Lord. Draw near to Him and fulfill all the things He has in mind for you during your break from the workplace. When you have done all that He requires you will find your new place of employment. Don't settle for anything less than the best God wants to give.

DECLARE THIS:

- I work for God and He directs my paths.
- By faith I claim God's blessing and expect to come out stronger than I was when I started my search.
- I thank God that I am living the gospel of unemployment in Christ Jesus.

MAY 5
CHOOSE YOUR BENEFITS

There are many who truly question if they'll ever find a job again or if they'll ever recover from the financial setback of unemployment. But we don't have to worry about that. The New Century Version of this scripture says that our God has promised that we will never be defeated. Don't lay awake at night worrying about this. Since He never sleeps, we can cast our cares onto His shoulders and get a good night's rest. If God is on watch, what sense is there in both of us being awake? While you rest, be assured that the same God that led the Israelites to freedom, destroyed the walled city of Jericho, and raised Jesus from the dead, will come through for you. Your victory is assured!

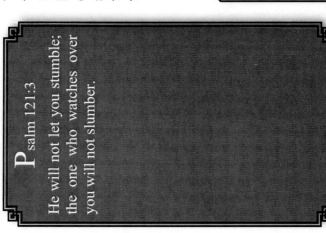

DECLARE THIS:

- I am guarded by Almighty God. He never takes His eyes off me.
- By faith I believe that I will never be defeated.
- I act with boldness in my job search knowing The Holy Spirit is backing me up.

P salm 121:3
He will not let you stumble; the one who watches over you will not slumber.

AUGUST 27
KNOCK AND OVERCOME

> Revelation 12:11
> And they overcame him by the blood of the Lamb and by the word of their testimony, and they did not love their lives to the death. (NKJV)

You've just completed an interview and you're excited. You've prayed and God has confirmed that this is the place for you. Then you're told a sudden hiring freeze has happened. How do you respond? Do you slide into depression or cry out to God, "Why did you lie to me? You said this was my job so why didn't you deliver what you promised?" Too many of us abandon our harvest just because storm clouds come up. Don't break before your breakthrough! The next time the enemy comes against something God has promised, rise up in your authority and release the hand of God over it. Stand in faith. When God tells you something you can count on it.

DECLARE THIS:

- I give generously and believe that I will receive as I have given.
- I spend time with God to receive His Word for my life.
- I thank God that the enemy cannot take what God has given me. I take my authority and cancel all the strategies of the devil.

MAY 6
Choose Your Work

That new job you're seeking, the one God has picked out for you, will most likely require you to learn new things in order to do it well. Kingdom life requires this too. In this scripture we are told to study God's book of instruction, His Word. The sooner we dive into our "owner's manual", to learn the ways of the Kingdom, the sooner we will prosper and succeed in all our endeavors. As we put the Word into our hearts, it will begin to do all the heavy lifting for us. The Word of God has the power in itself to bring itself to pass.

Joshua 1:8

Study this Book of Instruction continually. Meditate on it day and night so you will be sure to obey everything written in it. Only then will you prosper and succeed in all you do.

DECLARE THIS:

- I trust in the power of the living Word to transform my life.
- By faith I receive God's promise that I will prosper as I walk in the ways of the Kingdom.
- I accept the help and empowerment of the Holy Spirit to bring me into obedience to the Word.

> Proverbs 4:18-19
>
> The ways of right-living people glow with light; the longer they live, the brighter they shine. But the road of wrongdoing gets darker and darker — travelers can't see a thing; they fall flat on their faces. (Message)

You might be thinking, "Hey, I'm the one with needs here. Don't expect me to minister to others right now." On the face of it, that seems reasonable. But that's not what God says. He says you should glow with light, getting brighter every day! You have the mind of Christ to direct you and the Holy Spirit to teach and guide you. With God Almighty on your side, why wouldn't you be aglow? It helps to be reminded that we are righteous by God's grace, and we are being perfected by God Himself every day. Trust in the righteousness that you've been given and let that inner light shine out. Those who are walking in darkness need someone to show them the better way.

DECLARE THIS:

- Wherever I am and whatever my circumstances, Jesus is with me. I walk in His righteousness.
- The joy of the Lord fills me with love and light.
- By faith I am empowered to represent the Kingdom and show His light and love to the world.

MAY 7
CHOOSE YOUR PAY

God has a blessing, an empowerment, for us that will make us rich and there's no downside to accepting it. Take a moment and picture yourself fully satisfied and lacking nothing. Imagine yourself happy, secure and able to freely bless others as the Lord directs. When God bestows this blessing there is absolutely no pain attached to the gain. We won't get rich at the expense of our families. We won't become wealthy by compromising our integrity. We'll simply walk in the love of Christ, believe in His name and His promises, and experience prosperity. There's no catch. We are blessed to be a blessing. You won't find an offer like that anywhere else.

DECLARE THIS:

- I believe that God is good and only good and that He desires to bless me.
- By faith I receive God's blessing and am made rich.
- I know that God has the power to bless me no matter what is happening in the world and that He will!

Proverbs 10:22

The blessing of the LORD makes a person rich, and he adds no sorrow with it.

Matthew 14:28-30

Then Peter called to him, "Lord, if it's really you, tell me to come to you, walking on the water." "Yes, come," Jesus said. So Peter went over the side of the boat and walked on the water toward Jesus. But when he saw the strong wind and the waves, he was terrified and began to sink. "Save me, Lord!" he shouted.

This is almost funny. Peter has enough faith to get out and walk on water. Then he must decide that choppy water is harder to walk on than calm water so when the wind kicks up he starts to sink. Walking on water is walking on water, calm or choppy, right? And yet, so often our faith fails too — right in the middle of an interview process, or an offer negotiation, or the start of a new assignment. Without realizing what we're doing, we forget that God brought us to a place in order to bless us and that He will stay with us to get the job done. Exercise that faith of yours. Don't step out, holding your breath and hoping for the best. Step out and claim the best, and the victory, in Jesus name!

DECLARE THIS:

- I can do all things through Christ who strengthens me; I will not lose faith.
- My confidence is in God to see me through. I am never on my own.
- What God begins He is faithful to complete. I will not believe that He brought me this far to leave me now.

MAY 8

CHOOSE YOUR TRAINING

There's so much we need to learn about our identity in Christ and what God has in mind for us. It will take a while to understand how we've been created, what we're called to do and how to accomplish the plans of God. Fortunately the first step is simply to walk in love. We might become distracted and forget our first priority but, thank God, we've been given a Helper to ensure that we fulfill our mission as citizens of the Kingdom. Our sole task is show up for our training every morning, suited up and ready to learn.

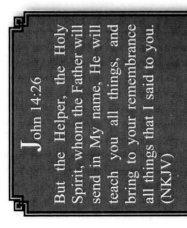

John 14:26

But the Helper, the Holy Spirit, whom the Father will send in My name, He will teach you all things, and bring to your remembrance all things that I said to you. (NKJV)

DECLARE THIS:

- I receive the Holy Spirit as my Helper, Teacher and Guide.
- By faith I receive all that God intends to give through His Spirit in me.
- I remember the teaching of Christ and the Word at all times.

Sometimes we think giving only applies to money and things. That's not true. We have love, time, energy, prayers and wisdom to share. Your financial resources might be scarce right now but don't let that stop you from living in a continual attitude of giving. Be a job seeker that stands out in a crowd because of the peace and joy you radiate. Look for opportunities to give encouragement and hope. Share your wisdom. Let your light shine so that the world can see the difference it makes to live in the Kingdom of God. The best part of doing this is our assurance that we cannot out-give God. As you pour out for others, He is released to give to you until it runs over.

Matthew 5:15

No one lights a lamp and then puts it under a basket. Instead, a lamp is placed on a stand, where it gives light to everyone in the house.

DECLARE THIS:

- I am a child of the King and my life reflects His presence in me.
- By faith I give my time, energy and resources to others as God directs and I expect a return on all that I give.
- I thank God for my abundant life and for the ability to receive all that He has for me.

MAY 9

CHOOSE YOUR BEHAVIOR

We believe God exists, certainly. But look at the rest of this scripture. We must also believe that He rewards those who diligently seek Him. Do you believe that? This is really important because faith begins where the will of God is known. When we know that it is God's will to reward us it becomes easier to expect the manifestation of His promises in our lives. Meditate on these thoughts: God is my rewarder. My reward is guaranteed. I expect reward in this life and in this unemployment experience.

Hebrews 11:6

And it is impossible to please God without faith. Anyone who wants to come to Him must believe that God exists and that He rewards those who sincerely seek Him.

DECLARE THIS:

- I believe that God is and that He rewards those who seek Him.
- By faith I seek the Lord in His Word and by the Holy Spirit and I expect His rewards.
- I send my faith forth to claim my reward because God desires to give it.

AUGUST 23
KNOCK WITH CONFIDENCE

> Isaiah 30:15
>
> This is what the Sovereign Lord, the Holy One of Israel, says: "Only in returning to me and resting in me will you be saved. In quietness and confidence is your strength. But you would have none of it.

In your most frantic, chaotic, and out-of-control moments, stop. Be quiet. Turn your thoughts back to the nature of our God and King — His majesty, awesome power, and perfect love. "Return to me", He says, or in others words "Turn to me once again." Then we are told to rest in Him. That's a great challenge, when the pressure is on and the whole world is shouting, "Do something!" Yet this is His direction and the path to our salvation in the storm of life. We just have to decide to obey. Turn to God and place all your cares and concerns at His feet. Be still, get centered in your heart and wait. In the quiet of your heart and mind you have just made a space that will be filled with confidence and strength.

DECLARE THIS:

- I return to the Lord every time I start to lose my peace and confidence.
- By faith I receive His strength and His salvation in every situation I face.
- I thank God that He carries my cares and deals with all my concerns as I wait in His rest.

MAY 10
CHOOSE YOUR BATTLE

We might be the only soldiers who carry our fortress with us into battle. We actually have a constant "hiding place" that the enemy cannot penetrate. We can fight until we're weary, and then leave the battlefield and go into a fortress to be revived and strengthened! Whenever the going gets too tough it's important to remember that we are hidden in Christ. When we retreat into Him the enemy cannot find us and cannot touch us. Wouldn't it be a wise battle tactic to conduct our job search by day and retreat into the Word of God and the presence of the Lord by night?

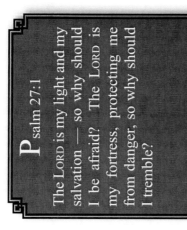

Psalm 27:1

The LORD is my light and my salvation — so why should I be afraid? The LORD is my fortress, protecting me from danger, so why should I tremble?

DECLARE THIS:

- I am safe and I am protected. I abide in the Lord.
- By faith I receive the light I need to see my path and the strong arm of the Lord to deliver me from harm.
- Men cannot with hold my good from me. I have nothing to fear.

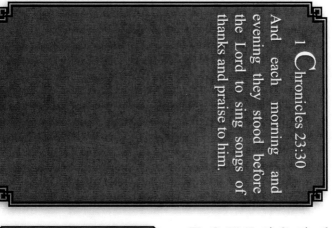

1 Chronicles 23:30

And each morning and evening they stood before the Lord to sing songs of thanks and praise to him.

We can genuinely stand before the Lord every morning and every night and sing songs of thanks, not just for what God has already done but also for what He has promised. There's a quote by Dag Hammarskjold that says it nicely — "For all that has been, 'thanks'; for all that will be, 'Yes!'" Whether we already possess the specific promise or not doesn't really matter because God's is always good for His word. We can believe that we have received it when we prayed and we can act accordingly. What God has promised, He will deliver. Go ahead — praise and thank God today as if you already have that perfect job. Get in practice for what is surely to come!

DECLARE THIS:

- I praise God every morning and every night for His great goodness and mercy towards me.
- By faith I give thanks for the manifestation of all that God has promised in His Word.
- I believe that God is well able to perform His Word and I am open to receive His promises.

MAY 11
ASK EXPECTING RESULTS

When we know God's plan for us surpasses anything we could ask, and then we'll ask what He wants us to ask for and make our requests right out of the heart of the Spirit within us. As Joel Goldsmith said, "Once you learn to open yourself to God without a desire that is a specific will or wish or chore to be performed, but only that God's will and God's grace be done through you, then you will witness the miracle of prayer fulfilled." The requirements for granted prayers are simple — a life in Christ and a heart filled with His love. Now that you know this, raise the level of your prayers. Tell God that you're no longer going to ask Him to follow your lead or grant selfish wishes. That's how miracles happen.

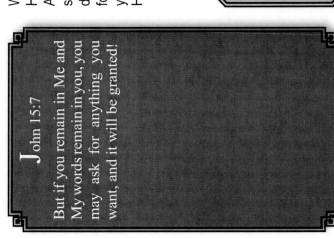

John 15:7

But if you remain in Me and My words remain in you, you may ask for anything you want, and it will be granted!

DECLARE THIS:

- I am willing to let my plans go and ask God to tell me what to ask for.
- I receive answers to all my questions and results whenever I pray because I ask according to the will of God.
- I trust that God is good and His will for me is better than my own.

Philippians 1:20

...according to my earnest expectation and hope that in nothing I shall be ashamed, but with all boldness, as always, so now also Christ will be magnified in my body, whether by life or by death.

When our highest goal and aspiration is only to get a job and pay our bills we cannot be bold and confident. But when we know that we are ambassadors for Christ and God is making His appeal to mankind through us, boldness comes naturally. Of course, God will guide us into prosperity because that will bring Him glory. We will find a great place to work because that gives us the opportunity to demonstrate the kind of life that results from being aligned with God's will. God's reputation is on the line, so we will never be put to shame. Pray for a full understanding of your kingdom identity and purpose. Allow the Spirit to work in your mind and heart until you truly know that you matter to God and He will bring you to victory for His sake.

DECLARE THIS:

- I am committed to bringing God glory by my words, actions and life.
- By faith I accept my Kingdom assignment and I boldly go forward to find my right place in the workplace.
- I am not alone in my job search. God is with me and I cannot fail.

MAY 12

ASK FOR FIRST THINGS FIRST

Proverbs 4:7 tells us "Wisdom is the principle thing; Therefore get wisdom. And in all your getting, get understanding." It helps to realize that wisdom is another name for the Word of God. Where true wisdom exists you'll find complete alignment with the Word and the character of God. If we're seeking after the highest and best things, wisdom needs to be at the top of the list. God tells us to ask for wisdom. When we do, He gives it to us freely. Look at the rest of the book of Proverbs to see what wisdom brings to us. For starters, Proverbs 3:16 says, "Length of days (long life) is in her right hand, in her left hand riches and honor." Given those free bonus gifts, we might want to make wisdom our first request.

DECLARE THIS:

- I eagerly seek God's wisdom in every part of my life. I hold nothing back.
- I trust that God will give me wisdom whenever I ask for it.
- By faith I receive the ability to recognize God's wisdom and put it into immediate action.

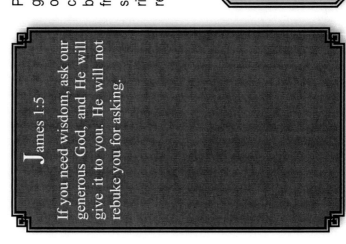

James 1:5

If you need wisdom, ask our generous God, and He will give it to you. He will not rebuke you for asking.

It so easy to get wrapped up in the activities of our job search and to completely forget that Jesus has said to us, "If you love me, feed my sheep." We need to see Jesus in everyone we meet. Remember that every person waiting in the unemployment line or sitting with you in the employment office is included in the flock that Jesus loves. We can offer an encouraging word, a friendly smile, and some form of assistance to show His love. We can bring a blessing wherever we go, and in so doing show our love for the Lord.

Matthew 25:39-40

When did we ever see you sick or in prison and visit you?' "And the King will say, 'I tell you the truth, when you did it to one of the least of these my brothers and sisters, you were doing it to me!'

DECLARE THIS:

- I care for and love others because I love the Lord.
- By faith I sow my love to others and claim a harvest in my life.
- I lack nothing and look for opportunities to give to others.

MAY 13
ASK ABOUT YOUR GIFTS

Ephesians 4:16

From Him the whole body, joined and held together by every supporting ligament, grows and builds itself up in love, as each part does its work.

This is such a beautiful picture — each believer finding his or her gifts, and bringing the best they've got into the Body of Christ. Then, as we all grow up together in faith and in love, we do the work of the Kingdom. When all the gifts are used together, when each part does its work, then we will truly become the body of Christ as God designed it to be. There's a key message here — gifts are not to be held for selfish purposes. Our gifts weren't given just to prosper us; they were given to build up the whole body. Unemployed or employed, what are we doing to use our gifts and do our part in the Church, the body of Christ?

DECLARE THIS:

- I am an essential part of the body of Christ and I am here to do my part.
- By faith I receive a revelation of my place in the body and I join my efforts with others for God's glory.
- I am called to serve in the church. There's an assignment there with my name on it.

AUGUST 19
SEEK HIDDEN TREASURES

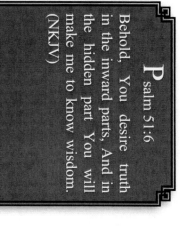

Psalm 51:6

Behold, You desire truth in the inward parts, And in the hidden part You will make me to know wisdom. (NKJV)

The world is pretty impressed by the human mind. People think man's ability to reason is his greatest feature — that the human mind is what sets us apart from animals. But while the mind is an amazing creation, the Holy Spirit dwelling in the human heart is what is truly awesome. In the deepest, most hidden part of a believer's heart the Spirit of God has taken up residence. We have the ability to receive the Truth directly from God's heart to ours, to share in His wisdom and His love. Talk about a hidden treasure!

DECLARE THIS:

- I am a temple of the Holy Spirit. The presence of God is hidden in me.
- By faith I receive the wisdom of God. I can know the mystery of God.
- I thank God, the source of love and wisdom that fills my heart, for His presence.

MAY 14
ASK ABOUT YOUR DESIGN

Psalm 8:4-6

What are mere mortals that you should think about them, human beings that you should care for them? Yet You made them only a little lower than God and crowned them with glory and honor. You gave them charge of everything You made, putting all things under their authority

God has crowned us with glory and honor. He has made us in His image and likeness and we are positioned to behave like gods. That's a radical, almost unacceptable, thought for many. The idea that we could be like God and that He would crown us with honor and glory just doesn't fit many people's self-image. But how can we argue with this scripture? "You gave them charge of everything you made, putting all things under their authority." We're the ones this scripture is referring to. So how will we behave now that we know we're in charge?

DECLARE THIS:

- I accept the authority God has given me and I behave like He designed me to behave.
- By faith I receive God's view of me, that I have been positioned beneath Him to serve in glory and honor.
- I take my authority and make a Kingdom difference in the workplace.

Proverbs 11:14

Where there is no counsel, the people fall; But in the multitude of counselors there is safety.

There is safety in a "multitude of counselors" but don't make the mistake of running around to take a poll or collect votes about the way that you should go. This is not God's way of leading us. Instead, seek Him. Ask the Holy Spirit for specific guidance. Praying in the Spirit will produce amazing results. Then, when you think you have been given an answer, ask some trusted believers to pray about the issue with you. Wait to see what counsel they have for you. The Holy Spirit never contradicts Himself. You will hear your confirmation or you will get a "check" that tells you to keep listening. There is no need to be rushed or to race to a decision. Trust God to provide just what you need and right when you need it.

DECLARE THIS:

- I know God will answer all my prayers and provide all the answers I need.
- By faith I receive wisdom for all my decisions.
- I receive the counsel of faithful believers to support and confirm my decision making process.

MAY 15

Ask About Your Purpose

Perhaps you're thinking, "Now is not the best time to go after God. I need to settle down into a job and bring in some money, and then I'll have the time to seek Him." Be honest — did you take the time when you had your last job? There are no good or bad times to go after God. There is simply this statement — that Hezekiah brought everything he had to offer as he went after God and he became very successful. Notice that he wasn't going after the things of God, he just wanted God. How many of us have that as our purpose in times of challenge and crisis? We may have just discovered a key to success!

2 Chronicles 31:21

In all that he did in the service of the Temple of God and in his efforts to follow God's laws and commands, Hezekiah sought his God wholeheartedly. As a result, he was very successful.

DECLARE THIS:

- I seek God with my whole heart, too; not for what He can do for me, I just want to know Him.
- By faith I receive a deep and personal relationship with God.
- All my needs will be met. I succeed as I serve and obey God.

Romans 5:5

And this hope will not lead to disappointment. For we know how dearly God loves us, because he has given us the Holy Spirit to fill our hearts with his love.

We can get our minds so fixed on a particular outcome that we place all our hope in to solve our problems. Then, if it doesn't come to pass as we expected, the disappointment is great. But God offers a different hope. He gives us the Holy Spirit to fill us completely with His awesome and perfect love. When we experience that love we know that all is well and we will be victorious. Will you put your hope in the fact that God loves you perfectly and is making a way for you, or are you going to put your hope in getting that particular job, or selling that project? If we choose to place our hope in the Holy Spirit, we will know with confidence that we will not be disappointed.

DECLARE THIS:

- I have a hope that will not disappoint.
- By faith I receive a revelation of God's love for me and my heart is filled with His presence.
- Because I keep my hope in God alone as I look for my next job, I will not experience disappointment.

MAY 16
SEEK SELF AWARENESS

Your spirit acts as the Lord's lamp, searching the depths of your heart to find those old and broken things you've pushed down and forgotten. Now is the time to pull them up and dump them. Ask Jesus to come into your heart and heal the old, festering wounds. Don't continue to suffer condemnation over things in the past. Take action right now and ask God to forgive you for the times you turned from Him or acted in sin. Ask the Holy Spirit to show you if you're listening to the enemy's lies instead of God's Word. It's time to turn on all the lights and clear out the cobwebs. You have important things to do in the future

DECLARE THIS:

- I willingly empty the contents of my heart before the Lord and receive His forgiveness and healing.
- I trust in the finished work of Christ and by faith I receive His righteousness, purchased for me at Calvary.
- I am filled with the love of God and completely made whole.

Proverbs 20:27
The spirit of a man is the lamp of the LORD, searching all the inner depths of his heart. (NKJV)

AUGUST 16
SEEK SELF AWARENESS

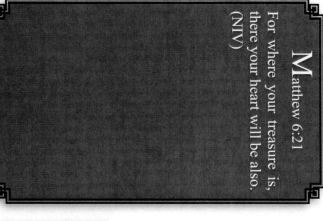

Matthew 6:21

For where your treasure is, there your heart will be also. (NIV)

Pull out your checkbook and calendar for the last few months when you were still employed. Take a look at how you spent your money and your time. That will show what really matters to you. Where did the Kingdom of God figure in? How did you spend your free time when it was in short supply? Did you invest in the Kingdom? What did you do with your paycheck? Could it be that you are being held back even now by wrong priorities? Now is the time to settle your heart on things of eternal worth. Ask God where He wants you to place your focus. Decide now how you will spend your treasure when you get a new job. Make plans to anchor your heart in Kingdom priorities.

DECLARE THIS:

- I claim Jesus as the Lord of my life and the King over all that concerns me.
- My treasure is in the Kingdom of God.
- By faith I receive a heart that is fixed on the plans and purposes of God alone. My life reflects His rule in it.

MAY 17

SEEK THE DIRECTION OF THE HOLY SPIRIT

Notice the cooperation and partnership between God and man here. We are not puppets. In fact, we have been invited to co-labor with God. He wants us to tell Him the things we are passionate about and what we want to do for the Kingdom. It's likely that the things we care deeply about are the very desires that God placed in our hearts before the foundation of the earth. God expects us to contribute to His plan using our ideas and creativity. We're His children, destined to rule for all eternity, so let's start get started. As we dream great dreams, He will show us how to accomplish them. What's more, He has promised to work right alongside us. What a partnership!

DECLARE THIS:

- I work for the Lord and He labors with me to accomplish great things.
- By faith I trust God to reveal how I can contribute to His kingdom with my energy and creativity.
- I trust that the Lord will show me how to accomplish whatever I set my hands to do.

Proverbs 16:9

A man's heart plans his way, but the LORD directs his steps.

AUGUST 15
ASK ABOUT YOUR PURPOSE

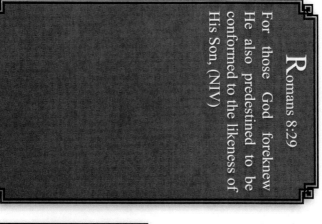

Romans 8:29

For those God foreknew He also predestined to be conformed to the likeness of His Son, (NIV)

We're called to be lighthouses in the storm of economic chaos. Now, while so many are watching to see how we're doing in our job searches, would be the time to shine the brightest. Long after we're working in our next job there will still be a lost, hurting world that needs to know Jesus, and an enemy who seeks to steal, kill and destroy. We can't afford to get so caught up in our job search and temporary things that we lose sight of our eternal Kingdom purpose. Make it a priority to be conformed into the likeness of Jesus. Stand strong against the devil and show the love of God to those who are lost.

DECLARE THIS:

- I have been chosen by God for such a time as this and I have a Kingdom purpose to fulfill.
- By faith I receive all the provisions I need so that I might demonstrate God's love and provision to those who don't yet know Him.
- My purpose is not my job. My purpose is to be like Jesus and to do the works He did.

MAY 18
SEEK DIVINE CONNECTIONS

When we openly love and accept our fellow Christians, we get to share in the blessings God has for them. He called some to be prophets and all of us to be righteous people. Then He tells us that if we will receive and honor those He sends and those He calls righteous, we will be given a reward just like theirs. As we give them our prayers and financial support, we participate in their anointing and blessing! Even if you're unemployed and unable to reach the world for Christ, your support of those doing God's work will bring their reward to you! When you bless others God always returns a greatly multiplied blessing to you.

DECLARE THIS:

- I thank God for the body of believers and for the shepherds and prophets He has ordained.
- By faith I receive the ability to discern God's prophetic voice when I hear it.
- I receive God's blessing and participate in His divine reward program!

Matthew 10:41

If you receive a prophet as one who speaks for God, you will be given the same reward as a prophet. And if you receive righteous people because of their righteousness, you will be given a reward like theirs.

AUGUST 14
ASK ABOUT YOUR DESIGN

We were never designed to function alone. Each of us is only one part of an entire body. We have been designed to connect with other believers and work in harmony with them. This is not optional — this is our design and our God-given destiny. The world thinks that talents and skills are to be used to further a career and promote oneself. We know that they are gifts from God to build His Kingdom. Have you dedicated your gifts and talents to that purpose?

> **Romans 12:4-6**
>
> For as we have many members in one body, but all the members do not have the same function, so we, being many, are one body in Christ, and individually members of one another. Having then gifts differing according to the grace that is given to us, let us use them: (NKJV)

DECLARE THIS:

- I am designed to serve in the body of Christ.
- By faith I bring my gifts and talents to God. He gave them to me and He knows how I am to use them.
- I am perfectly designed to work with others for the benefit of the Kingdom.

MAY 19
SEEK HIDDEN TREASURES

The world can't see or hear the Holy Spirit, and doesn't even recognize that He exists. But in truth He may be the greatest "hidden" treasure of all. Because of the Spirit of God living inside us, we are equipped to handle and overcome every one of life's challenges. The Holy Spirit will tell us things we never learned through studying. With the leading of the Spirit we will always escape every snare the enemy may set and we'll confidently pursue the opportunities God has prepared for us. Beyond success, the Holy Spirit will also connect us with the power to heal the sick and brokenhearted, and set captives free. The Holy Spirit will tell us exactly when and where to release that power. Now that's a treasure, but hopefully it won't remain hidden!

John 14:16-17

And I will ask the Father, and he will give you another Advocate, who will never leave you. He is the Holy Spirit, who leads into all truth. The world cannot receive him, because it isn't looking for him and doesn't recognize him. But you know him, because he lives with you now and later will be in you.

DECLARE THIS:

- I have the Holy Spirit inside me to empower me in all things.
- By faith I receive the supernatural insight and wisdom that comes directly to me through the Spirit of God.
- I thank God for this life-transforming gift of Christ in me.

AUGUST 13
ASK ABOUT YOUR GIFTS

Leviticus 23:37-38

'These are the feasts of the LORD which you shall proclaim to be holy convocations, to offer an offering made by fire to the LORD, a burnt offering and a grain offering, a sacrifice and a drink offerings, everything on its day — besides the Sabbaths of the LORD, besides your gifts, besides all your vows, and besides all your freewill offerings which you give to the LORD. (NKJV)

If we don't want to continuously bless God and bring Him gifts, perhaps it is because we don't fully comprehend what He has done for us. We probably haven't fully realized what our Kingdom citizenship means in our lives. When we really get this, like the woman in Matthew 26:7, we'll look around for our "alabaster box of precious ointment" and bring it to Jesus. In an act of adoration we will pour out our gifts on His children because He said, "If you love me, feed my sheep." As God cares for you throughout this time of unemployment, as He sustains you and directs your steps, be aware of the gifts you have to offer and look for ways to bless Him back by loving others.

DECLARE THIS:

- I have the gift of love and the authority of Jesus. I will bless others wherever I go.
- By faith I bring a sacrifice of praise to God in this challenging time and I seek to bless Him with my gifts.
- I freely give to God and worship Him by loving His children.

MAY 20

SEEK TO STAY FOCUSED ON JESUS

There are many who accept Jesus as their Savior without ever realizing that He is also their Lord and Master. Upon receiving His salvation we committed our lives to His service. We owe obedience to Him. The great news is that the reward for following Him is awesome! As we let our roots grow down into Him we secure our lives from being battered by the storms we face, including unemployment. Grow roots. Build upon Him. Then our job search will be built on a solid foundation and we'll have unshakeable confidence. Life built on the Rock will cause us to "overflow with thankfulness!"

Colossians 2:6-7

And now, just as you accepted Christ Jesus as your Lord, you must continue to follow him. Let your roots grow down into him, and let your lives be built on him. Then your faith will grow strong in the truth you were taught, and you will overflow with thankfulness.

DECLARE THIS:

- I thank God that my life is rooted and grounded in Him.
- By faith I receive Christ as my Lord and the Holy Spirit as my guide.
- I am so grateful that I don't have to struggle. My life is built on Him.

P salm 51:10

Create in me a clean heart, O God, and renew a steadfast spirit within me. (NKJV)

As we seek to pray for the most important things first this scripture suggests that we ask for a "heart cleaning." Invite Jesus to come into your heart and cleanse you of everything that doesn't suit Him. It's time to get rid of all the baggage we've been carrying. Time to let go of resentments, shame, offenses and guilt. Now — imagine going on interviews or selling your services knowing that God is with you and that everything about you is aligned with His will and purpose. That's how we'll get a steadfast spirit and the strength to make it through this journey and into the promised land.

DECLARE THIS:

- I know that God is working in me and I want to cooperate with everything He desires to do.
- My heart is open to the love of God and His healing.
- By faith I accept the cleansing, perfect work that Christ has already accomplished and look forward to its manifestation in my life.

MAY 21
KNOCK WITH BOLDNESS

We need confidence and boldness as we go into the job market. That means we need to connect with God's presence and discover His will before we begin our day's activities. Notice the pattern here — they prayed, were filled with the Holy Spirit, and then spoke with boldness. Every job seeker needs this empowerment. Without boldness, we'll run out of gas before the day is half over. All it takes is one bad report, one unfavorable judgment about our skills and abilities, and we struggle to hang onto self-esteem and confidence. Thank God we aren't on our own. We have the presence of God within us and that's the wind in our sails that can carry us victoriously throughout the day.

Acts 4:31

And when they had prayed, the place where they were assembled together was shaken; and they were all filled with the Holy Spirit, and they spoke the word of God with boldness. (NKJV)

DECLARE THIS:

- I am bold because the Spirit of God fills me.
- By faith I receive the guidance and empowerment of the Holy Spirit and I know I cannot fail.
- I go out into the job market "prayed up" and powered by love.

AUGUST 11
ASK EXPECTING RESULTS

> P salm 35:27
>
> Let them shout for joy and
> be glad, Who favor my
> righteous cause; And let
> them say continually, "Let
> the LORD be magnified, Who
> has pleasure in the prosperity
> of His servant." (NKJV)

How would you behave today if you knew that you would soon be working again, in a job you enjoyed, with all your needs met? Well, what are you waiting for? That's exactly how your job search experience is going to turn out. God's reputation is on the line with you. Haven't you've been telling people that you are trusting God for a great outcome and that you are following His lead because you know that He is good and only good. Do you think there's any chance He will allow you to stumble or fail with everyone watching to see what happens? No! God has pleasure in the prosperity of His servants so just imagine what His intentions must be towards His children! Shout for joy. Your new job is on its way.

DECLARE THIS:

- I give thanks to the Lord for giving me a victorious job search.
- By faith I receive the revelation that God desires to prosper me. My days of lack are over.
- I am so happy that God loves me and guarantees my success.

MAY 22
Knock With Thanksgiving

The full awareness of God's grace towards us makes us fall to our knees to worship Jesus, too. But unfortunately, we get so caught up in our pursuit of employment and our attempts to supply our own needs that we allow what we don't yet have to crowd out all that we already possess. Today, before you begin your job search activity, sit still and recount all that the Lord has done for you. Thank Him and praise Him. Then be refreshed, knowing that God is good and only good. His love and mercy towards us is boundless. Bask in thanksgiving and go forth in peace and confidence. The God who has blessed us in the past is forever in the "blessing business."

Luke 17:16-18

He fell to the ground at Jesus' feet, thanking him for what he had done. This man was a Samaritan. Jesus asked, "Didn't I heal ten men? Where are the other nine? Has no one returned to give glory to God except this foreigner?"

DECLARE THIS:

- I give thanks for all that Jesus has done for me. I am saved, healed, prosperous and complete.
- By faith I receive God's blessing and expect it to manifest in every part of my life.
- With the help of the Holy Spirit, I make thanksgiving and praise my continuous response to God.

Joshua 10:8

"Do not be afraid of them," the Lord said to Joshua, "for I have given you victory over them. Not a single one of them will be able to stand up to you."

It's easy for job seekers to believe that they have some fatal flaw that will prevent them from ever securing a good job. We all have to face our own personal "giants" — I'm too fat, too old, too uneducated, too shy, you name it. But not one of those giants will be able to stand against us. We have to remember that nothing in our lives is a surprise to God. He has seen our lives from the end to the beginning. More than that, He has a perfect and wonderful plan that has already taken all of our flaws into consideration. Hear what He tells us — "I have given you victory over them." Count on it, and by faith, expect it.

DECLARE THIS:

- I expect a great conclusion to my job search. God guarantees my victory.
- Nothing will be able to keep my good from me. My Father is the King over all kings.
- By faith I face my limitations and flaws knowing that, in Christ, I am perfect and complete, lacking nothing.

MAY 23
KNOCK WITH CONFIDENCE

When we grasp the full revelation of the authority we've been given in this world, we'll take dominion over our workplace. It belongs to us. Christ is the head, we are the body and all things have been placed under our feet! We need to believe God when He says the things of this world are under our rule! As you look for your next job, start thinking about the place that you want to influence for the Kingdom. Declare your willingness to assume responsibility for the workplace. God views us as sons and heirs, not servants. He wants us to rise up in confidence. Let's claim what God has given us and be bold about our claims, knowing that the Kingdom of God has need of us.

DECLARE THIS:

- I am part of the body of Christ and I claim authority over the workplace.
- By faith I receive my Kingdom assignment from God and look for a place where I may serve Him by blessing others.
- I move in confidence because I serve the King of Kings who rules from within me.

Ephesians 1:22-23
And God placed all things under His feet and appointed Him to be head over everything for the church, which is His body, the fullness of Him who fills everything in every way. (NIV)

AUGUST 9
CHOOSE YOUR BEHAVIOR

Matthew 7:13 – 14

Enter through the narrow gate; for wide is the gate and spacious and broad is the way that leads away to destruction, and many are those who are entering through it. But the gate is narrow (contracted by pressure) and the way is straitened and compressed that leads away to life, and few are those who find it.

Imagine a person trying to fit through a narrow passage carrying an armload of luggage. To make it through will require a choice to leave it behind or to stay outside. That's us with all our past baggage. We can't carry our sinful behavior, bad habits, wounds, resentments and offenses into the Kingdom. If you've been hanging onto something other than what God has for you, let it go. Invite Jesus into your heart to heal your broken places so you can go forward. Then you will be ready to receive new blessings from God. Those who decide to travel this path are glad they did, for this is where abundant life is found.

DECLARE THIS:

- I am willing to let go of anything that would prevent me from traveling on the way of Life.
- By faith I believe that I am one of the few who will go through the narrow gate to the fullness of God's blessing.
- I don't follow the ways of this world for I know they lead to destruction.

MAY 24
KNOCK AND BRING GIFTS

Think about all the places you might go during your job search. Chances are you'll be driving around your city and the surrounding areas a good bit. Why not spend your travel time praying for the entire area and releasing God's hand over it? Every workplace you enter could use a blessing too, couldn't it? Bless the business leaders and ask for wisdom for them. Bless all the workers you see, that they might come to know the Lord and grow strong in their faith and love. See yourself as a Kingdom employee on assignment as a "blessing giver" right now. Your prayers will produce results that are desperately needed in the workplace. Will you accept this assignment?

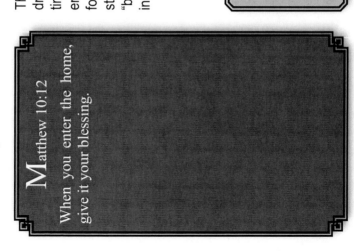

DECLARE THIS:

- I am on assignment for the Lord and I bring blessings wherever I go.
- By faith I receive guidance from the Holy Spirit to know how and when to pray for the workplace.
- I know my prayers will produce results.

Matthew 10:12

When you enter the home, give it your blessing.

AUGUST 8
CHOOSE YOUR TRAINING

In all the years I spent growing up in the church I was never taught about the Holy Spirit. Finally, as an adult, I experienced the baptism of the Holy Spirit and my life was radically changed. Alive and active in me now is the mind of Christ, the power of God, and the source of everything I will ever need. We truly do have a far more excellent covenant than the Old Testament saints, for the Holy Spirit of God now dwells within us. With the baptism of the Holy Spirit He will be released to add His "super" to your "natural" for supernatural results. If you haven't had this experience, go after it! Your life will never be the same.

John 16:7

Nevertheless I tell you the truth. It is to your advantage that I go away; for if I do not go away, the Helper will not come to you; but if I depart, I will send Him to you. (NKJV)

DECLARE THIS:

- I am the temple of the Holy Spirit of God. He lives in me.
- By faith I receive the full revelation of the Holy Spirit that I might walk in power and authority.
- With the very presence of God in me, I expect to do the works that Jesus did. Signs and wonders will follow me.

MAY 25

KNOCK AND EXERCISE YOUR FAITH

Did you ever wonder why those people had to walk around the city of Jericho seven times, or why you had to do ten job interviews that amounted to nothing? God is doing something. He has already prepared a new assignment for you so that's not the issue. The truth is that this part of the process is about your faith, your obedience and your patience. Don't try to skip the important work that's being accomplished in you right now, the strengthened faith and confidence you are developing in the Lord. Your job search testimony just might become a lifesaver for someone else. So hang in there. Do whatever God asks for as long as He asks and you'll be positioned for greatness.

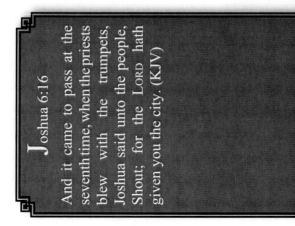

Joshua 6:16

And it came to pass at the seventh time, when the priests blew with the trumpets, Joshua said unto the people, Shout; for the LORD hath given you the city. (KJV)

DECLARE THIS:

- I am building patient endurance and confidence in the Lord.
- All eyes are on me and I do not waver in my faith. I trust in the Lord.
- By faith I receive the confidence that I hear from God and He will not let me miss His directions.

AUGUST 7
CHOOSE YOUR PAY

Psalm 34:10
...those that seek the Lord lack no good thing. (NIV)

Right now you may be wondering how this scripture can possibly be true. Perhaps you are lacking some good things in your life so you're thinking the Word must be wrong somehow. But the requirement for success here is clear — "seek the Lord." He knows where your next job is. He has the wisdom and instruction you need in order to grow in faith and love. He really does desire to banish lack from your life, once and for all. Be convinced that God wants you to live in prosperity. Then, if you're not experiencing prosperity, check yourself. Are you seeking Him in His Word, through spiritual teachers, and in prayer? Park yourself on His doorstep every morning, seek him diligently, and discover all the good He has already procured for you.

DECLARE THIS:

- God is my top priority for I know my answers will be found in Him.
- I trust that I will find Him when I seek Him and I will recognize His voice.
- I know it is God's desire to prosper me for He is good and only good.

MAY 26

KNOCK AND WITNESS FOR THE KINGDOM

Job seekers are in a perfect position to bring the good news. Many eyes will be focused on you, from family and friends to former coworkers, watching to see how you'll fare in this time of unemployment. There are hurting and frightened people out there who need Jesus. Let them see your joy and your peace. They'll want to know your secret and you will be able to tell them. It's Jesus. Lean on the Lord, exercise your faith and demonstrate the power of God in the life of a believer. You can make a Kingdom difference while you're looking for work. Those you touch will bless you for sharing the really good news of Jesus.

DECLARE THIS:

- I want to bring the good news to others so I trust the Holy Spirit to lead me to the right people.
- By faith I accept my assignment to demonstrate the power of God's blessing in the life of a believer.
- I move in faith and confidence every day, living out the good news of Jesus in my life.

Romans 10: 14-15

But how can they call on Him to save them unless they believe in Him? And how can they believe in Him if they have never heard about Him? And how can they hear about Him unless someone tells them? And how will anyone go and tell them without being sent? That is why the Scriptures say, "How beautiful are the feet of messengers who bring good news!"

AUGUST 6
CHOOSE YOUR WORK

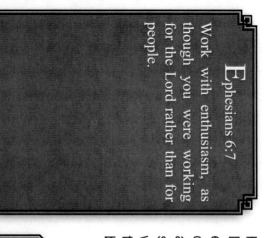

Ephesians 6:7

Work with enthusiasm, as though you were working for the Lord rather than for people.

How can job seekers work with enthusiasm when they're not working? Don't be fooled. Looking for a job is work. So maybe enthusiasm would be calling a recruiter back and expressing interest. Maybe it would be offering to work as a contractor to help the company out while they're interviewing. Perhaps it's investing energy to research a company and arriving fully prepared for the interview. It's easy to get depressed and lazy in the job search... and so hard to keep your energy up. But, oh, the difference it makes! People will notice you. Perhaps they'll even ask why you act the way you do. Then you'll be able to tell them that it's because you work for the Lord and He pays so well, He deserves the best you've got.

DECLARE THIS:

- I work for the Lord and I cannot be unemployed.
- I receive joy, energy and enthusiasm to fuel my job search efforts.
- You can tell that I work for the Lord by the way I approach my job search with excellence.

MAY 27

KNOCK AND OVERCOME

Maybe you think you aren't blessed with a strong faith like some people. You're just you and you have just enough faith to believe that Jesus saved you and no more. Well, that's not what the Word says. Romans 12:3 tells us that God has given each of us the measure of faith that we need. It would be unfair of God if He failed to give us enough to sustain us, wouldn't it? No, the problem isn't the amount of faith that we have, it's the amount of exercising we've done. Faith muscle requires stretching. So act in faith and believe this Word — we overcome the world, unemployment, poverty, failure, disease, through faith in the work and love of Jesus. The victory is promised but we have to take it by faith.

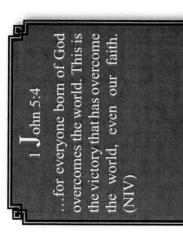

1 John 5:4

...for everyone born of God overcomes the world. This is the victory that has overcome the world, even our faith. (NIV)

DECLARE THIS:

- I am born of God and I overcome the circumstances of this world.
- By faith I declare that Jesus is more than enough and in Him I have victory.
- I thank God that I have the faith I need to overcome all of life's challenges.

AUGUST 5
CHOOSE YOUR BENEFITS

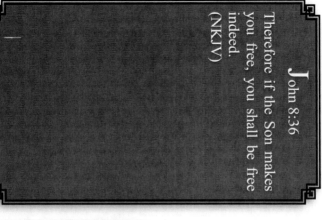

John 8:36

Therefore if the Son makes you free, you shall be free indeed.
(NKJV)

When we get bogged down in the world's systems and way of thinking we become ensnared by the devil. Those who don't know Jesus have no other option, they are stuck — but believers are not. Jesus offers us a radically different way to live. We have the choice to stay in bondage to the world systems or to accept the freedom Jesus purchased for us at Calvary. If your choice is freedom, then turn off the reports of doom and gloom and turn to the Word. Choosing freedom means no more talking about your problems... only about your promises. There's no wiggle room here — WE ARE FREE INDEED and we need to walk in our liberty. This is one benefit that's too good not to accept.

DECLARE THIS:

- I am free from the systems of this world for I belong to the Kingdom of God.
- By faith I receive the liberty Christ has given to me. I walk like one who is completely free.
- I trust in the Word of God and the completed work of Christ Jesus. The world has no hold on me.

MAY 28
KNOCK AND FAINT NOT!

We admire Job for his steadfastness, Joseph as he endured prison and Paul as he experienced all the hardships of a life in service to God. Their strength and endurance is worthy of respect and admiration. But how do we behave when it's our turn? Are we living like modern day believers of God's faithfulness? When this season ends and you're in your new job, don't you want to look back on this time and feel good about how you handled it? Decide today that you will give yourself something to be proud of because you, too, endured like Job without wavering and without turning against God. Let others honor you for the way you endured the suffering and stood fast on the promises of God until you obtained the victory.

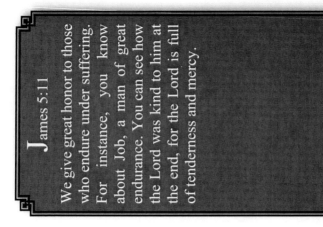

J ames 5:11

We give great honor to those who endure under suffering. For instance, you know about Job, a man of great endurance. You can see how the Lord was kind to him at the end, for the Lord is full of tenderness and mercy.

DECLARE THIS:

- I will endure all the challenges of this season and I steadfastly trust God.
- By faith I receive the ability to see God working on my behalf and I know He is the source of good in my life.
- I will witness before powers and principalities that I serve God and put my faith in Him to save me.

AUGUST 4
CHOOSE YOUR BOSS

Deuteronomy 3:24

'O Sovereign Lord, you have only begun to show your greatness and the strength of your hand to me, your servant. Is there any god in heaven or on earth who can perform such great and mighty deeds as you do?

As Moses stood at the edge of the Jordan river, after all he had seen and experienced in the wilderness, he said to God, "You have only begun to show your greatness and strength." If that was just the beginning of God's greatness can you imagine the full scope of it? With just this example, we can see that this mighty and great God, the Ruler over all, stands ready to extend the strength and greatness of His hand to His people. But now comes the best part of the scripture — What God has done for any of His children He will do for you personally. Release His hand over your circumstances and stand in faith. He will perform great and mighty deeds for you too.

DECLARE THIS:

- I know my God is willing and able to sustain and bless me.
- By faith I release the Hand of God over all that concerns me.
- I go forward in the greatness and the strength of the Spirit of God who dwells in me.

MAY 29
KNOCK AND BE ENCOURAGED

Recall the story in 1 Samuel 30:6 — "David was greatly distressed, for the men spoke of stoning him because the souls of them all were bitterly grieved, each man for his sons and daughters. But David encouraged and strengthened himself in the Lord his God." That's exactly what we have to do for ourselves. You may experience the anger and disappointment of others. They might criticize you because they think you're not trying hard enough. They might even blame you for your circumstances. That's when unemployment becomes very difficult. But David's strategy will work for us too. Turn your attention to verses like this one, and encourage yourself in the Lord. We are called to be joyful, because Almighty God is with us. See yourself surrounded with goodwill and favor! Sing praises to God, rejoice in His goodness, and stay in His Word! Soon you will feel His strength.

DECLARE THIS:

- I encourage myself when times are tough. I know the Lord is with me.
- By faith I believe that God rescues, defends and covers me.
- I am righteous in Christ and I know God is blessing me with favor.

Psalm 5:11-12

But let all those who take refuge and put their trust in You rejoice; let them ever sing and shout for joy, because You make a covering over them and defend them; let those also who love Your name be joyful in You and be in high spirits. For You, Lord, will bless the [uncompromisingly] righteous [him who is upright and in right standing with You]; as with a shield You will surround him with goodwill (pleasure and favor).

(The Amplified Bible)

Matthew 5:44-45

But I say to you, love your enemies, bless those who curse you, do good to those who hate you, and pray for those who spitefully use you and persecute you, that you may be sons of your Father in heaven; (NKJV)

Love your enemies, including those who fired you, let you go or caused your termination. Pray for those who treated you badly and persecuted you. Bless the very people who spoke against you and sought to do you harm. If you get the opportunity, do good to the very people who hated you. There's nothing easy about this command. I've been so hurt that I just couldn't pray for the people who wronged me. That's when I found that God would empower me to bless and forgive them. Don't allow yourself to be chained to people who have hurt you. Forgive, bless, love and release them all. If not for the power of God inside us, this would be impossible. But with the help of the Holy Spirit you can do this too.

DECLARE THIS:

- By faith I forgive everyone who has hurt me or caused me harm.
- I release God's blessing and His love over all my enemies and pray that they too will experience the Love of God.
- I have the Holy Spirit in me to give me the ability to love my enemies with the love of Christ.

MAY 30
Knock And Keep Knocking

Sometimes we forget that the Lord is with us everywhere we go, observing our behavior and listening to everything we say. So often, when we do think about His presence, we're distressed because we just did or said something we regret. But what about when you are encouraging others and giving of yourself? What about when you are thinking about Him and standing in faith believing for a promise? He's watching and listening then, too. He's delighted with your commitment to Him. This scripture says He's actually writing it down, making note of your desire to honor His name with your life. As you walk this life out and continue to honor Him, remember that He considers you His special treasure. He will bring you victory in this life and eternally.

DECLARE THIS:

- I think about the Lord and ways to bring Him honor with my life.
- By faith I receive the promise that He will spare me from judgment because Christ has paid for me.
- I know that the Spirit of God dwells in me and I live in the awareness of His presence.

Malachi 3:16-17

Then, those who feared the LORD spoke with each other, and the LORD listened to what they said. In His presence, a scroll of remembrance was written to record the names of those who feared him and always thought about the honor of his name. "They will be my people," says the LORD of Heaven's Armies. "On the day when I act in judgment, they will be My own special treasure. I will spare them as a father spares an obedient child.

Luke 5:38-39

New wine must be stored in new wineskins. But no one who drinks the old wine seems to want the new wine. 'The old is just fine,' they say."

Does this sound like anyone you know? "My old job wasn't great but I could have lived with it" or, "I know this isn't where I belong but the job market is bad and I can't risk making a change right now." It's easy to put trust in a job or a paycheck, no matter how paltry or dissatisfying. All our lives we've been taught to think there is security in this world. In fact, "job security" still shows up as one of the top things that workers want from employers. Unfortunately, it doesn't exist in today's world. Those who think they have it are sadly mistaken. Our only security is in God. If we rely on His promises, God will provide all the security, both physical and spiritual, that we could ever need or want.

DECLARE THIS:

- I am willing to be changed by God into a new creation.
- I am ready to do God's will and fulfill my Kingdom purpose.
- The past was not that great — I can let it go to make room for the greater things God has for me.

MAY 31
KNOCK AND BE AT PEACE

Isn't it good to know that God wants us to get a good night's sleep? Take this great comfort as a gift from your Father in Heaven. However your day goes — no matter if you had good interviews or no interviews, excellent employment prospects or no clue what you'll be doing tomorrow — this fact never changes: our Lord is our Shepherd and He will keep us safe. It is safe to lie down and cast your cares onto His shoulders. He can handle the burden while we sleep. Let Him!

DECLARE THIS:

- I am safe in the care of the Good Shepherd.
- By faith I receive good sleep every night and energy every day.
- I thank God that He orders my steps and keeps me in His perfect will.

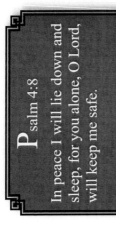

P salm 4:8
In peace I will lie down and sleep, for you alone, O Lord, will keep me safe.

AUGUST 1
CHOOSE YOUR KINGDOM

Matthew 2:2

...and asked, "Where is the one who has been born king of the Jews? We saw his star in the east and have come to worship him." (NIV)

The wise men understood. They had been studying and they knew a king was coming. More than that, they were prepared to pay a great price to come into His presence. Their journey to find Him took months, maybe years. The treasure that they brought to Jesus was substantial. They let nothing stand in their way as they journeyed to worship the King. We could learn from their example. Let's put our focus on finding the King and worshiping Him too. The Bible promises that if we seek Him first, every other thing we need will be provided for us. Make your journey believing that you will find the King. Finding Him will be the most magnificent outcome of your job search.

DECLARE THIS:

- I know that Jesus is the King and I choose to worship Him.
- My life reflects my love of Jesus as my king.
- I worship you, Lord, and thank you for who you are and for how you love me.

JUNE

GOOD NEWS

AUGUST

GOOD NEWS

JUNE 1
CHOOSE YOUR KINGDOM

This promise assures us we will find His kingdom and His way of doing and being right, if we keep our hearts stayed on that objective. But don't expect things to happen immediately. Some believers think that when things don't happen right now it means that God has not answered their prayer. That's just not true. We have to keep knocking, and keep seeking. A job search is usually a time-consuming process, not a single event that happens overnight. So again we must choose to keep on until we have the victory. Whether this process is painful or joy-filled is up to us. Know this, and stand on God's promise that the door will be opened and you will have the victory.

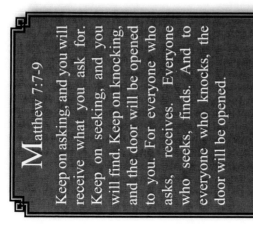

Matthew 7:7-9

Keep on asking, and you will receive what you ask for. Keep on seeking, and you will find. Keep on knocking, and the door will be opened to you. For everyone who asks, receives. Everyone who seeks, finds. And to everyone who knocks, the door will be opened.

DECLARE THIS:

- By faith I exercise the "ask, seek, and knock strategy" of the Kingdom.
- I know that the right door will open for me.
- I am determined to seek the Kingdom and its King first, and to receive what God has for me.

JULY 31
KNOCK AND BE AT PEACE

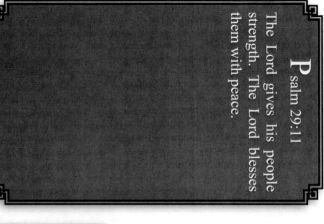

Psalm 29:11

The Lord gives his people strength. The Lord blesses them with peace.

You might feel like you have no strength left and you might be right. Maybe you don't. But the Lord always has the strength we need and He will give it to us. When we receive His strength, we receive peace along with it. Don't try to go in your own strength. You will fail. We need Him and He's there with the free gift of strength and peace. Keep your eyes on the Lord and receive by faith this promise of strength.

DECLARE THIS:

- I bless others by remaining at peace.
- By faith I receive strength from the Lord so that I can run my race.
- I thank God that He meets all my needs and sustains me.

JUNE 2
CHOOSE YOUR THOUGHTS

Do you realize that you might be carrying a heavy load in your heart? Hurts, offenses, unhappy memories... it's all unnecessary baggage. Most of us don't have a clue what we've hidden deep in our hearts. Now would be a great time to unpack. Ask Jesus to come into your heart and find things you've hidden away that you no longer need. Let the baggage go so you'll have plenty of room for the full, wonderful and perfect love of God. Invite God to do a work in your heart, and in your mind, and get you lined up with the Kingdom way of life. It'll make the journey so much easier, and the experience of unemployment one of the best times of your life.

P salm 51:10

Create in me a clean heart, O God, and renew a right, persevering, and steadfast spirit within me.
(The Amplified Bible)

DECLARE THIS:

- I willingly release all the baggage from my past.
- I invite Jesus to come into my heart and heal all my past wounds and hurts.
- I forgive freely because I have been freely forgiven.

Malachi 3:2-3

"But who can endure the day of His coming? And who can stand when He appears? For He is like a refiner's fire And like launderers' soap. He will sit as a refiner and a purifier of silver; He will purify the sons of Levi, And purge them as gold and silver, That they may offer to the LORD an offering in righteousness. (NKJV)

Who could possibly like the thought of being refined in fire and washed with laundry soap? But consider the result. When we allow the Lord to purify us, all the addictions, bad habits, character flaws and things that have held us back get burned away, never to return. As God works on us he will do for us what we could not do for ourselves. When our Maker can see His reflection in us, His work will be complete. Let's confess our sins and shortcomings to God and tell Him about the things that seem to be hindering our progress and preventing our success. Then let's trust the Refiner who loves us. As we become more like Him we will be able to give ourselves to Him, a true and righteous offering.

DECLARE THIS:

- I bring all that I have and all that I am to the Lord for His refining process.
- I receive God's promise that He will complete the work He began in me.
- I receive the righteousness of Christ and will surrender all that does not match my true nature in Him.

JUNE 3
CHOOSE YOUR FUTURE

If we've been wronged, the Word is clear that we are to trust God to handle the situation. We are to turn the other cheek, kick the dust off our shoes, and walk away. There's no telling how many believers have been derailed in their job searches by the desire to seek revenge against their former employers. Can you see the snare of the enemy here? If you pursue revenge you'll be focused on the past and prevented from obtaining the wonderful promises before you. Let your anger go and put your attention on your future. There is peace and joy there. Trust God to take care of any repayment that is due. Isn't that a welcome change from hurt, anger and revenge?

DECLARE THIS:

- I am free of the past and it has no hold on me.
- By faith I forgive all those who have wronged me and I leave them in God's hands.
- My heart and my energy are directed to the future God has planned for me.

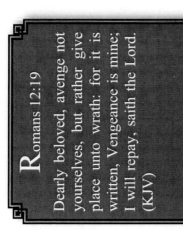

Romans 12:19

Dearly beloved, avenge not yourselves, but rather give place unto wrath: for it is written, Vengeance is mine; I will repay, saith the Lord. (KJV)

JULY 29
KNOCK AND BE ENCOURAGED

> ## Acts 9:31
>
> The church then had peace throughout Judea, Galilee, and Samaria, and it became stronger as the believers lived in the fear of the Lord. And with the encouragement of the Holy Spirit, it also grew in numbers.

With the encouragement of the Holy Spirit the Church grew in strength and in numbers. Today, you and I are the church of Jesus Christ and we have been given an awesome gift — the Holy Spirit inside us. We can release this power in us through the baptism of the Holy Spirit. The same power that set the early church on fire is the power that can encourage and empower you in the workplace. If you need encouragement, power, and victory in your life, seek the baptism of the Holy Spirit. If you've never exercised the power of praying in tongues, now is the time. Build yourself up by praying in the Spirit every day and give the Spirit the freedom to move in your life.

DECLARE THIS:

- I have the Spirit of God dwelling in me.
- By faith I receive the baptism of the Holy Spirit as evidenced by the gift of tongues.
- I thank God that the Holy Spirit in me will guide, comfort and teach me and that I will walk in power and victory as a result.

JUNE 4
CHOOSE YOUR BOSS

Isn't it great to know that you work for the Ruler of all? Ultimately everything falls under God's dominion. But while He owns the earth, He has given it to us to rule and to govern. In Genesis, Adam took this authority and handed it to the devil. In Christ the authority was reclaimed and handed to believers. Now, as God's special treasure, we are to obey Him and rule as He originally planned for us to rule. Why not get connected to God, learn to rise up in your Kingdom authority, and command victory into your life starting today? Go for it! He the ultimate King over everything and He has declared that you have the power and authority to do it!

DECLARE THIS:

- I am God's special treasure and He has given me the authority to rule over my circumstances.
- By faith I have the ability and commitment to obey the voice of God and walk in His covenant.
- The blessing of Abraham is mine in Christ and I will see prosperity in this life in Jesus name.

Exodus 19:5

Now therefore, if you will indeed obey My voice and keep My covenant, then you shall be a special treasure to Me above all people; for all the earth is Mine. (NKJV)

JULY 28
KNOCK AND FAINT NOT!

> **I**saiah 50:7
>
> Because the Sovereign Lord helps me, I will not be disgraced. Therefore, I have set my face like a stone, determined to do his will. And I know that I will not be put to shame.

I've often listened to job seekers speaking doubt and unbelief. When I confront them about it they say, "I'm only human. I can't help it if I get down." That's not true. We must set our faces like stone and determine to do God's will. We have to make a once-and-for-all-time decision to believe our God is sovereign and that His promises to deliver, protect and provide for us are true. No matter what the circumstances look like, if we fill our hearts and minds with faith in Him we will make room for God to move on our behalf. Then we can have confidence that we will not be put to shame or disgraced.

DECLARE THIS:

- I have decided to place all my trust in the Word of God.
- By faith I receive God's help in this season of unemployment and I know He is more than able to meet my needs.
- I am not ashamed to be unemployed for I am a child of God and joint heir with Jesus. There is no disgrace in my situation.

JUNE 5
CHOOSE YOUR BENEFITS

How many people do you know who have peace in troubling times? Believers have been given this gift. We simply have to keep our eyes on Jesus. The same Jesus that walked in peace and confidence on the earth has sent His Spirit to live inside us. If He had power, we have power. If He had peace and confidence in God, so do we. Jesus trusted in God to meet all His needs, and so can we. You have a right to that peace, so claim it. Don't allow any doubt or questioning thoughts to enter your mind. We have every reason to trust God and no reason not to. When we make a quality decision to trust God, we put ourselves in the place of peace. Let's dwell there.

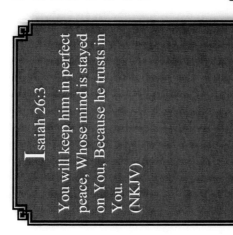

Isaiah 26:3

You will keep him in perfect peace, Whose mind is stayed on You, Because he trusts in You.
(NKJV)

DECLARE THIS:

- I trust God and by faith I dwell in peace.
- Doubt and despair can not stand up to the Word of God.
- I am determined to keep my eyes on Jesus and His Word. So shall I be saved from my enemies.

JULY 27
KNOCK AND OVERCOME

> E xodus 15:2
>
> The Lord is my strength and my song; he has given me victory. This is my God, and I will praise him — my father's God, and I will exalt him!

Some mornings you might wake up and wonder if you'll ever get another job. After a while it can seem that searching for a job just might become your new career. That's when you need to remember what God has to say about the matter. According to this scripture, "He has given me the victory." That isn't just something God did for the writer. That is something God does for all His children. Today dwell on these truths — you will overcome, you have the Lord to strengthen you, and your job search victory is assured. Picture yourself walking into a great new job, and give praise to God. But don't wait until it happens, praise and exalt Him now for the victory that is sure to come.

DECLARE THIS:

- I receive God as my strength and I sing praises to His name.
- By faith I receive victory in my job search and I know that I will overcome this challenge.
- I thank God that I will come out of this season of unemployment with a stronger faith and freedom from fear

JUNE 6
CHOOSE YOUR WORK

You've heard this before but it bears repeating. God has constructed all of creation to operate in Love. Success is the by-product of love. This scripture provides a surefire strategy for achieving success in our Kingdom assignment. As we unselfishly put the interests of others first, God is released to look out for our interests. Try it out. As you interview for a position, put the interest of the employer before your own. If you aren't able to do the job, say so. Let the employer keep looking until they find the perfect match for their opening. You will be amazed at how often this behavior is rewarded by employers who will remember you and call when your perfect job suddenly becomes available.

DECLARE THIS:

- I trust that God has me covered as I focus on what others need.
- By faith I receive a selfless attitude and the courage to look out for others before myself.
- I am blessed to be a blessing. As a worker I look for an employer that I can bless.

Philippians 2:4

Let each of you look out not only for his own interests, but also for the interests of others. (NKJV)

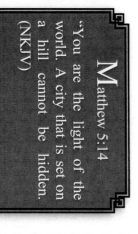

Matthew 5:14

"You are the light of the world. A city that is set on a hill cannot be hidden. (NKJV)

Now that you're unemployed don't you feel like you're under a microscope? Everyone in your family is talking about you and checking in to see what's happening. Friends are calling to see how you're doing. You're on display and everyone is wondering what will happen next. Well, tell them! Start declaring the promises of God for everyone to hear. Don't let a negative word come out of your mouth. Don't plant one negative seed. Make a quality decision to line up with the Word of God and be bold. Remember, God is with you as you do this. It's His reputation that's on the line here, not yours. He will honor you for honoring Him. Make the most of this time when the spotlights are on you. You can shine a light in a very dark world and send the enemy packing.

DECLARE THIS:

- I am in the spotlight to bring God glory.
- By the help of the Holy Spirit I will shine forth the light and love of God.
- I trust in the promises of God and I declare them to be true.

JUNE 7
CHOOSE YOUR PAY

God wants us to prosper, and He's done everything to make this possible. God tells us in Proverbs to seek wisdom above all else. Then in the book of James He tells us that if we lack wisdom we can ask for it, and He will freely give it to us. Finally, in this scripture He promises that His wisdom will give us good sense, strength and knowledge, which in turn will produce precious riches and valuables. No wonder He tells us to "Seek first the Kingdom." That's His master plan for getting wealth and prosperity to His children. To prosper in a time of unemployment, to unleash the promises of wisdom in your life right now, read God's Word with a passion and watch how He will reward you.

P roverbs 24:3-4

A house is built by wisdom and becomes strong through good sense. Through knowledge its rooms are filled with all sorts of precious riches and valuables.

DECLARE THIS:

- I am a seeker of the wisdom of God and believe in the power of His living Word to bless me.

- I trust in the promises of God in His Word. I expect to be given the way out of unemployment and into prosperity.

- I receive all the wisdom I need to handle my present circumstances.

Judges 6:12-13

And the Angel of the LORD appeared to him, and said to him, "The LORD is with you, you mighty man of valor!" Gideon said to Him, "O my lord, if the LORD is with us, why then has all this happened to us? And where are all His miracles which our fathers told us about, saying, 'Did not the LORD bring us up from Egypt?' But now the LORD has forsaken us and delivered us into the hands of the Midianites." (NKJV)

Gideon didn't think of himself as a mighty man of valor. He was hiding out, threshing wheat under cover, when the angel found him. Of course, Gideon had good reason to be afraid. He thought God had abandoned him and his people. But God knew Gideon to be a man of valor because that's how God designed him. So God called Gideon, the two of them spent some time getting acquainted, and then mighty exploits were accomplished. That can be your story too. You might feel that God has abandoned you. Make a quality decision right now, today, to trust His Word. Declare His promises and seek His face. Together you will accomplish great things.

DECLARE THIS:

- I am filled with the power of the Holy Spirit and led by God.
- I am not moved by what I see or by what I feel. I am only moved by the Word of God.
- I can do what God says I can do and I have what the Word says I have.

JUNE 8
CHOOSE YOUR TRAINING

We haven't begun to live at the level God intends. If we will allow it, God is ready to train us to be supernatural. This doesn't mean we'll leap tall buildings in a single bound, but we will speak to a mountain of debt and cast it into the sea, by the authority of Christ. Living inside each believer is One who is ready to reveal all of the things that God has already freely given to us. We can go inside ourselves to find out how to live every moment of our lives in power, authority and love. We will be able to command negative circumstances to turn around and they will have to do as we say! With our ears tuned to the Spirit within, we will rule on earth. Let the training begin.

---

1 Corinthians 2:12-14

Now we have received, not the spirit of the world, but the Spirit who is from God, that we might know the things that have been freely given to us by God. These things we also speak, not in words which man's wisdom teaches but which the Holy Spirit teaches, comparing spiritual things with spiritual. But the natural man does not receive the things of the Spirit of God, for they are foolishness to him; nor can he know them, because they are spiritually discerned. (NKJV)

DECLARE THIS:

- I am open to behaving supernaturally.
- By faith I receive revelation knowledge directly from the Spirit of God and I recognize it when I hear it.
- I expect to receive insights that the world doesn't have and that will make all the difference in my life.

JULY 24
KNOCK AND BRING GIFTS

Giving is a Kingdom law — it never fails. When we need to open up a flow of resources in our lives, we can do this by giving. A dried-up well can be coaxed into giving water by priming it. Priming is the act of pouring water into the well first, in order to get water out of it. That seems like an odd way to get things started, but it works. Right now, while you are without a job, give away your work and your time for the sake of the Kingdom. Somewhere there is a need that you can meet. And as you sow your time and energy, tell God that it is your seed planted in His Kingdom and that you claim a harvest of work opportunities and provision.

Acts 20:35

And I have been a constant example of how you can help those in need by working hard. You should remember the words of the Lord Jesus: 'It is more blessed to give than to receive.'"

DECLARE THIS:

- I am a giver and I look for ways to meet the needs of others.
- By faith I trust that God will care for me as I give to others.
- I know that I cannot out-give God. He will always care for me.

JUNE 9
CHOOSE YOUR BEHAVIOR

This isn't the way most of us read the Bible. Look at this scripture and compare it to your personal practice. First, we're told to look at the scripture very carefully, making sure not to miss a single thing, as if it's a research process rather than a casual read. Then we're instructed to be faithful to it — to put it to work in our lives. Next we're told to go back and read it again to find added insights, and keep up this process to get better and better at it. That's the behavior that delivers the blessing. That's where our success will be found. Anything less than that and the wisdom we receive is likely to be in one ear and out the other. Heedless listener or active doer — you choose!

James 1:25

But he who looks carefully into the faultless law, the [law] of liberty, and is faithful to it and perseveres in looking into it, being not a heedless listener who forgets but an active doer [who obeys], he shall be blessed in his doing (his life of obedience). (The Amplified Bible)

DECLARE THIS:

- I look carefully into the Word of God expecting to find my answers there.
- By faith I will concentrate on the Word and apply what I learn in my life.
- I ask the Holy Spirit to reveal the meaning in the Word as it applies to me personally.

JULY 23
KNOCK WITH CONFIDENCE

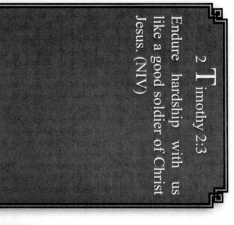

2 Timothy 2:3
Endure hardship with us like a good soldier of Christ Jesus. (NIV)

Hardship is just something to be dealt with on the way to a much higher and more important goal. Soldiers don't talk about hardship — they talk about progress towards the end objective. Not so for many job seekers. They talk about the length of the search, the number of unanswered resumes, their shortage of money, and the things they've lost. Where's the high purpose that's driving them in their search? We were told to expect trials and tribulations. If we choose we can allow these hardships to build our faith, and we can reap a harvest of steadfastness and confidence from our continued endurance. So fight on, soldier!

DECLARE THIS:

- I am prepared for hardship and willing to go through it to get to the promise.
- By faith I believe that God works all things together for my good.
- I thank God that I am empowered by the Holy Spirit and can stand strong in times of adversity.

JUNE 10
CHOOSE YOUR BATTLE

Chances are we won't encounter too many snakes and scorpions in the employment office, but the point here is we've been given authority over ALL the power of the enemy. There's nothing he can throw at us that we can't crush. So how does that apply to the job search? No bad references will be able to injure your chances of employment. A lost or misplaced resume will not hold you back. No nasty recruiter or hiring freeze will be able to keep you out of the position God has for you. But this authority we've been given has no value if we don't rise up in our authority if we don't exercise it and release it effectively. We will only rise up in our authority if we study Jesus to see how He did it because it's His power and authority that we've been given.

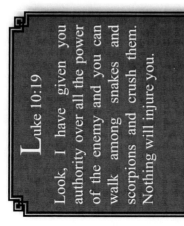

Luke 10:19

Look, I have given you authority over all the power of the enemy and you can walk among snakes and scorpions and crush them. Nothing will injure you.

DECLARE THIS:

- I am not afraid because nothing can harm me.
- By faith I receive the power and authority of Jesus. It's in His name and I have the right to use it.
- Because I am in Christ and He is in me, I walk in His authority on earth.

JULY 22
KNOCK WITH THANKSGIVING

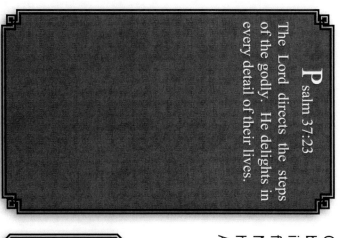

P salm 37:23

The Lord directs the steps of the godly. He delights in every detail of their lives.

God misses nothing about us and He is delighted with what He sees. But can the same be said about us? Do we look for all the details that reveal that God is actively involved in our lives? Do we delight in all that He does for us every day? Begin to actively search for the blessings in your life. Seek them in every experience and person you encounter. Notice how God is directing your steps, how He is arranging for provisions to flow to you, how He is setting up chance encounters and coincidences to help you in your job search. As you see His hand on your life, delight in Him and give thanks!

DECLARE THIS:

- I am a hunter of the blessings of God. I know He continuously cares for me.
- By faith I receive God's love and His direction.
- I am so glad that God is delighted with the details of my life!

JUNE 11
ASK EXPECTING RESULTS

I used to feel like some of my prayers never made it past the ceiling of my room. I had this idea that I had to send them all the way to a heaven somewhere far above me. Imagine my relief when I discovered that He was inside me and I could whisper right into His ear whenever I bowed my head. Isn't it great to know that He hears us, that He can't possibly miss a word, because He lives in our hearts? Then the Word gives us an even more amazing promise — He will give us what we ask for! Let's just make sure that our requests will bring glory to God and be aimed at the best He has to offer. That's why it's such a good idea to ask Him to be the author of our prayers.

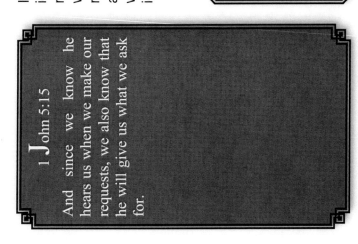

DECLARE THIS:

- I am so glad that God hears my every prayer.
- By faith I trust that the Holy Spirit will direct my prayer s for the highest good of all concerned.
- Knowing that God will grant my requests makes me careful to seek His will before I ask.

1 John 5:15

And since we know he hears us when we make our requests, we also know that he will give us what we ask for.

JULY 21
KNOCK WITH BOLDNESS

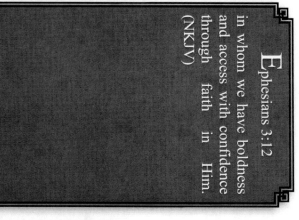

Ephesians 3:12 in whom we have boldness and access with confidence through faith in Him. (NKJV)

"We have boldness" because through faith in Jesus we have become righteous. We can approach God to talk about anything that concerns us. Do you see yourself as righteous and fully pleasing to God? Do you know that what Jesus did was more than enough to cover all your shortcomings? Do you know that God is love and only love? Finally, are you absolutely persuaded that all power and authority in heaven and earth has been given to us in the name of Jesus? These truths are essential to a victorious Christian life. If you aren't walking in this revelation take the time to get these truths into your heart and mind. Boldness is sure to follow.

DECLARE THIS:

- I am fully persuaded that God loves me and Jesus died to give me an abundant and victorious life.

- By faith I receive confidence and boldness through my faith in the works and life of Jesus.

- I go out in boldness because I go with Christ in me to do the work of the Kingdom. I have God's backing in my job search.

JUNE 12
ASK FOR FIRST THINGS FIRST

Let's be absolutely clear about the basis for our faith. It isn't about anything we've done — it's only about what Christ has done for us. Ask for a full revelation of this truth. It's all about Jesus. It's nothing about you. Everything we ask has to be based on our faith in the name of Jesus and the work He has done. He successfully completed His royal assignment and now He's freely giving His power and authority to us; it's our inheritance in Christ. When we fully understand this we'll be able to go forward in confidence and expect a victory because that's what Jesus deserves for the price He has paid. It's that simple and that wonderful. Ask for the faith to believe this awesome truth.

DECLARE THIS:

- My confidence for every good thing is in Christ alone.
- Nothing I want or need depends upon me.
- Jesus paid the price for my inheritance and I am prosperous.

2 Peter 1:10-11

So, friends, confirm God's invitation to you, his choice of you. Don't put it off; do it now. Do this, and you'll have your life on a firm footing, the streets paved and the way wide open into the eternal kingdom of our Master and Savior, Jesus Christ. (Message)

Matthew 14:31

Jesus immediately reached out and grabbed him. "You have so little faith," Jesus said. "Why did you doubt me?"

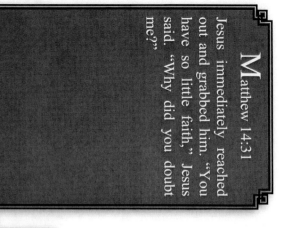

Peter took his eyes off Jesus. He forgot that it was Jesus who told him to come. Seriously, would Jesus have invited him out of the boat so that he could sink beneath the waves and get soaked? In fact, we see that even when Peter took his eyes off Jesus and started to flounder, the Lord was right there to grab him and bring him to safety again. So it is with us. We take our eyes off Him, we forget His promises, we believe the lies of the world and we too start to go under. That's when we find that Jesus is still ready to save us, no questions asked. Start anew today and put your focus back on the Word. You are designed to be a "water walker!"

DECLARE THIS:

- I can do all things through Christ who strengthens me.
- By faith I receive the power of Christ in me and I am an overcomer.
- I trust that nothing I do will ever put me out of the reach of Jesus who loves me.

JUNE 13
Ask About Your Gifts

Not only does God give us our gifts but He also provides the wisdom we need to use them in an excellent manner. For example: there's no chance that He designed you to be a writer only to refuse to give you wisdom about what to write and how to get your work published. In fact, His Word says that He labors with us, as it is written here: "I have filled the gifted artisans with the spirit of wisdom." So don't be confused about how and where to use your gifts. Ask the One who gave them to you. He promises to give wisdom to anyone who asks.

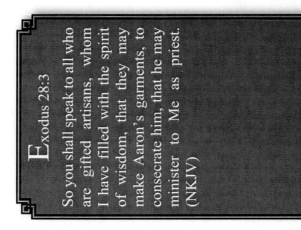

DECLARE THIS:

- I know that I am gifted by God's design.
- I have a great contribution to make to the Kingdom.
- By faith I receive the ability to recognize my gifts and the wisdom to use them as God intended.

Exodus 28:3

So you shall speak to all who are gifted artisans, whom I have filled with the spirit of wisdom, that they may make Aaron's garments, to consecrate him, that he may minister to Me as priest. (NKJV)

Psalm 91:11-12

For He will give His angels [especial] charge over you to accompany and defend and preserve you in all your ways [of obedience and service]. They shall bear you up on their hands, lest you dash your foot against a stone. (The Amplified Bible)

Unfortunately, many believers were never taught about angels and so they've categorized them as fairy-tale beings, or discounted their presence entirely. Make no mistake — angels are real and they are extraordinary, hidden treasures. They were there to minister to Jesus after His days in the desert where He was tempted by Satan. They were present throughout the Old Testament. In the book of Acts we read about an angel that walked into a locked prison, handed Peter his cloak, and walked him right out into the street. They are definitely real, and God has made them available to minister to us and to care for our needs. They're waiting to go to work for you. Accept this wonderful, unseen gift as another of His hidden treasures for you.

DECLARE THIS:

- I am covered and protected by angels.
- I receive angelic support as just one more way that God cares for me.
- I accept all the promises of Psalm 91 and know that nothing shall by any means harm me.

JUNE 14
Ask About Your Design

Before you go into the workplace to look for your next position, get clear about who you really are. "I have begotten you, you are my offspring. I am the King of Kings and you are designed to be royalty — to rule the earth." Notice the change in our status. We are no longer just His servants; we are His sons. God has given us all the nations of the world as our inheritance in Christ Jesus. We are to rule as His royal offspring. This is a tall order for us to fulfill, but it is our design. If we are not willing to receive this revelation of our true identity we will never realize the destiny God has planned for us.

DECLARE THIS:

- I am a child of the Most High God; not a servant, but a son (daughter.)
- By faith I receive my true identity and my assignment to rule in the earth.
- I receive the power of the Holy Spirit to show me where and how I am to take dominion.

Psalm 2:7-8

I will declare the decree: The LORD has said to Me, 'You are My Son, Today I have begotten You. Ask of Me, and I will give You The nations for Your inheritance, And the ends of the earth for Your possession. (NKJV)

The enemy uses the tactic of isolation to cut job seekers out of the fellowship of others, because he can do so much harm when the believers are on their own. Don't fall for this. Now is a great time to get into a group of fellow believers and experience the power of community. Sheep are meant to be in the sheepfold. We are not designed to be alone. Ecclesiastes 4:12 tells us "Though one may be overpowered, two can defend themselves. A cord of three strands is not quickly broken". So find a small group to connect with and experience God's gift of relationships.

H ebrews 10:25

Not forsaking the assembling of ourselves together, as is the manner of some, but exhorting one another; and so much the more as you see the Day approaching. (NKJV)

DECLARE THIS:

- I am open to the possibility of fellowship and look for a group of like minded believers to connect with.

- I know that I am never alone and that God has provided others to pray with and support me at this time.

- I declare by faith that I am not alone and I will not be snared by the enemy who tries to isolate me.

JUNE 15
ASK ABOUT YOUR PURPOSE

We know that God gives us the desires of our hearts, but many of us have completely lost the ability to hear from our hearts. We think a heart's desire must be anything we really, really want. If our hearts have been broken we may think anything that lessens the hurt is a heart's desire. If we're struggling financially we might think a steady income is a heart's desire. But these may not be true desires of the heart at all. Before we can get to our destiny and the true purpose of our lives we have to allow the Lord to help us recover our hearts. Then we'll clearly hear the voice of the Spirit and come to know the deepest desires of our heart... and be led by those desires to the fulfillment of our life's purpose.

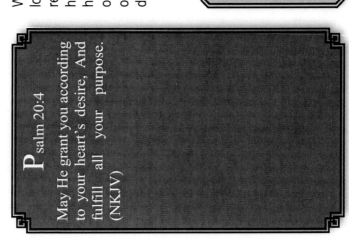

DECLARE THIS:

- I listen for the voice of my spirit speaking from my heart.
- By faith I receive the complete restoration of my heart with the help of Jesus who heals me.
- I trust that God will lead me to the fulfillment of my purpose as I come to know my heart's desire.

P salm 20:4

May He grant you according to your heart's desire, And fulfill all your purpose. (NKJV)

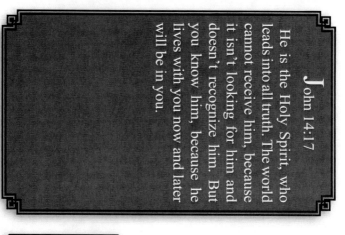

John 14:17

He is the Holy Spirit, who leads into all truth. The world cannot receive him, because it isn't looking for him and doesn't recognize him. But you know him, because he lives with you now and later will be in you.

The Spirit of Christ is inside each and every one of us. This is an awesome power that the world doesn't know about, and unfortunately neither do many Christians. The power, insight and ability of Christ have been placed in us. We ought to expect favor and victory in absolutely everything we do, particularly in the job market, for Jesus Christ walks through every door with us! If you haven't yet received the baptism of the Holy Spirit, receive it now. Let His spirit loose to rise up in you and take the lead. Unleash the secret weapon you've been given and watch what happens.

DECLARE THIS:

- By faith I receive the baptism of the Holy Spirit as evidenced by speaking in tongues.
- I know that the spirit of Christ dwells in me and gives me power.
- I choose to be led by the Spirit of Truth in every area of my life.

JUNE 16
SEEK SELF AWARENESS

What kind of steward have you been? Have you faithfully handled the things that have been entrusted to your care? How about in the workplace, in your past jobs? This is sometimes hard to face, but the message is clear. Jobs that offer increased authority and compensation will only come when we demonstrate faithful stewardship over our current positions. We aren't permitted to give less than our best to jobs that we deem to be "beneath us," or act disrespectfully to supervisors we judge unworthy. If we haven't behaved as good stewards in our past jobs, now is our chance to confess it and repent. Determine to behave in your next position as if you are working directly for God himself. Start now in your job search by being grateful and careful with every blessing and opportunity you receive. Then watch God as He rewards your faithful stewardship.

DECLARE THIS:

- I acknowledge that every good thing I have is a gift from God.
- I am God's steward. By the Holy Spirit I will serve Him faithfully.
- By faith I receive increased responsibility and increased blessing as God's faithful servant.

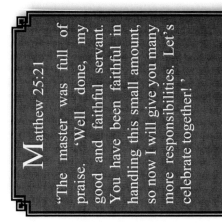

Matthew 25:21
'The master was full of praise. 'Well done, my good and faithful servant. You have been faithful in handling this small amount, so now I will give you many more responsibilities. Let's celebrate together!'

JULY 16

SEEK SELF AWARENESS

Mark 11:22-24

Then Jesus said to the disciples, "Have faith in God. I tell you the truth, you can say to this mountain, 'May you be lifted up and thrown into the sea,' and it will happen. But you must really believe it will happen and have no doubt in your heart. I tell you, you can pray for anything, and if you believe that you've received it, it will be yours.

Think about the last bad report you heard. How did it affect you? When a surprise bill showed up in your mailbox, how did you feel? If you got swamped with despair or lost a night's sleep to panic, there's still doubt in your heart. So before you ask for anything else, ask for victory over doubt. Remember the man in the bible who said this to Jesus, "Lord, I believe. Help my unbelief." That same request will work for you. Then find every promise in the Word that drives out fear and doubt. You can get to a place of complete confidence. This scripture promises that freedom from doubt is God's will for you. Believe that you have received it and it will be yours!

DECLARE THIS:

- I believe the Word of God.
- By faith I receive complete freedom from doubt.
- My confidence is in God alone. I can do all things through faith in God.

JUNE 17

SEEK THE DIRECTION OF THE HOLY SPIRIT

Daniel alone was able to tell the King what he had dreamed. None of the other wise men or magicians could do that. Clearly Daniel had insider information to truths that the others could not see. What was his edge? The visitation of the Spirit of God. This is the very same Spirit that indwells every believer! You may not know where to look for opportunities and you may not know where to find job openings, but for you that's not a problem. With the Holy Spirit there is no mystery too great to be solved. Nothing is hidden from Him, so ask and allow Him to reveal the mysteries to you.

DECLARE THIS:

- I know that God knows all things and there are no mysteries to Him. He sees the way I should go.
- By faith I receive the ability to hear and to trust what the Spirit tells me.
- As I walk by the Spirit, secrets are revealed to me and all mystery surrounding my job search is solved.

Daniel 4:9

"I said to him, 'Belteshazzar, chief of the magicians, I know that the spirit of the holy gods is in you and that no mystery is too great for you to solve. Now tell me what my dream means.

ASK ABOUT YOUR PURPOSE

Proverbs 20:24

The Lord directs our steps, so why try to understand everything along the way?

Sometimes confusion comes when we try to make the Lord's guidance fit into our insistent belief that purpose must somehow be tied to work. For a believer, life purpose is not connected to type of work. Our purpose is to take authority over the workplace and demonstrate the Kingdom way of life. Wherever we work we are to bring God glory. We simply have to commit to follow God and go to work for the Kingdom, and He will open the path before us. Don't try to understand where He's taking you. Just show up and trust. Then knock as you are led, and boldly walk through every open door. God will handle the rest.

DECLARE THIS:

- I trust the Lord to lead me in the way I should go.
- By faith I receive direction and wisdom. All that I need to know will be provided to me at exactly the right time.
- I know that I don't understand everything that is going on around me or even what to pray for sometimes, so I trust the Holy Spirit to pray through me.

JUNE 18
SEEK DIVINE CONNECTIONS

It's so valuable for job seekers to find others who know the Word of God and who will stand in faith with them until the promises of God are realized. There are plenty of people who think they're qualified to offer advice to job seekers, but so many of them do not, as a habit, meditate in the Word of God, nor do they have His mind on the matter. Surround yourself with those who really do walk in faith and who show the fruit of it in their lives. Just as importantly, avoid people who discourage, demean or distract you. Now is truly a time when you need to guard your heart and your mind. Stay far away from anyone who is not intent on encouraging your walk with the Lord.

DECLARE THIS:

- I seek godly counsel and faith-filled associates through this journey.
- By faith I receive the blessing of others to encourage and support me.
- I trust the Holy Spirit to alert me to any voice that does not align with God's Word and I refuse to listen to ungodly counsel.

Psalm 1:1-3

BLESSED (HAPPY, fortunate, prosperous, and enviable) is the man who walks and lives not in the counsel of the ungodly [following their advice, their plans and purposes], nor stands [submissive and inactive] in the path where sinners walk, nor sits down [to relax and rest] where the scornful [and the mockers] gather. But his delight and desire are in the law of the Lord, and on His law (the precepts, the instructions, the teachings of God) he habitually meditates (ponders and studies) by day and by night. (The Amplified Bible)

JULY 14
ASK ABOUT YOUR DESIGN

We have been designed just like Christ. We're called to behave just like Christ on this earth. There will be a day of judgment on this earth but we'll only be there as spectators. Why? Because we have been made perfect, complete and righteous in Christ, who now dwells within us. We can start practicing for that day now. The greed, selfishness and pride at the foundations of so many businesses and institutions are already bringing judgment upon them. But we don't need to participate in that either. We can walk in love and integrity wherever we are called to serve. As systems crash around us we will stand firm in our identity in Christ and be unshaken by what we see around us.

> ### 1 John 4: 17
>
> Love has been perfected among us in this: that we may have boldness in the day of judgment; because as He is, so are we in this world. (NKJV)

DECLARE THIS:

- I am not moved by what I see or what I hear. I am bold in Christ.
- By faith I receive my identity — as Jesus is, so am I in this world.
- I am created in the image of God to bring His Kingdom on earth.

JUNE 19
SEEK HIDDEN TREASURES

It is sad that the world is filled with believers who have never experienced the fullness of joy found in the presence of God. If you're in that group, today is the day for you to hear the truth. God wants to bring you into the path of abundant life. He wants you to come into His presence and experience the fullness of His love for you. Tell Him "Yes." Then, and this is important, expect a unique relationship with Him that no one else will ever have… just you and God in perfect communion. Seek to build Him a throne room in your heart, a hidden place where just you and He can talk. Don't stop until you find intimacy with Christ. Truly, that promises to give you the most priceless experience you'll ever have.

DECLARE THIS:

- I am determined to know God personally.
- I receive by faith God's promise that He will draw near to me as I draw near to Him.
- In the presence of God I experience fullness of joy and eternal pleasure.

Psalm 16:11
You will show me the path of life; In Your presence is fullness of joy; At Your right hand are pleasures forevermore. (NKJV)

JULY 13
ASK ABOUT YOUR GIFTS

Genesis 2:19

Now the LORD God had formed out of the ground all the beasts of the field and all the birds of the air. He brought them to the man to see what he would name them; and whatever the man called each living creature, that was its name. (NIV)

This scripture tells us that from the very beginning God intended us to co-create with Him. We alone have been designed to be just like our Father in likeness and in image. Knowing that you are a "chip off the divine block" should help you to see yourself through new eyes. This earth is the Lord's and we work in the family business so let's act in the very likeness of God and fill the workplace with His love.

DECLARE THIS:

- I am one of God's sons (daughters). The world is my inheritance.
- By faith I receive a revelation of my true identity as God's offspring.
- I have been given dominion over the earth and I stand in my Kingdom authority. I will not be moved.

JUNE 20

SEEK TO STAY FOCUSED ON JESUS

The time has come for believers to claim the promises that come with salvation. Whether we are employed in the workforce or not, we have a secure future and a provider. Whether we get a job offer or not, we have an identity in Christ and an inheritance beyond measure. Jesus is our foundation stone. Keep yourself centered on that firm and immovable cornerstone, and you'll never get shaken. Keep your focus on what is real and eternal and do not be moved. There's a hurting world that needs to see the Children of God standing firm and reflecting His light like radiant lighthouses in a fierce storm.

Isaiah 28:16

Therefore, this is what the Sovereign Lord says: "Look! I am placing a foundation stone in Jerusalem, a firm and tested stone. It is a precious cornerstone that is safe to build on. Whoever believes need never be shaken."

DECLARE THIS:

- I am at peace and I cannot be shaken.
- By faith I place my confidence in the finished work of Christ.
- I thank God that the storms of life cannot move me. I am safe in Him.

Psalm 27:4

One thing I have desired of the LORD, That will I seek: That I may dwell in the house of the LORD All the days of my life, To behold the beauty of the LORD, And to inquire in His temple. (NKJV)

Listen to this request of King David — "Let me dwell in your house all the days of my life." I'll bet you're wondering how that will help you get a job, right? Can these two things be even remotely related? Well consider Psalm 91. It tells us that if we dwell in the shelter of the Most High "nothing shall by any means harm us." There's perfect protection in the house of the Lord. There's joy in seeing how wonderfully and beautifully He loves and cares for us. Go out today knowing that you dwell in the house of the Lord and that He's watching over you. See what that does for you.

DECLARE THIS:

- I desire to love God with everything I am.
- I dwell with the King of Kings. I am His dearly beloved child.
- By faith I receive the favor of the Lord in everything I do.

JUNE 21
Knock With Boldness

Boldness of speech and great hope are a matched set. We can't have one without the other. It's helpful to go back a few verses in this scripture and read about our hope and the source of our confidence. Among other things we are reminded, "Not that we are competent in ourselves to claim anything for ourselves, but our competence comes from God." That should give every job seeker confidence. All we have to offer are our skills and abilities, but we are backed by a competence that comes directly from the Creator. That's our basis for both hope and boldness. God is with us, and in us. When we go into the workplace we bring supernatural competence with us. Go in the strength of the Lord and go with boldness in that knowledge!

2 Corinthians 3:12
Therefore, since we have such hope, we use great boldness of speech — (NKJV)

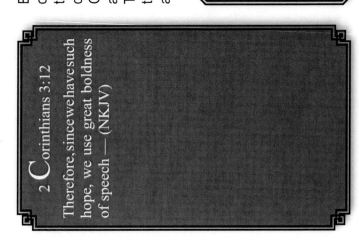

DECLARE THIS:

- I am complete in Christ. There is nothing that I need for my next job that has not already been supplied.
- By faith I speak and act with boldness knowing that God's Word is true and victory is mine.
- I have great hope and I will never let it go.

JULY 11
ASK EXPECTING RESULTS

Psalm 127:1-2

Unless the LORD builds a house the work of the builders is wasted. Unless the LORD protects a city, guarding it with sentries will do no good. It is useless for you to work so hard from early morning until late at night, anxiously working for food to eat; for God gives rest to his loved ones.

Have you ever tried to untangle a really snarled up pile of string? The more you pull at it the tighter the knots become. That's exactly what happens when we start trying to solve our own problems. We can work like crazy and get absolutely nowhere. We can do everything to land a good job and still fail to get the offer. Hear this word. "It's useless to work so hard and so anxiously." The solution is simple — turn the whole thing over to God and receive His rest in return. Why waste another night fretting about something over which you have no control? When you get tangled up in your problems, be still. God wants us to let go so He can untangle the knots.

DECLARE THIS:

- I put my trust in the Master builder. He will help me to build the house of my dreams if I will follow His lead.
- By faith I receive direction from the Lord for every question I have and everything I undertake to do.
- I receive rest from the Lord as He makes my path clear.

JUNE 22
KNOCK WITH THANKSGIVING

This is a tall order for our prayer time. Be earnest, unwearied, steadfast, alert, and intent. But notice the last phrase — "with thanksgiving." That tells us that thanksgiving is an essential ingredient influencing the effectiveness of our prayers. Most of us know how to be earnest and steadfast when we are really after one of God's promises, but do we mix those ingredients with thanksgiving? For the duration of your job search why not try a little experiment? Every time you pray, do so upon the foundation of praise and thanks for all you have already received. Let your requests to God ride in on a cloud of thanksgiving and watch your results. Remember — the fervent effectual prayers of the righteous (that's us!) avail much!

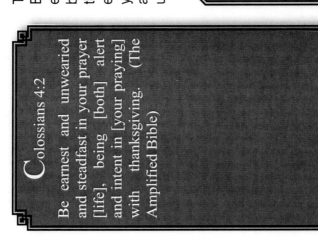

DECLARE THIS:

- I expect results from my prayers because I pray according to God's rules.
- By faith I give thanks for all that I have and all that is promised because I know God's Word is true.
- I do not grow weary in praying because I know my requests will be granted as I stand in faith.

Colossians 4:2

Be earnest and unwearied and steadfast in your prayer [life], being [both] alert and intent in [your praying] with thanksgiving. (The Amplified Bible)

JULY 10
CHOOSE YOUR BATTLE

> Isaiah 45:5
>
> I am the Lord, there is no other God. I have equipped you for battle, though you don't even know me,

Before we even knew there was a battle going on, God was making all our preparations for us. Even when we haven't built a good relationship with Him — "though you don't even know me" He says — He has positioned us for success. This is what Abraham experienced as God made a covenant with him. Knowing that Abraham would never be able to fulfill his part of the covenant, God put him to sleep, and then took both halves of the covenant upon Himself. We don't have to worry that we haven't done enough or prayed enough, or performed perfectly. Our God has equipped us for battle and for victory in Him. Praise God!

DECLARE THIS:

- I serve the one true God and He is with me in the battle.
- By faith I receive all that I need to win in every challenge I face.
- My desire is to seek and to know the Lord who has taken such care of me.

JUNE 23
Knock With Confidence

Confidence is a close relative of courage. Our confidence and courage are rooted not in ourselves and our abilities, but in God's empowerment within us. Nothing has more power and authority than the name of Jesus. We can go into the job search every day knowing that He who is good and who loves us perfectly will never leave us. So don't quit. It's confidence in Him that enables us to keep moving forward when there is no other evidence that our efforts are producing any good results. It will take courage to stay the course to the very end. Just remember: "Courage doesn't always roar. Sometimes it is a quiet voice at the end of the day saying, "I will try again tomorrow." (Mary Ann Rademacher)

DECLARE THIS:

- I boldly declare that I will not quit. I will keep going until I find the job I have been promised by God.
- By faith I receive a good work assignment so that I may be blessed to be a blessing.
- I have more than enough in Christ and abundant life is my promised inheritance.

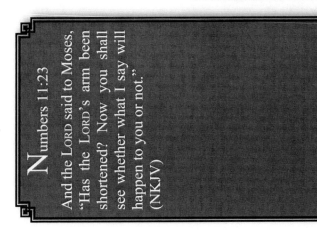

Numbers 11:23

And the LORD said to Moses, "Has the LORD's arm been shortened? Now you shall see whether what I say will happen to you or not." (NKJV)

JULY 9
CHOOSE YOUR BEHAVIOR

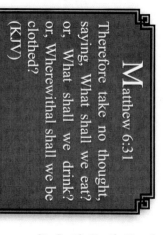

Matthew 6:31

Therefore take no thought, saying, What shall we eat? or, What shall we drink? or, Wherewithal shall we be clothed?

(KJV)

When the enemy brings us a lie we have the ability to simply say, "No, I don't believe that and I won't let it into my mind." Furthermore, we are warned to not speak out loud the lie we've just heard. Those negative thoughts can cause you to wonder out loud "How will I survive this crisis?" or "How could they pull that job out from under me like that?" You have the power to respond, with your mind and mouth, to the enemy's lies. Catch your thought, decide if it agrees with the Word of God, and determine what you will allow into your mind and your mouth. Then speak the Truth. Stay in line with the Word on every matter.

DECLARE THIS:

- I am in charge of my thoughts and what goes into my mind.
- By faith I guard my mind and heart from anything that does not line up with God's Word.
- My mouth speaks only words that align with God's Word.

JUNE 24
KNOCK AND BRING GIFTS

No matter what our circumstances might be, we all have seed to plant. Even those who have been out of work for an extended period still have something they can sow. We all need to keep planting so that God can grant us a harvest as the increase on our sowing. You might plant your time, your expertise in some area, or, as this scripture suggests, a shirt from your closet or some canned goods from your pantry. If you need a harvest, you will have to put some seed in the ground. When you don't know what to plant, seek God's guidance in prayer. Then let your faithfulness multiply your seed into a magnificent harvest!

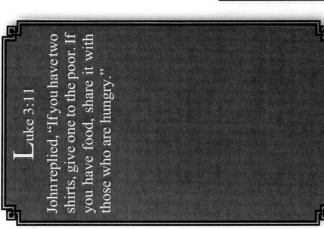

Luke 3:11

John replied, "If you have two shirts, give one to the poor. If you have food, share it with those who are hungry."

DECLARE THIS:

- I am a giver and I know that I will receive a return on all that I give.
- By faith I receive God's promise that I will receive in the same measure that I give.
- I look for opportunities to give because that is the Kingdom way of life.

JULY 8
CHOOSE YOUR TRAINING

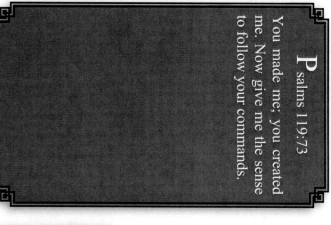

Psalms 119:73

You made me; you created me. Now give me the sense to follow your commands.

This is the best piece of training advice I've ever heard. "Give me the sense to follow your commands." We've done foolish things and we've survived by the grace of God. Now it's time to take our lives to a whole new level — the spiritual realm. It's time to get totally committed to this truth. God made us. He knows what we're best designed to do and He knows how to make us prosperous. All we need do is to seek Him completely and do whatever He says. The sense we need sounds like common sense, doesn't it?

DECLARE THIS:

- I am ready to follow God's direction.
- By faith I receive the sense to obey as the Spirit leads.
- I trust that the One who made me knows exactly what to do with me so I choose to follow His lead.

JUNE 25

Knock And Exercise Your Faith

I can't tell you how many times I've heard job seekers declare that they will not be able to make it financially for one more week or one more month. They are absolutely sure that they are out of resources and going under. Yet week after week and long past their supposed meltdown date, they are still alive and sustained. So do you believe that you cannot make it another week if you don't get a job? This would be a great time to see what God will do about your situation. The only way to grow faith is to hang on to it to the very end of your supplies, your money, and your hope. When you get there tie a knot in the rope of faith and hold on! If you purpose to stand forever, no matter what comes, you won't have to stand for long.

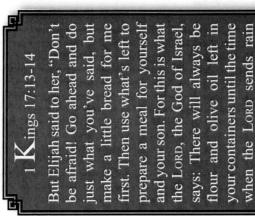

DECLARE THIS:

- I believe in the goodness of God and His love for me.
- I know God asks for my sacrifice only to give me better things and greater prosperity.
- By faith I surrender all that I have to God who cares for me.

1 Kings 17:13-14

But Elijah said to her, "Don't be afraid! Go ahead and do just what you've said, but make a little bread for me first. Then use what's left to prepare a meal for yourself and your son. For this is what the LORD, the God of Israel, says: There will always be flour and olive oil left in your containers until the time when the LORD sends rain and the crops grow again!"

JULY 7
CHOOSE YOUR PAY

Deuteronomy 30:9, 15-16

Then the Lord your God will make you most prosperous in all the work of your hands... See, I set before you today life and prosperity... For I command you today to love the Lord your God, to walk in His ways, to keep His commands, decrees and laws; then you will live and increase, and the Lord your God will bless you.... (NIV)

If we want a paycheck from God, this is our assignment: love the Lord, walk in His ways, and keep His commands. Jesus has commanded us to love as He has loved. He's waiting for us to make Him a priority in our lives and to fill our hearts with love and only love. After we achieve this, He is able to "make you most prosperous in all the work of your hands." Would you like to prosper during your job search? Drop all offense, resentment and unforgiveness. Grow in love, and expect a harvest of blessings. God is always ready to bless us when we become ready to receive.

DECLARE THIS:

- I am filled with the love of God and I choose to release it to the world.
- By faith I trust that God is making me most prosperous in all that I do because I walk in the ways of His Kingdom.
- I believe that God wants to bless me and I receive His blessing by faith in Christ who bought it for me.

JUNE 26

Wherever God sends us He expects us to represent Him and His Kingdom. He is our Master. Other job seekers might talk about the economy, spread doom and gloom, and have pity parties, but we can't go there. When we talk it needs to bring encouragement and hope. It's our job to bring God glory and to demonstrate that Kingdom citizenship makes all the difference in our lives. If you're not there yet, get deeper into the promises of God and seek more instruction in the Word. Get understanding and wisdom from the Holy Spirit. Become so filled with His love that it just spills out of your mouth. There's more than enough negative talk in the world. Be the one to offer hope and encouragement.

DECLARE THIS:

- I speak words that line up with the truth of God.
- By faith I have the power to speak only what is good and helpful.
- My mouth speaks the truth because my heart is filled with the Word and God's love.

Ephesians 4:29

Don't use foul or abusive language. Let everything you say be good and helpful, so that your words will be an encouragement to those who hear them.

JULY 6
CHOOSE YOUR WORK

> ### 2 Timothy 2:15
>
> Study and be eager and do your utmost to present yourself to God approved (tested by trial), a workman who has no cause to be ashamed, correctly analyzing and accurately dividing [rightly handling and skillfully teaching] the Word of Truth.
> (The Amplified Bible)

Study and preparation in God's Word is precisely what we need to do if we are to "present ourselves to God approved." Look again at the definition of "approved" — it's tested by trial. The workman has no reason to be ashamed, because he passed the test. He learned the Word and then he correctly applied it and was successful. That's our blueprint. If we want to be successful, we need to study the Word of truth, walk confidently into the test and apply the Word effectively. Isn't that the way you want to handle the job search? When your search is over and you look back on the unemployment experience, wouldn't it be great to say that you passed the test with flying colors?

DECLARE THIS:

- I give God my utmost as I apply His Word in my life.
- By faith I receive the ability to rightly handle and skillfully teach His Word.
- My life is victorious and I am thrilled as I experience the wonder-working power of the Word in my situation.

JUNE 27
KNOCK AND OVERCOME

If you know anything about gardening, you know there is always a period of time between the planting and the reaping, a time when it looks like nothing is happening. But despite appearances, there is always a harvest. Look at the promise — "My elect shall long enjoy the work of their hands." The meaning is clear, isn't it? Though we may have to wait for the timing to be right, we will reap a harvest for all the seed we've planted during our job search. Never forget that Christ has made us children of God. In Him we have every blessing and promise made by God. Be patient and stand in faith until you see this promise fulfilled.

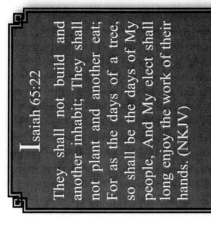

Isaiah 65:22

They shall not build and another inhabit; They shall not plant and another eat; For as the days of a tree, so shall be the days of My people, And My elect shall long enjoy the work of their hands. (NKJV)

DECLARE THIS:

- I expect to be victorious in my job search. I will enjoy the work of my hands in the place God has prepared for me.
- By faith I receive God's promise that others will not take what is mine. I expect to find and secure a great job that will bring me joy.
- I thank God that I am blessed with work so that I can be a blessing.

JULY 5
CHOOSE YOUR BENEFITS

> ## Romans 8:26
>
> Likewise the Spirit also helps in our weaknesses. For we do not know what we should pray for as we ought, but the Spirit Himself makes intercession for us with groanings which cannot be uttered.
>
> (NKJV)

Imagine starting a new job and finding out that you've been assigned a Helper to compensate for any abilities you do not have. Instead of being told to fix your weaknesses, you are told that help is available if there's anything you can't do! This is exactly what your employer, God, has arranged. Each of us has been given a Helper to take over whenever we need it. Get to know your Helper and learn to use Him every day. There are so many things we cannot see and so many times we need intercession. Don't wait for a problem to arise. Ask for help in the morning for whatever might come up. Let's not allow the Spirit to be unemployed! Put Him to work.

DECLARE THIS:

- By faith I receive the gift of the Holy Spirit and ask for help to cover all my weaknesses.
- I know that I don't always know how to pray but I pray in the Spirit who always knows how to pray perfectly.
- I am a Spirit-led believer and I trust God to come through with strength in my areas of weakness.

JUNE 28
KNOCK AND FAINT NOT!

Faith begins where the will of God is known. Until we know something is God's will for us we can't have confidence in it. We can see in this Word that confident faith is required if we are going to be able to stand strong in a time of testing and challenge. If you find yourself wavering, if panic and anxiety are finding a way into your mind, fight back. You don't need more faith, you need firm faith. That comes from pouring in more Word, a greater infusion of the promises of God. A mind renewed by God's Word produces a transformed life. Fill your mind with His Word and your heart will follow. Then God can make you stand firm until the day of your victory.

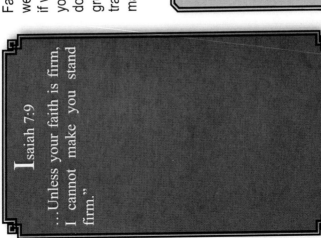

DECLARE THIS:

- I have firm faith. I have made the decision to trust God and I will not be moved by what I see or feel.
- By faith I receive God's promise that He will use my faith to make me stand firm.
- I thank God for freedom from fear and doubt. My confidence is in the Word of God.

Isaiah 7:9

…Unless your faith is firm, I cannot make you stand firm."

JULY 4
CHOOSE YOUR BOSS

> **P**salm 46:1-2
>
> God is our refuge and strength, always ready to help in times of trouble. So we will not fear when earthquakes come and the mountains crumble into the sea.

As we go through this season of challenge and uncertainty, we go in God's strength. He's always ready to help us in times of trouble and most of us would consider unemployment a time of trouble. Notice what God offers — strength and refuge. His supernatural strength is our strength. Whenever we feel lost and insecure we can return to Him as our shelter and dwell in peace. Remember this as you go through the job hunt. God wants us to rely on His strength, not ours. He wants us to run to Him for shelter and to expect His miracle-working help whenever we encounter trouble. No economic earthquake or mountain of debt can harm us now that we belong to Him. Now that's a great employer!

DECLARE THIS:

- I trust in the strength of the Lord and the Hand of God to help me.
- By faith I invite God to help me in my times of trouble and I know He will answer my prayers.
- When I encounter trouble I run to the Lord who shelters me.

JUNE 29
KNOCK AND BE ENCOURAGED

Our discomfort and challenges are not the most important parts of the job search experience. God is perfecting us and achieving something in us that surpasses our wildest imaginations. That's why Paul's words in this scripture can offer a great strategy for us. We need to keep our focus on the Kingdom and our eyes on Jesus. This doesn't mean that we live in denial of the facts we are dealing with in the natural realm. But it does mean that we need to trump those facts with the eternal truth and promises of God. It's up to us to keep our minds filled with the Word and our hearts filled with love, and to keep ourselves encouraged and moving forward. Only a right and eternal perspective will enable us to do that.

DECLARE THIS:

- I am a spiritual being on a journey towards the Kingdom of God.
- By faith I receive the truth that God is producing and achieving an ever lasting weight of glory for me.
- My focus is on eternity and I live now as a citizen of the Kingdom of God.

2 Corinthians 4:17-18

For our light, momentary affliction (this slight distress of the passing hour) is ever more and more abundantly preparing and producing and achieving for us an everlasting weight of glory [beyond all measure, excessively surpassing all comparisons and all calculations, a vast and transcendent glory and blessedness never to cease!], Since we consider and look not to the things that are seen but to the things that are unseen; for the things that are visible are temporal (brief and fleeting), but the things that are invisible are deathless and everlasting. (The Amplified Bible)

JULY 3
CHOOSE YOUR FUTURE

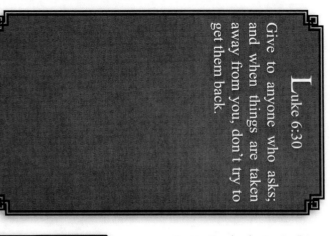

Luke 6:30

Give to anyone who asks; and when things are taken away from you, don't try to get them back.

Here is a radical thought that you may have never considered in the context of an employment situation, but it fits. If your job is taken from you, don't try to get it back. Let God take you a new place where you can perform and contribute again. But what if you loved what you were doing? That's great — because it means that you have the capacity to love your work. What if you felt safe and secure there? That was wrong — because there is no such thing as job security in the world any more. God alone is our security. So never offer to take any old job if they'll just let you stay. You are a child of God, and you are not desperate! This could be the most important, faith-growing time of your life. Decide to put your hand in God's hand and see where He'll lead you.

DECLARE THIS:

- I know I am not alone and that my security is in God.
- I release the past and look forward to my future in Christ.
- By faith I receive all that I need to find my next place of employment.

JUNE 30
KNOCK AND KEEP KNOCKING

The term perfection, as used here, means completeness and it comes via a path of endurance. I admit that this was never one of my favorite scriptures. I don't like troubles and I have never been fond of patience. But like it or not, patient endurance is an important characteristic for believers. The average job search is not a sprint, it's a marathon. Most job searches take months, and they really put faith to the test. But look at what happens as we walk this path — we reach a place of needing nothing. By the end of this experience, if we stay in faith and remained fixed and patient, we will have the full assurance that God really has everything covered and that we are secure!

James 1:2-4

Dear brothers and sisters, when troubles come your way, consider it an opportunity for great joy. For you know that when your faith is tested, your endurance has a chance to grow. So let it grow, for when your endurance is fully developed, you will be perfect and complete, needing nothing.

DECLARE THIS:

- I accept this experience as a test of faith and opportunity for growth.
- By faith I believe that God will perfect me and make me complete in Him.
- In faith I release the joy within me and make the determination to endure with patience until I have the victory.

JULY 2
CHOOSE YOUR THOUGHTS

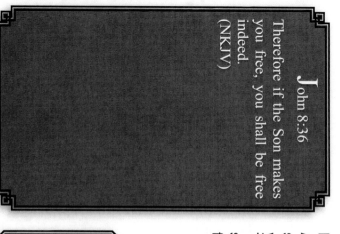

John 8:36

Therefore if the Son makes you free, you shall be free indeed.
(NKJV)

Do your own thoughts trouble you? What is it that plays in your mind for hours on end? Are you thinking about how frustrated you are at the circumstances in your life? Are you still struggling to keep fear at bay? If you are experiencing thoughts and beliefs that cause you distress and pain, now is the time to shed them! That's what God wants for you. That's what Christ did for you. Receive your freedom! With the help of the Holy Spirit, seek out the enemy strongholds in your mind and destroy them with the Word. Don't settle for anything less than complete freedom.

DECLARE THIS:

- I receive my freedom because Jesus died to get it for me.
- I let go of anything that stands between me and my freedom in Christ.
- By faith I declare to powers and principalities that I have been freed of addictions, bad habits and wrong thinking. I am free indeed!

JULY

GOOD NEWS

JULY 1
CHOOSE YOUR KINGDOM

The Amplified Bible really shows how much commitment the apostle Paul placed on getting to know Jesus. Many of us have never realized that we could truly know Jesus as a person, perhaps as our best friend. Consequently, many of us have settled for simply knowing about Jesus. But a key objective that the Lord has for all believers during a time of unemployment is to establish an intimate relationship with them. Think about that. Jesus Christ, who walked on the earth, experienced life as a man, was crucified for the sins of all mankind, died and was resurrected, wants to get to know you personally! He's called you to be a disciple just like Peter, James and the others. Don't miss this opportunity. Don't let your job search go forward without committing to build a beautiful, personal relationship with Jesus.

DECLARE THIS:

- I love the thought of knowing Jesus as my friend.
- By faith I accept that I can have a personal relationship with God.
- I seek Jesus so that I can come to know the power of His resurrection